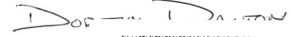

How to Run an Academy School

HOW TO RUN AN ACADEMY SCHOOL

The Essential Guide for Trustees, School Leaders and Company Secretaries

Second edition

Katie Paxton-Doggett FCIS

icsa

The Governance
Institute

Published by
ICSA Publishing Limited
Saffron House
6–10 Kirby Street
London EC1N 8TS

First edition published 2014

© ICSA Publishing Limited, 2016

Typeset in 9½ on 12½ pt Kuenstler by Hands Fotoset, Bexhill, East Sussex
Printed in Great Britain by Hobbs the Printers Ltd, Totton, Hampshire

British Cataloguing in Publication Data
A catalogue record for this book is available from the British Library.

ISBN 978 1 86072 682 8

Contents

Foreword	ix	
Preface	xi	

1	**What are academies?**	1
	Background	1
	What is an academy trust?	3
	Continuing obligations	5
	Freedom of 'academisation'	5
	Charity status	6
	The trustee	8
	Regional Schools Commissioners	9
	National Leaders of Education	9
	Teaching schools	10
	Collaborative arrangements	10
	National Governors' Association	14
	Ofsted	14

2	**Governance structures**	17
	Single academies	17
	Multi-academy trusts	19
	MAT funding	20
	Governance and delegation	23
	Church schools	25
	Umbrella trust	28
	Free schools	29
	Independent schools	29
	Studio schools	29
	University technical colleges (UTCs)	30

3	**Becoming an academy**	31
	Free schools	31
	University technical colleges (UTCs)	32
	Forced academisation	33
	Sponsorship	34
	Converting to a single academy trust	35
	Converting to a multi-academy trust	36
	Outline of the academy conversion process	37
	TUPE	39

	Pensions	40
	Stakeholder management	41
	Marketing	42
	Land transfer	43
	PFI schools	44
	Role of the local authority	45
	Mergers and acquisitions	46

4	**MATs and due diligence**	47
	Centralised services	48
	Church schools	49
	Performance tables	51
	Due diligence	51
	Expansion and staff	60

5	**Funding agreement**	61
	General obligations	62
	Running of the academy	62
	Grants funding	66
	Financial and accounting requirements	68
	Land clauses	70
	Complaints	70
	Termination	70
	Other contractual arrangements	72
	Annexes to the funding agreement	73
	MATs	74

6	**Memorandum and Articles of Association**	77
	Memorandum of Association	77
	Articles of Association	77
	Changes to the Articles	89

7	**Statutory registers and Companies House**	91
	Register of members	91
	Register of secretaries	91
	Register of directors/trustees	92

Register of directors'/trustees'
    residential addresses   92
Register of directors'/trustees'
    interests   92
Single alternative inspection location
    (SAIL)   93
Inspection of the registers   94
Register of gifts, hospitality and
    entertainments   94
Register of People with Significant
    Control   95
Company registers and Companies
    House   96
Companies House   97
The public record   97
Filing hard copies   98
WebFiling   99
Annual report and accounts   102
Change to the accounting
    reference date   103
Change of registered office address   103
Appointing a director/trustee   104
Appointment of a company
    secretary   105
Change of trustee's or
    secretary's details   105
Termination of appointment of
    trustee or secretary   105
Notification of single alternative
    inspection location (SAIL)   106
Removal of auditor   106
Special resolutions   108
Powers and duties of Companies
    House   109
Late filing   109

8   **Members**   111
Multi-academy trusts (MATs)   111
Responsibilities, rights and
    remedies   114
Ceasing to be a member   116
General meetings   117
Decision making at general
    meetings   120
Annual general meeting   123
Drafting the minutes of general
    meetings   125
Companies House filing   126

9   **Directors, governors and
    trustees**   127
Role of the board   127
Structure   128
Directors   128
Eligibility for directorship   130
Directors' duties   131
Appointment of trustees   131
Finding the right trustee   133
Skills audits and analysis of
    training needs   135
Induction and training   135
Payment of trustees   137
Termination of office   137
Disqualification of directors   138
Shadow and de facto directors   139
Liability   140
LAAPs   141
Chair of the board   142
Governors   142
Trustees   144

10 **Board meetings and trustee
    decision making**   145
Calling board meetings   145
Managing the meeting   151
ICSA Code for Good Boardroom
    Practice   158
Written resolutions   160

11 **Minutes of trustees'
    meetings**   163
Practical considerations   163
Drafting the minutes   166
Confidential items   175
Preparation of minutes   175
Storing minutes   176

12 **Financial management**   177
Accounting reference date   177
Accounting officer   178
Chief financial officer   178
Exempt charity status   179
Subsidiary trading companies   179
Gift aid   180
Tax relief   180
Investment policies   181

Value Added Tax 184
Capital funding 187
Procurement 190
Financial monitoring 190
Financial management and
    governance self-assessment 195

13 Accounts 197
Annual report and accounts 198
Reports 199

14 Corporate governance 219
Corporate governance
    mechanisms 220
Conflict of interest 225
Delegation of authority 229
Vision and strategy 232
Clerks and company secretaries 235

15 Risk management 243
Health and safety 246
Safeguarding 250
Business continuity and disaster
    recovery plans 250
Insurance 251
Dealing with complaints 254
Appeal panels 254
Review of board effectiveness 255

16 Policies 259
Statutory policies 259
Policy drafting 263
Access to policies 265
Review 265
Social media 266

17 Information management 271
Website 271
Edubase 275
Freedom of Information Act
    2000 276
Data protection 279
Risk management 283

Appendices
1   Example registers 285
2   Skills audit 287
3   The minute-taker's reminder
    checklists 290
4   Finance processes for month-end
    reporting 296
5   Board of Directors (BoD)
    Decision Planner 299
6   Example strategic objectives and
    key indicators 305
7   Risk assessment form 307
8   Example risk register 311
9   Committee self-evaluation 313
10 360° review of chair's
    performance 315
11 Data protection 319
12 Website review 336

Glossary 341

Directory 347

Index 349

Foreword

On behalf of the National Governors' Association (NGA), I am very pleased to be able to write a foreword for this publication. ICSA is the chartered membership and qualifying body for people working in governance, risk and compliance, including company secretaries. Its work is therefore complementary to that of the NGA: the membership organisation for all state-funded school governing boards and academy boards of trustees.

The past ten years have seen seismic changes in how schools are run, managed and governed, and of course the pace of that change continues to increase: a version of Moore's Law for school organisation, perhaps? There has been a significant increase in the number of schools that are academies, and particularly in the number of academies that are now within a multi-academy trust (MAT), the government's preferred model.

The majority of secondary schools and an increasing proportion of primary and special schools are now academies, many of whom are 'Gold Members' of the NGA. Academies are independent state schools, answerable to the Secretary of State for Education via Regional Schools Commissioners, both through statute and by the school's individual funding agreement.

The NGA has always championed the need for governing boards, as the accountable body of the school, to be strategic. In academies that accountable body is the board of trustees, but those leading in academies also need to understand the different responsibilities of trustees, directors, members and 'local governors' – although the NGA prefers an alternative title for these academy-level bodies in MATs to clarify that their role is a committee of and answerable to the trustees, not 'governors' in the traditional sense.

It is apparent to the NGA from the numerous questions asked of our advice team and the details on the ground work of our consultancy teams that there is a level of confusion and misunderstanding about the different roles of trustees, directors, members and governors, particularly within MATs. This publication distinguishes these differences and provides a template of how an academy should be run corporately. It is vital that everybody involved in its management and leadership understands their different roles and responsibilities.

Confusion and misunderstanding will inevitably lead to problems within the corporate governance of an academy and detract from the effective running of any school.

This publication details this not only from the standpoint of a trustee and of a governor, but more especially from the point of view of the clerk or company secretary of the organisation. Again, professional clerking is something that the NGA has actively pushed for a number of years. We know that this is a critical element of the good governance of any school: a respected professional clerking all trustee and governing board meetings, who can provide advice, but who is independent of the school. The NGA offers specific support for clerks through its guidance centre and holds topical meetings for clerks. Please do also look out for the NGA's biannual awards, where we celebrate outstanding clerking as well as outstanding governing boards.

Ofsted quite rightly focuses on the leadership and governance of a school and the effectiveness of governors/trustees in holding senior leaders to account. Without professional clerking, with minutes of meetings that show an equal measure of support and challenge, trustees and governing boards will struggle to attain or retain the necessary accolade of 'Good' or 'Outstanding'.

The constant theme of this book is that the right people must be around the table to ensure effective governance of an academy. This, again, is something that the NGA will always support: indeed it is the first of our 'eight elements of effective governance'. The second is that everybody around the table understands their roles and responsibilities, followed by good chairing, professional clerking and leading on to a commitment to asking challenging questions followed by courageous conversations. All of these elements of effective governance are dealt with in detail here. I commend also the chapters on risk assessment, risk management and skills audits – areas with which many trustees and governors are not as familiar as they should be.

An element of governance that has increasingly come under the spotlight as the landscape changes is how other players make their voice heard and how their account is rendered. Academy-level committees can have an extremely important role in ensuring both that the voices of parents, pupils, staff and the wider community are heard by the executive leadership and the board of trustees, and that reports are made to them. The challenge to those that govern at academy level is to embrace this role, rather than mourning what has gone before.

This book contains many examples of good practice from existing academies and MATs. These move the publication from being a theory-driven book to a practical day-to-day application of the legal and regulatory compliance necessary for good governance of any organisation.

While the NGA cannot trace its history back to 1902 (the year that ICSA was granted its Royal Charter), the commonality of approach around the detail of corporate governance is gratifying. The NGA sees this publication as an essential guide to the legal and regulatory compliance to fulfil the company secretary role in an academy.

Ian Courtney MBE
Chair, National Governors' Association
July 2016

Preface

There have been significant changes around academies since the publication of the first edition of *How to Run an Academy School*. At that time the majority of academies were single academy trusts where a school had become a standalone trust. Now the majority of schools become academies as part of a new or existing multi-academy trust.

Academy trusts have become increasingly complex organisations as governance structures have developed and evolved and individual trusts have adopted arrangements and processes that work for them. What this means is that the trusts have been able to take an approach to governance that complies with legal and regulatory requirements but which is completely personalised. This is good news for academies and the people that run them.

However, this flexibility also means that it can be difficult to generalise about the internal arrangements within trusts. This, coupled with the fact that there have now been numerous revisions of the model documentation which form the constitutional basis, means that almost every trust is slightly different.

The content of the book is based on the versions of the model documentation available at the time of writing and focuses on mainstream academies. I have taken a fairly generic approach. However, the specific terms will differ according to the type of trust, as well as when the documentation was drafted and agreed. It is, therefore, absolutely essential that reference is made to the original documentation: it should be the first task of anyone involved in the administrative function of a trust to read and be familiar with the contents of the funding agreement and Articles of Association for their own academy.

The terminology around academy trusts is confusing and it is important that anyone working in this area is clear about what the various expressions mean. Most confusion arises around the terms 'member', 'trustee', 'director' and 'governor'. Members are not trustees. In fact, the last three terms apply simultaneously to the same group of people: by virtue of their roles as charitable trustees, directors of a limited company and governors of a school, they have a number of different responsibilities. However, generally the roles are indistinguishable. This book clarifies the terms in current usage within academies and helps the officers fulfil their roles effectively. In this book I generally refer to them as 'trustees' in line with the DfE's practice.

A well-run academy offers great opportunities both for those running it and for the students passing through it. The key to good outcomes for both groups is ensuring that the administrative function both supports and enables a fantastic learning experience for pupils.

This book is intended as a practical guide for those involved in the day-to-day administration of an academy. It provides real-life case studies along with useful precedents that the reader can use. It is the book that I would have liked if I had found myself required to do the job without any experience.

I would like to thank all the talented and committed people working with academy trusts who have contributed to the book as well as my four beautiful daughters who are my constant reminder of why it's so important to get the governance of academies right!

Katie Paxton-Doggett
September 2016

1 What are academies?

Background

The idea for publicly funded schools free from local authority (LA) control was initially introduced by the Conservative government in the Education Reform Act 1988. City Technology Colleges (CTCs) specialise in subjects such as science, mathematics and technology and were intended to be located in urban areas. One-fifth of capital costs were to be met by private business sponsors.

However, the programme was met with significant opposition from local authorities who failed to identify suitable sites so that the schools were built on the outskirts of cities rather than centrally as planned. The cost of building the new schools was also much more expensive than anticipated, requiring a much higher level of government funding. The programme was abandoned after only 15 CTCs had been created.

In 2000, the Labour government introduced city academies which were intended to replace failing schools in deprived areas. The legislation for CTCs was amended by the Learning and Skills Act 2000. Again, sponsors were appointed, although the financial commitment was halved from that under the CTC scheme. Although the schools were independent of LA control, city academies were bound by the schools admission code. CTCs were encouraged to convert to city academies and the majority did so. In 2002, the name was changed to 'academies' by an amendment enacted by the Education Act.

David Cameron's Coalition government expanded the programme and streamlined the process to enable more schools to become academies. The first academies had been failing schools which were sponsored; the new academies were excellent schools which wanted autonomy. The Academies Act 2010 opened the way for all maintained schools, both primary and secondary, to become academies. Unlike the earlier 'Mark 1' academies, no external sponsor was required. Initially, only schools assessed as 'Outstanding' by Ofsted were able to convert; the first schools became 'converter academies' in September 2010. In an effort to help raise achievement more widely, these converter academies were required to support at least one weaker school.

The Academies Act 2010 was a watershed in the move to a fully independent, yet state-funded, education system. Prior to this, only poorly performing secondary schools were covered by the academies programme. However, as only 'outstanding' schools could convert, the Act meant that suddenly academy status was something to aspire to, an indicator of quality.

Following the comprehensive spending review announcement on 20 October 2010, the programme was further expanded so that schools assessed as 'Good' with one or more outstanding features were able to convert to academy status. Other schools were also eligible if they were working in partnership with an 'Outstanding' or 'Good' school which had committed to assisting them with improvement. In January 2011, the policy was expanded to allow 'Outstanding' special schools to convert.

Since then, the programme has continued to grow exponentially with all schools now being given the opportunity to convert to academy status. Schools can apply to convert as single academy trusts (SATs) or as part of a multi-academy trust (MAT). However, the DfE has stated its preference for the MAT structure and any school wishing to convert as a single academy will need to show:

- the latest Ofsted rating is 'outstanding' or 'good with outstanding features';
- pupils' attainment and progress are above the national average; and
- the schools' finances are healthy.

In addition, the converter school would be expected to support at least one other local school.

The government made clear its intention in November 2015 when it stated:

> 'The Spending Review and Autumn Statement represents the next step towards the government's goal of ending local authorities' role in running schools and all schools becoming an academy.'

The subsequent white paper 'Education Excellence Everywhere', published in March 2016, set out that all remaining maintained schools would be required to convert to academy status or be in the process of converting by 2020. All schools would be academies by 2022, giving a definitive end to the role of local authorities in maintaining schools. It further confirmed the expectation that most schools would convert into 'dynamic MATs'.

However, the white paper was not warmly welcomed and after fierce lobbying the Secretary of State announced in May 2016 that the proposals contained in the white paper regarding compulsory academisation would not go ahead. The DfE confirmed that the earlier proposal to convert all schools to academy trusts by 2022 was now an 'aspiration' rather than a promise.

Despite the apparent U-turn, the government has re-stated its 'continued determination to see all schools become academies in the next six years'.

The Education and Adoption Act 2016 came into effect from 18 April 2016. This, together with the statutory guidance, Schools Causing Concern, requires governors and local authorities to take active steps to convert schools into trusts if they are failing, underperforming or 'coasting'.

Furthermore, the government has stated its intention to legislate to convert all schools (including those rated 'good' or 'outstanding') in a local authority where:

- a 'critical mass' of schools in the LA area have converted, with the result that the local authority can no longer viably support its remaining schools; or
- the LA consistently fails to meet a minimum performance threshold across its schools, demonstrating an inability to bring about meaningful school improvement.

What is clear is that the academies programme is here to stay. Introduced by the Conservative government and embraced and developed by successive Labour, Coalition and Conservative governments, there is no formal opposition from any of the main political parties. With the funding to LAs declining rapidly and cutbacks in the services they provide, schools are left with little choice about whether to convert to academy status.

▓ What is an academy trust?

A trust is a state-funded independent school. It is not under LA control and has greater freedom than a maintained school, particularly in relation to delivery of the curriculum and the ability to set its own pay and conditions for staff.

Trusts are charitable companies limited by guarantee. They must be regis-tered as a company with Companies House and governance must be undertaken in the same way as any other company. They are exempt charities, so are not required to register with the Charity Commission. Compliance with charities law is regulated by the DfE as the Secretary of State for Education is the 'principal regulator' for trusts.

Trusts receive their funding directly from the Education Funding Agency (EFA), the DfE agency specifically tasked with funding and compliance. Funding is calculated on a per-pupil basis in the same way as maintained schools. With the move to a national funding formula, inconsistencies between schools should reduce. Trusts also receive additional funding to account for services that were previously provided by the LA. At the outset of the academies programme, this additional funding was significant, but it has already reduced. Initially, this addi-tional funding was identified separately but it is now subsumed within the grant funding. Perhaps the most important feature of funding for trusts is the increased freedom as to how budgets are utilised to best benefit their pupils.

The DfE has a series of model documents which schools are expected to use when the trust is created. This documentation forms the constitution and sets the rules for the business operations of the trust. There are several versions avail-able depending on whether the trust is to stand alone or will join with others in a

MAT; the status of the converting school will also affect this choice, particularly if faith schools are involved. There is also a cooperative version of the documentation for free schools, studio schools and university technical colleges (UTCs).

Only a few years ago, converting schools were able to decide whether they should become (or join) an umbrella trust. In this case, the over-arching body, or umbrella, is a charitable trust in its own right with its own board. Each of the individual academies is a SAT. The umbrella trust allowed schools of different status such as community, VC and VA to work together in a formal structure without having to alter their governance structure or change the representation by a faith or other foundation body. Unfortunately, umbrella trusts have not been hugely successful – the flexibility inherent in the structure has generally not encouraged academies to work jointly and collaborate but to remain relatively independent. The umbrella trust is no longer favoured by the DfE and new applications are highly unlikely to be successful.

New model documents have been, and continue to be, introduced reflecting changes in policy and legislation. Any deviation will only be approved in 'exceptional circumstances'. This does mean that trusts already formed may have versions of the documentation which differ from the current models.

In the Mark 1 academies, underperforming schools were sponsored by an external sponsor who provided funding as well as taking responsibility for improvement in performance. Schools are rarely sponsored in this way now. A range of organisations, such as successful schools, businesses, universities, charities and faith bodies, can act as a 'sponsor'.

In many cases, an existing MAT or SAT (including a SAT within an umbrella trust) takes over responsibility for a failing school through a 'sponsorship' arrangement. The terminology is not terribly helpful; in these situations, the failing school becomes legally part of the MAT rather than just being supported by it. This is an onerous task and MATs are unlikely to take it on if they do not believe they can genuinely offer the support required.

In addition to SATs and MATs, there are other structures: free schools, studio schools and UTCs. Although they offer different educational provision and come into being in different ways, they operate along the same lines as trusts. Furthermore, new schools must either be a new academy or a free school.

All the necessary documentation and relevant provisions are explored in detail in this book. There are common themes throughout as, once up and running, sponsored and converter academy trusts, SATs and MATs, free schools, studio schools and UTCs operate, on a legal basis, in much the same way. However, the details will differ and it is absolutely essential that all involved in the management of a trust are fully aware of the provisions contained within their own funding agreement and Articles of Association. It will be no defence to any potential action to be unaware of the requirements!

Trusts sign a funding agreement which is essentially a contract with the Secretary of State. The trust must meet the requirements in the funding agreement to qualify for ongoing public funding. Despite its name, this document contains no details of funding that will be granted to the trust.

Continuing obligations

The governing body of a school is part of its leadership and management whether the school is maintained or a trust. However, the responsibilities borne by the governors, who now become the trustees of the trust, are greatly increased. The role of 'governor' needs to be 'professionalised' and nowhere is this clearer than in a trust where strict legal obligations already exist.

Trustees are not only to be entirely focused on developing and operating an outstanding school with excellent pupil progress and achievement, they are also responsible for running a charitable company! Whereas previously, the LA took overall responsibility for many aspects relating to property, staffing or general legal requirements, now the trust must do so alone.

Funding for a trust comes directly from the EFA. Although the requirements of a trust are more onerous in terms of accounting functions, the financial year is brought into line with the academic year rather than the situation under the maintained system where budgets ran from April to March, straddling two academic years. Academies must comply with Companies Act, Financial Handbook, Accounts Direction, charity SORP and charity law in a complex inter-relation of rules unique to academies coupled with a reporting deadline equal to that of listed companies.

Freedom of 'academisation'

According to the DfE, trusts benefit from 'greater freedoms to innovate and raise standards' which include:

- freedom from local authority control;
- the ability to set their own pay and conditions for staff;
- freedoms around the delivery of the curriculum; and
- the ability to change the length of terms and school days.

'Academisation' offers schools an opportunity to recreate themselves and become the organisation that they wish to be. The single biggest difference is the control over funding. Trusts can allocate budgets as they wish, shop around to get better value and, in the case of MATs, take advantage of economies of scale.

> **COMMENT**
>
> Bob Wintringham, Chair of the Board of Directors, Faringdon Academy of Schools, expresses what becoming a MAT meant for them:
>
> 'The structure of a community multi-academy trust provides a mix of local expertise and knowledge, but also adds in a real desire for success born out of a sense of ownership.
>
> Directors experience tangible empowerment that drives and focuses improvement and staff are set free to work together across the academy, unhindered by notional school boundaries that can stifle innovation.
>
> Academies have a golden opportunity to take the best of the old system and combine it with radical thinking and bold initiatives. The new freedoms allow us to think differently – but there are no guarantees of sure-fire success.'

The trust becomes the employer of all staff and, in theory, has the freedom to set its own pay and conditions. However, all staff who had previously worked for a school which has converted to trust status will be protected by the Transfer of Undertakings (Protection of Employment) Regulations 2006 (TUPE) (see Chapter 3). This means that those employees automatically transfer on the same terms and conditions. There are also specific TUPE obligations in relation to notification to, and consultation with, unions and employee representatives.

Irrespective of the TUPE arrangements for existing staff, the trust is free to set its own terms and conditions for new members of staff and has the opportunity to pay a premium to attract and retain high-quality staff.

Following conversion, any subsequent changes to terms and conditions for staff who transferred under TUPE may only be put into effect following formal consultation with staff and their union representatives.

Charity status

Since 1 August 2011, all trusts are automatically classified as exempt charities (s. 12(4) Academies Act 2010) and do not need to apply for charitable status. This means that they are exempt from registration and direct regulation by the Charity Commission; any trusts previously registered must stop using their charity number and should be removed from the register. Trusts must, however, inform HMRC that the company is charitable. Otherwise, they will have to complete tax returns, which will increase their administrative burden. A written application to HMRC for recognition as a charity for tax purposes should be made using Form ChA1.

According to the Charities Act 2011, a charity must:

- be established for charitable purposes only; and
- have a purpose that is for the public benefit.

For trusts, the charitable purpose is 'the advancement of education'.

Charities must be independent and must not be controlled by another organisation. At present, this means that trusts cannot be run by a profit-making organisation.

The basic responsibilities of trustees are the same as those of a registered charity, but some Charities Act requirements do not apply.

The Secretary of State for Education is the principal regulator for academies, which means that the DfE is responsible for overseeing compliance with charity law. This role is undertaken by the EFA with support from the Charity Commission. According to the Charity Commission, principal regulators can provide information about charity law requirements and use their existing monitoring arrangements to check whether charities are complying with charity law. They have no additional powers, but can involve the Charity Commission if they have concerns about the way a charity they supervise is operating. In particular, the DfE, as principal regulator, will ensure that trusts:

- comply with requirements in the governing document;
- act responsibly and in the interests of the charity and its beneficiaries;
- manage any conflicts of interest; and
- exercise reasonable care and skill, taking professional advice where necessary.

Endowments and other funds set up by the founders of a trust to provide additional funding may also benefit from this exempt status. If that fund is a charity, controlled by the trust and for one or more of the purposes of that trust, it will also be exempt. In these cases, where the administrative links are very close, the funds should be included in the trust's accounts.

Parent Teacher Associations (PTAs) are independent of the trust and are not exempt. They must register with the Charity Commission if they wish to benefit from charitable status. Alternatively, PTAs may choose to operate as a club or committee.

COMMENT

Chloe Brunton, Senior Associate with Veale Wasbrough Vizards, explained:

'All academies are operated by charitable companies called "academy trusts". Academy trusts are exempt charities, which means that whilst they are charities, they are not regulated by the Charity Commission nor are they required to be registered with them. Instead, they are regulated by their "Principal Regulator" the Secretary of State for Education (supported by the Education Funding Agency).

Despite their exempt charity status, academy trusts remain subject to the key principles of charity law. The trustees (directors) of an academy trust have the same general duties and responsibilities as trustees of other charities. These are summarised by the Charity Commission in their guidance entitled *The Essential Trustee: What you need to know* (CC3):

> Trustees have and must accept ultimate responsibility for directing the affairs of a charity, and ensuring that it is solvent, well-run, and delivering the charitable outcomes for the benefit of the public for which it has been set up.

Being a charity means that certain additional restrictions apply to the academy trust's operation, including restrictions around non-charitable trading and payments being made to trustees or to connected parties. Academy trusts are also required to prepare accounts under the Charities' Statement of Recommended Practice (SORP).

The Department for Education and the Charity Commission have entered into a memorandum of understanding which details how they will work alongside one another including, for example, the circumstances when the Secretary of State might invite the Charity Commission to use its powers of intervention and investigation under the Charities Act 2011.'

The trustee

A director of a trust is also regarded as a trustee for the purposes of charity law. In a single academy, this will be the governors of the academy trust. In a MAT, the charity trustees are the directors of the academy trust; any governors sitting on an individual school's local governing body are akin to committee members and do not have trustee responsibility.

Trustees are required by law to 'have regard' to the public benefit guidance produced by the Charity Commission 'when exercising any powers or duties to which the guidance is relevant'. This means that trustees should be able to show that they are aware of the guidance and have taken it into account when making any decision to which it is relevant and have good reasons if they depart from the guidance. The Charities (Accounts and Reports) Regulations 2008 (SI 2008/629) also require trustees to confirm that they have done so in their annual report.

Trustees have ultimate responsibility for the charity and its property and must:

- make sure the charity complies with the law and its governing document;
- act responsibly, in the interests of the charity and its beneficiaries;
- manage any conflicts of interest; and

- exercise reasonable care and skill – using relevant personal knowledge or taking professional advice where appropriate.

It is paramount that trustees remember that their duty is owed to the charity, which must be uppermost in any decision making; despite the method of appointment or election, trustees do not represent any specific body or group. Trustees must not forget that the trust controls public funds. This introduces a further layer of regulatory requirements.

Regional Schools Commissioners

There are eight Regional Schools Commissioners (RSCs) appointed to eight regions across the country: East of England and North-East London; East Midlands and the Humber; Lancashire and West Yorkshire; North of England; North-West London and South-Central England; South-East England and South London; South-West England; and West Midlands. The RSCs act on behalf of the Secretary of State for Education and are accountable to the National Schools Commissioner. They work with school leaders to take action in underperforming schools, and their main responsibilities include:

- taking action where academies and free schools are underperforming;
- intervening in academies where governance is inadequate;
- deciding on applications from local-authority-maintained schools to convert to academy status;
- improving underperforming maintained schools by providing them with support from a strong sponsor;
- encouraging and deciding on applications from sponsors to operate in a region;
- taking action to improve poorly performing sponsors;
- advising on proposals for new free schools;
- advising on whether to cancel, defer or enter into funding agreements with free school projects; and
- deciding on applications to make significant changes to academies and free schools.

Each RSC is supported by a head teacher board (HTB) of between four and eight members who meet once or twice a month. HTB members are experienced academy head teachers, former head teachers, trustees and other sector leaders who advise and challenge RSCs on the decisions they make.

National Leaders of Education

Individuals who are executive head teachers, CEOs and head teachers can now apply to be appointed as a National Leader of Education (NLE). The individual must have experience of effectively supporting schools in challenging circumstances. If an individual is selected as an NLE, their school will become a national support school (NSS). Under the current criteria to become an NLE, the school must:

- be judged as outstanding by Ofsted;
- show consistently high levels of pupil performance and progress or continued improvement over the last three years;
- be above the current minimum standards set by the government; and
- have outstanding senior and middle leaders who have demonstrated that they have a strong track record and the capacity to provide significant support to underperforming schools.

NLEs usually work with schools identified as being in need of significant improvement by the DfE, Ofsted, a teaching school, an RSC or a local authority.

Teaching schools

Part of the government's plan to 'give schools a central role in raising standards by developing a self-improving and sustainable school-led system' was the introduction of teaching schools. Outstanding schools and academies can apply to become teaching schools if they meet the stringent criteria, which require them to:

- have an outstanding rating from Ofsted;
- provide evidence of successful partnerships;
- show excellent leadership with a proven track record of school improvement;
- have an outstanding head teacher with at least three years' experience; and
- have a leadership team with the capacity to lead the six core areas of the teaching school role.

Teaching schools work with others to provide high-quality training and development to new and experienced school staff. Teaching schools can also lead a teaching school alliance.

There are six core areas of responsibility for teaching schools:

1. school-led initial teacher training
2. continuing professional development
3. supporting other schools
4. identifying and developing leadership potential
5. specialist leaders of education
6. research and development.

Collaborative arrangements

The government believes that the move to academisation offers the opportunity for a self-improving system which can be sustained. One way of doing this is through collaborative arrangements.

Informal collaborative arrangements may be developed along the lines of partnerships to enable academies to work with each other and with maintained schools. It is possible to agree a memorandum of understanding between the various schools, but there is no shared governance. Each academy involved in such an arrangement will have its own funding agreement and Articles of Association, and the academy will need to ensure its own corporate governance structures and company law compliance.

There are significant difficulties with a collaborative arrangement where there is the intention to set up central support to employ staff or to get the benefits of joint procurement. A collaborative arrangement such as this would be regarded as a partnership, which could have significant repercussions in terms of risk. The parties in a partnership are regarded as having 'joint and several' liability. This means that each individual party is liable to the full extent of the obligation in respect of a liability; one party could find themselves liable to pay the full extent of a claim to a claimant and then take action against the other partners for their respective elements of liability and payment. Consequently, it is more difficult to employ staff and run central services in a collaborative arrangement.

It is also possible for maintained schools and academies to collaborate through a 'school company' (ss. 11–13 Education Act 2002):

- to provide services or facilities for any schools;
- to exercise relevant LA functions; or
- to contract for goods or services from third parties on behalf of member schools.

Not only is the importance of collaborative working recognised by the DfE, but it expects schools to support one or more other schools (which can be maintained or academies themselves). This measure is intended to raise standards as part of a 'self-improving school system'. Although this commitment is not regularly monitored by the DfE, it is clear that collaborative arrangements will be part of the educational landscape in the longer term.

COMMENT

Graham Burns, Partner with Stone King:

'Where a school is wishing to collaborate with other schools, it is recommended that the governors carefully consider the trust's intended purpose from the outset. Form should follow function – i.e. the schools should consider how they wish to work together, and what they want to achieve before considering what form their collaboration should take.'

Working with other schools enables a pooling of resources which can be used to improve performance, expand the curriculum or get better value for money.

COMMENT

Brian Walton, Head teacher at Headley Park Primary School, describes their collaborative arrangement:

'I am part of a collaboration called the Malago Learning Partnership (MLP and not to be confused with Malaga). We are a group of seven primaries and one secondary within South Bristol. Our schools have collaborated since 2011. All the primaries who joined the partnership have made significant improvements as illustrated through Ofsted inspections since 2012.

1 moved from good to outstanding.

1 from satisfactory to outstanding.

2 from satisfactory to good.

1 new academy (after a history of inadequate in its previous form) was graded good.

One school has an interim assessment deferring their inspection – good.

The last primary to join the partnership was at the time in special measures. It has since had, by far, its best ever results (high 80s and 90s L4+) and considering it has free school meals (FSM) at 80%+ and now has very stable leadership will be a strong school in its next full inspection.

Our secondary is currently graded "Requires Improvement" by Ofsted.

The schools sit in an area of social need with Pupil Premium figures on average at 49% compared to the Bristol average of 24%.

Our model of partnership involves:

- Two school improvement visits per year to each school
- Termly head's strategy meetings with three additional days of CPD
- MLP website to provide forums for CPD and share school led professional development
- Joint INSET training (Jan 2014 – Over 540 staff and 70 workshops (90% led by partnership staff))
- A joint Practice Development Group (JPDG) who identify and broker support within the MLP
- Joint analysis day leading to a risk matrix shared within the MLP and including production of a shared data pack and presentation to strategic partners
- Established clusters for specific areas including Early Years Foundation Stage (EYFS), Inclusion, Transition, ICT and NQTs.

I think what is most unique about the MLP is that it is a fully functioning system-led collaborative partnership (there's a mouthful!) which includes a sponsored academy (E-Act), CofE primary, maintained schools, independent academies and a secondary academy. It is a mixed bag and there is no law, we know of, that can bind us. Therefore, we are doing this because we see the impact it is having on our school communities. That is a VERY powerful incentive.'

CASE STUDY

Academies can also find themselves in a collaborative arrangement due to the nature of their governance structure. One company secretary acts for five of the grammar schools in Birmingham; these five schools are now academies:

- King Edward VI Aston School
- King Edward VI Camp Hill School for Boys
- King Edward VI Camp Hill School for Girls
- King Edward VI Five Ways School
- King Edward VI Handsworth School for Girls.

The company secretary's role ensures a robust and consistent approach to governance across each of these academies and items of common interest are shared across the five.

Although established as standalone academies, these schools enjoy a close relationship due to the underlying foundation and as a member of each academy trust may make appointments to the individual governing bodies.

The academies converted from former voluntary aided grammar schools and retain a selective admissions policy.

There has been a huge increase in the prominence of Business Manager groups or other collaborative arrangements, both to share best practice and also as a way of finding cost-effective procurement.

COMMENT

John Banbrook MA FCMI FNASBM, Business and Finance Director at the Faringdon Academy of Schools and elected Council Representative for the South East for ASCL:

'There has been a rise in the significance of groups like the Oxfordshire Academies Business Manager group. The group really came together when forced to find a solution to payroll. A procurement specialist was hired and the process overseen by a steering group. A suitable provider was sourced and then individual schools/academies contracted individually which avoided the OJU process.

The group has been formalised and we charge £350 for a MAT/academy which pays for the administration of hiring a clerk, finding a venue, etc. We meet six times per year and are looking at collaborating on further projects such as insurance, HR, etc. The value of the group is that it gives small MATs/academies the same leverage as larger MATs. It is also afford-able in terms of time.'

National Governors' Association

The National Governors' Association (NGA) is an independent charity repre-senting and supporting governors, trustees and clerks in maintained schools and academies in England. The NGA's goal is to improve the wellbeing of chil-dren and young people by increasing the effectiveness of governing boards and promoting high standards. It does this by providing information, advice, guidance, research and training. It also works closely with, and lobbies, UK government and educational bodies, and is the only campaigning national membership organisation for school governors and trustees.

The NGA has over 46,000 governor members and supports over a quarter of schools in England.

Ofsted

All state-funded schools are subject to inspection by Ofsted.

The Ofsted common inspection framework, effective from September 2015, exempts certain types of schools that are judged outstanding from routine inspec-tion unless there are concerns about their performance. This exemption will apply to academies and free schools judged outstanding, but also to schools that were judged outstanding before conversion to academy status.

Outstanding special schools and pupil referral units that convert to academy status will not be exempt from routine inspection but 'will be eligible for a short inspection under section 8 of the Education Act 2005'. Mainstream acad-emies whose predecessor schools were judged good will also be eligible for short inspection.

Short inspections of converter academies will be carried out approximately every three years.

The first inspection of new schools will usually take place within three years of opening. However, the guidance states that 'In most instances, we will not select new schools for a first inspection until they are in their third year of operation'. Converter academies and sponsored academies and free schools are technically new schools, and inspection will also be deferred until the third year of operation. However, Ofsted makes clear that it may inspect any new school at any time where information it holds or receives 'causes sufficient concerns'.

Where a school judged 'good' subsequently undergoes significant change, it will normally have a section 5 inspection rather than a short inspection. Examples of significant change could be a merger with another school which closes, or by adding a new phase or key stage.

2 Governance structures

Becoming an academy, either through conversion or as a new endeavour, involves decisions about the way that the school is going to operate and collaborate long before the first pupil has walked through the door. This is not a simple decision.

The first academies were standalone, single academies, where the school was one company. This meant that the first of the academy converters were large secondary schools with significant resources and manpower to support the additional workload. The very first converters also had the benefit of an external sponsor which contributed significant financial resources. Unfortunately, for many smaller schools (particularly with the removal of sponsorship funding) the reality of setting up alone was not an option. Consequently, as time has gone on, structures have evolved to enable schools to work together.

The Department for Education (DfE) is clear that schools cannot use the conversion process to change or remove their faith character, expand, become mixed or single sex or introduce selection.

Single academies

A single academy trust (SAT) is a separate legal entity which is responsible for one school. It has its own funding agreement and Articles of Association with the Secretary of State.

Becoming a single academy is an onerous responsibility for a school. As well as the practical aspects of running a school outside of the local authority (LA), it is necessary to demonstrate that the school has the capacity to maintain high levels of achievement and attainment.

The DfE has stated that each application will be considered on its own merits and the decision as to whether the school can convert into a SAT structure will be informed by various factors, including:

- the school's exam results from the last three years;
- the progress that pupils have been making over the last three years;
- the most recent Ofsted inspections;
- the school's capacity to be successful and sustainable as a single academy; and
- the school's finances.

Figure 2.1: Single academy governance structure

Stone King LLP

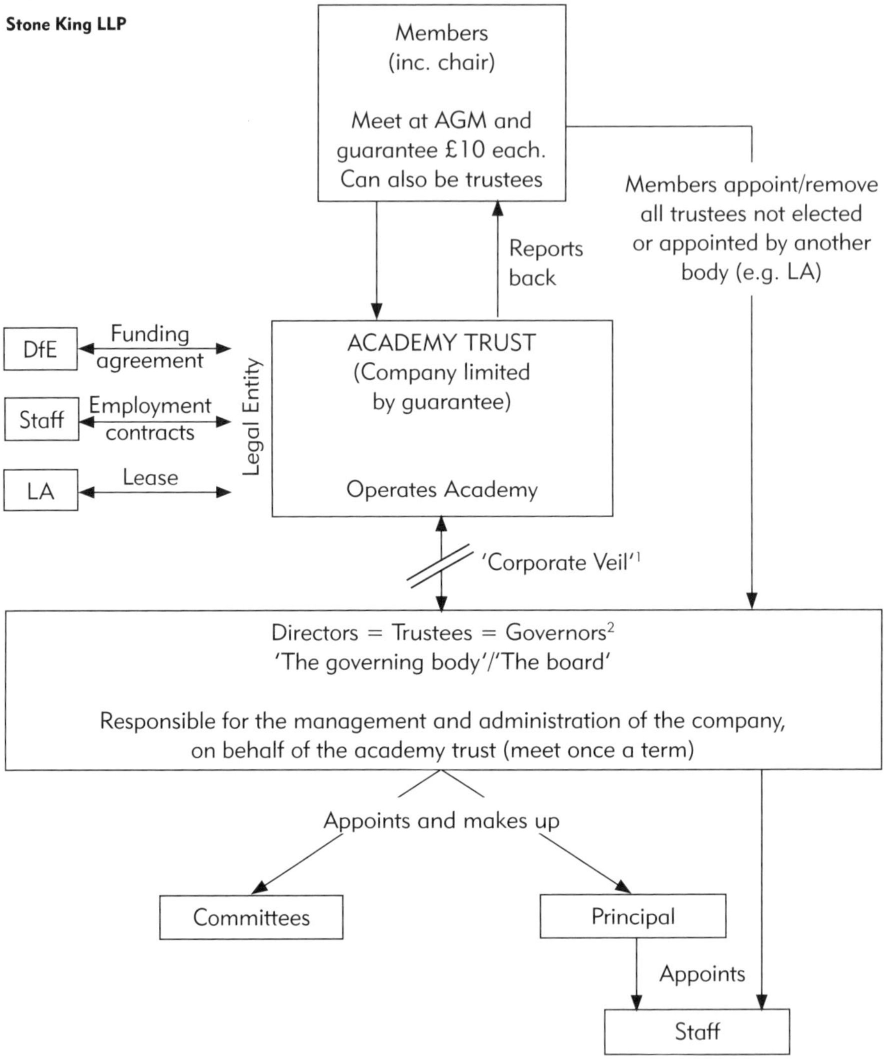

Notes:

[1]*Corporate veil*
The Directors/Trustees/Governors have no personal liability for their actions on behalf of the academy, unless they act outside their powers or continue to trade when they are aware the academy is insolvent. They may, however, be responsible for regulatory breaches.

[2]*Directors/Trustees/Governors*
The terms 'Directors', 'Trustees' and 'Governors' are interchangeable, as the role is essentially the same. The three terms are used as the responsibilities of the board are governed by three different branches of law – as the academy trust is set up as a company limited by guarantee and a charity, and the academy is an educational establishment. In education terminology, they are known as 'governors' of the school. In company law terms, they are 'directors' of the academy trust as a company. Under charity law, they are known as 'trustees' of the academy trust as a charity. Whatever terminology is chosen, they have the same duties and responsibilities.

Any school converting as a SAT is also expected to 'commit to support at least one weaker school'. Care should be taken as to choices made as, in the current climate, it seems likely that, in due course, that school may become part of a MAT with the original SAT.

The early converters generally adopted a 'flat' governance structure, where all trustees were also members. This is no longer the DfE's favoured structure and a 'two-tier' structure is preferred. In this case, the members are a group distinct from the trustees and have the authority to make a small number of decisions without consulting the board.

Part of the reason for the two-tier structure being the DfE's current preferred approach is that the DfE has been resistant to the head teacher or other school employees being members (as recorded in a footnote to the DfE model articles). On this basis, it should be anticipated that as a matter of policy the DfE may request that the head teacher and any school employees are excluded from the membership.

Multi-academy trusts

The government has indicated that schools will generally be expected to convert into a multi-academy trust (MAT), although they have said that they will not put pressure on 'successful and sustainable stand-alone academies' to 'subscribe to a different model'.

COMMENT

In the application to convert to academy status, the DfE states:

'We believe all schools, including those performing well, will benefit from being in a multi-academy trust. We want schools to operate in strong, resilient structures which raise standards. Multi-academy trusts bring together leadership, autonomy, funding and accountability in a single structure, and are the best long-term formal arrangement for schools to collaborate and support each other.

Because of these benefits, we expect that most schools will form or join multi-academy trusts as they become academies. Effective schools can apply to become single academy trusts, but will need to demonstrate that they are performing well and can be successful and sustainable alone. We expect most small schools will be part of a multi-academy trust, helping to secure their long-term success.'

In any event, many schools will feel that they would be better working with others in a MAT, particularly where they have enjoyed a close relationship as part of a partnership arrangement. If schools are in a hard federation, it will be necessary for a conversion to cover all member schools.

In a MAT, a number of schools are combined to form a single legal entity. There is one board of trustees which is accountable for the performance of each of the individual academies.

All staff employed either in central services or within one of the academies are employed by the MAT, which can also facilitate the sharing of expertise and transfer of personnel across sites. Ultimately, the MAT must be able to provide effective support to any of the academies that require it.

Efforts have been made to enable schools with different governance structures to work together in MATs (i.e. community, foundation and faith schools in a single MAT).

As a single legal entity, the MAT will have a single vision and strategy which will apply to all academies subject to agreed flexibilities and variation.

COMMENT

Graham Burns, Partner with Stone King:

'In the MAT model, the academy trust is responsible for operating a number of academies. The MAT enters into a master funding agreement with the Secretary of State which sets out the overarching terms and conditions which apply to all of the academies the MAT operates.

The MAT also enters into a supplemental funding agreement with the Secretary of State for each of its academies. Each supplemental funding agreement sets out terms and conditions which are specific to that academy. Each academy must be run in accordance with the terms of the master funding agreement and the terms of the academy's supplemental funding agreement.

The members of the MAT are not involved in the day-to-day management, but will usually have the power to appoint a certain number of directors to the MAT and have certain constitutional powers under company law (such as amending the company's articles or changing the company's name).' (See Figure 2.2 below.)

MAT funding

There is a master funding agreement between the Secretary of State and the MAT with each individual school having a supplemental funding agreement.

Funding is calculated based on pupil numbers in relation to the individual schools. However, the MAT has the flexibility to set up central services such as HR, facilities management, finance and business support which are utilised by

Figure 2.2: Multi-academy governance structure

Stone King LLP

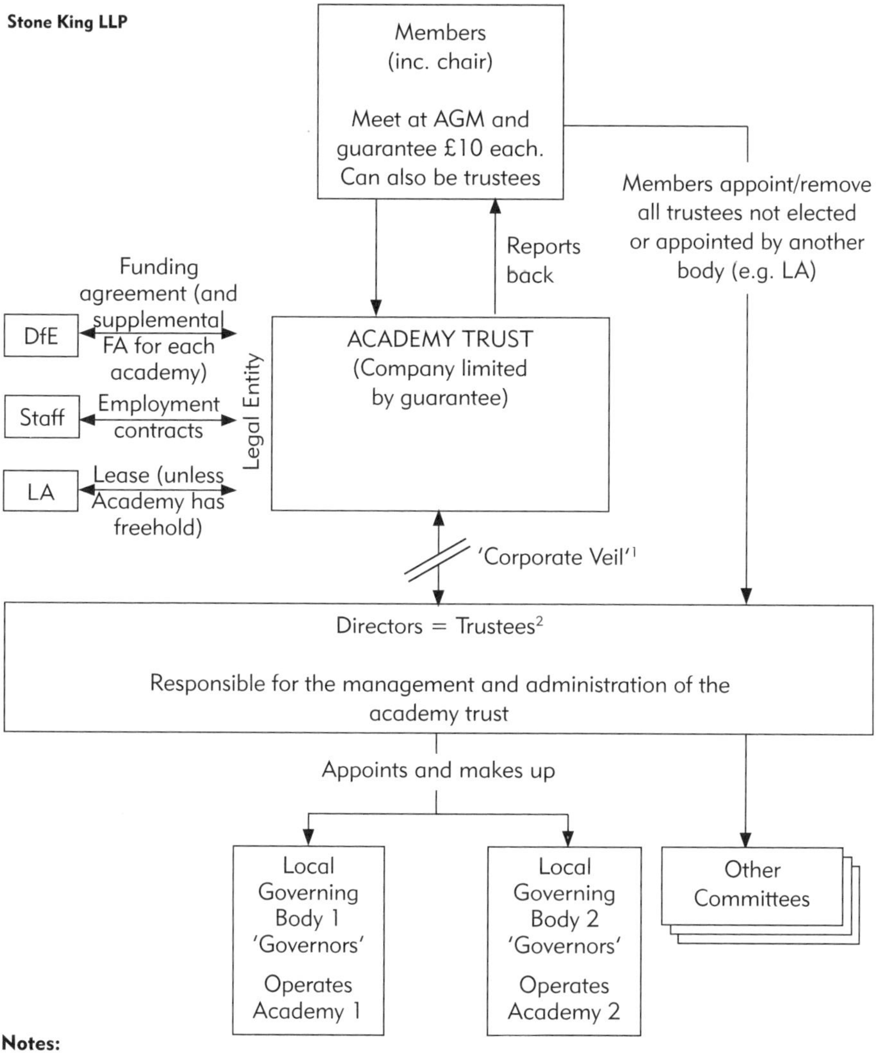

Notes:

[1]*Corporate veil*
The Directors/Trustees/Governors have no personal liability for their actions on behalf of the academy, unless they act outside their powers or continue to trade when they are aware the academy is insolvent. They may, however, be responsible for regulatory breaches.

[2]*Directors/Trustees/Governors*
The terms 'Directors', 'Trustees' and 'Governors' are interchangeable, as the role is essentially the same. The three terms are used as the responsibilities of the board are governed by three different branches of law – as the academy trust is set up as a company limited by guarantee and a charity, and the academy is an educational establishment. In education terminology, they are known as 'governors' of the school. In company law terms, they are 'directors' of the academy trust as a company. Under charity law, they are known as 'trustees' of the academy trust as a charity. Whatever terminology is chosen, they have the same duties and responsibilities. They may, however, be responsible for regulatory breaches.

all schools in the MAT. Depending on the size of the MAT, many services which were previously provided by the LA can be secured on a cost-effective basis.

The funding for these central services will be sourced from a contribution often based on a percentage of the individual schools' budgets (see Chapter 4). The MAT now has flexibility in the way that the general annual grant (GAG) is applied across schools.

This does mean that MATs take on responsibility for managing the budget across all academies.

COMMENT

John Banbrook MA FCMI FNASBM is Business and Finance Director at the Faringdon Academy of Schools and elected Council Representative for the South East for ASCL. FAoS is a MAT in Oxfordshire consisting of one secondary school (the Community College), five primary, one junior and one infant school. He explained:

'We applied for emergency funding for Faringdon Infant School as the costs of rectifying the building problems were more than the academy's reserves. The EFA agreed that there was a need and approved the solution, but it regarded the academy as part of a stable MAT with sufficient funds. Even though the individual school had not got the money, the EFA expect the MAT to cover the costs. It requires a more mature approach to dealing with reserves and a bit of a leap of faith.

One of the MAT academies went into RI. The MAT approved a deficit budget to address teaching and learning which would be effectively "paid back" to the MAT as pupil numbers increased in the manner of a loan.

We maintain individual charts of accounts for each school so that we can identify the position in relation to income/deficit/carry forward. This means that individual schools have identified reserves and these are considered in the overall MAT reserve figure. There would be a problem if all schools spent all their reserves. Centrally, we prepare 3–5-year plans which are scrutinised by the Academy Resources Committee. If the cost of delivering the plans would reduce the level of reserves considered acceptable by the MAT, then the Committee would prioritise spending across the schools.'

Underperforming schools are usually sponsored, which means that the lead sponsor will have majority control of the academy and be able to appoint the majority of members.

Historically, sponsorship meant an injection of capital to help turn around the fortunes of the failing school. However, this is no longer necessarily the case, and the majority of sponsorship situations now relate to the provision of school improvement services or school-to-school support within a MAT structure. NCSL research published in *The Growth of Academy Chains: Implications for Leaders and Leadership* identified eight different types of academy sponsor:

- successful school
- charitable non-faith-based organisation
- charitable faith-based organisation
- philanthropic individual
- further education college
- higher education institution
- corporate.

Successful converter academies are now the most common sponsors and it may not be terribly useful to talk in terms of sponsors. Where a failing school converts to join a MAT, the school is subsumed into the governance structure of the overall company; the MAT is responsible for its performance in the same way as any other school, whether struggling or 'Outstanding'.

Furthermore, any academy can choose to involve a sponsor who can bring specialist expertise or knowledge. This is particularly apparent in the studio school and UTC format where employers and university sponsors may bring valuable input.

Governance and delegation

The governance structure put into place must be appropriate to the circumstances and strategic vision of the MAT to facilitate effective school improvement support for all academies.

It is particularly important to have a clear governance structure which is understood by everybody, together with a schedule of delegation setting out what functions and authorities have been delegated by the board to local governing bodies, head teachers in the schools or other individuals.

Local governing body

A MAT can establish a local governing body (LGB) in each academy to which it delegates some governance functions. This is a common structure in a MAT which has developed out of a collaborative arrangement or the formalisation of a partnership. Generally, the LGB is delegated the responsibility for oversight of teaching and learning and ensuring that the individual academy remains on track. Whether the LGB has responsibility for finance, health and safety or other matters will depend on the individual circumstances and the level of centralisation of services within the MAT. However, whether the responsibility is delegated to the LGB or not, the board remains accountable and must ensure that it is confident in the systems and processes in place as well as the individuals appointed as LGB governors.

The LGB does not have a legal personality and is akin to a committee of the MAT. Individuals appointed as governors of the LGB are not directors by virtue of the position (though they could also be appointed as a director).

The articles of association of MATs which include both church and non-church schools require any LGBs constituted to include 25% of its members to be appointed by the Diocesan Board of Education. Any such governors must also sign an undertaking to the Diocesan Board of Education 'to uphold the designated religious character of the said academy'.

Advisory councils/bodies

Some MATs engage with schools through an advisory body which acts as a mechanism for gathering information from academies for board consideration and decision making. Such advisory bodies can also act as a way of disseminating information to the individual academies in the MAT. Advisory bodies in this context do not have any delegated authority.

Cluster governing bodies

As MATs grow in size, the logistics of managing large numbers of academies becomes more cumbersome. Some MATs set up governing bodies organised on a cluster basis where powers are delegated to the cluster governing body which is made responsible for the performance of all academies within that group.

Scheme of delegation

The board of trustees can choose to delegate their powers or functions to a LGB or advisory body. The model Articles state:

> 'Any such delegation shall be made in writing and subject to any conditions the directors may impose, and may be revoked or altered.'

They can also delegate such powers or functions to any individual trustee, committee, chief executive officer/head teacher or, in fact, any other holder of an executive office. That person or committee must report to the board:

> 'in respect of any action taken or decision made with respect to the exercise of that power or function at the meeting of the directors immediately following the taking of the action or the making of the decision'.

Despite any delegation, the board remains accountable and it is essential that the communication mechanisms are set up to ensure seamless reporting.

The remit of powers and functions delegated need not be the same for all academies within a MAT. In many models, responsibilities are delegated on a case-by-case basis according to the strengths of the particular academy. This means that an academy which is graded Good or Outstanding and with good ongoing performance can be delegated a great deal more power than an academy which needs ongoing support or which has joined the MAT as it was regarded as a failing school. This scenario is often known as 'earned autonomy'.

A scheme of delegation setting out what decisions have been delegated by the board needs to be agreed. This will define the lines of responsibility and accountability and should be clear enough so that everyone involved in the MAT knows how and where decisions can be made.

The NGA has worked with MATs to develop a series of Model Schemes of Delegation which can be adopted.

Schools converting to join a MAT should consider the Schemes of Delegation in place and the level of responsibility, if any, that is delegated to any LGB and whether this accords with their wishes. However, schools should bear in mind that the board of trustees decides on the level of delegation appropriate and can decide to change that level or remove it entirely at a later date!

Church schools

Formal agreements between the DfE and the Church of England and the Catholic Church have been developed and set out in memoranda of understanding. The memoranda contain the agreed approach to academisation of church schools and both the National Society and the Catholic Education Service have been involved in their development.

COMMENT

Howard Dellar of Lee Bolton Monier-Williams outlines the requirements on church schools joining MATs:

'The manner in which church schools should convert to academies as part of a MAT is governed by Memoranda of Understanding made between the Department for Education and respectively the National Society (for the Church of England) and the Catholic Education Service (for the Catholic Church) dated April 2016. Schools which have a non-denominational "Christian" character and schools belonging to other Christian and religious groups are not covered, but the principles set out in the Memoranda may be of relevance to those. For both Church of England and Catholic Schools the model documentation agreed between the Department for Education and the churches must be used. Do ensure that all necessary consents (e.g. from site trustees) have been obtained.

For Church of England schools the shared expectation is that church schools that wish to convert will do so as part of a MAT with governance arrangements that reflect, at member and director level, no dilution of the level of church governance and involvement as it was immediately prior to conversion. Where a Voluntary Aided (church majority governance) school enters a MAT, there are church majority model articles for this. Where a Voluntary Controlled (church minority governance) enters into a MAT, either with other VC schools, or with schools without a religious designation, there are church minority model articles for that scenario.

A Diocesan Board of Education may, in a small minority of circumstances, support church schools joining an existing MAT which has up to that point had no church involvement in governance (e.g. a MAT which has not previously had a church school). The Church of England and the DfE have agreed a special model form of articles for this situation which is available only with the prior agreement of the relevant diocese and Regional Schools Commissioner. A Church of England diocese may also occasionally support a VA school going into a church minority-governed MAT. In both these cases, the Church of England Memorandum of Understanding requires appropriate safeguards to be put in place for the church school including the members of the MAT entering into an approved form of Members' Agreement which will (inter alia) confirm the members and directors' various responsibilities for protecting the church school's character.'

Catholic schools

The Catholic Church is responsible for some 1,811 primary schools, 377 secondary schools and 49 all-age schools, making up some 10% of state-funded schools across England and Wales.

The majority of the board will be foundation governors appointed on behalf of the church. They have a legal duty to preserve and develop the Catholic character of the school and must sign a declaration to that effect when they are appointed.

This means that Catholic schools can only convert in MATs with other Catholic schools. This is in line with the decision of the Catholic Bishops' Conference of England and Wales and the underlying strategy that all schools are based on 'an educational philosophy in which faith, culture and life are brought into harmony'.

The memorandum provides that communication of policy changes must be made nationally through the Catholic Education Service rather than through RSCs on a local level. The first point of contact for any matter concerning any Catholic school is the Diocesan Schools Commissioner, appointed in individual dioceses to fulfil the rights and responsibilities of the Archbishop.

Any Catholic schools wishing to convert to academies must obtain the prior consent of the Diocesan Bishop.

Where any Catholic school is causing concern, an 'appropriate solution' will be sought 'in consultation with the Diocese' which must 'reflect and protect its existing designation and the ethos of that school'. A sponsor may be agreed 'where local circumstances indicate that this would be an appropriate way forward and in consultation with the relevant Diocese'. The presumption in such cases will be that the 'Diocese's preferred sponsorship arrangements will be accepted if the Secretary of State is satisfied that the sponsorship package contains the appropriate capacity and expertise to address the needs of the particular school causing concern'.

A Catholic academy cannot become a sponsor without the express consent of the Diocesan Bishop and the DfE acknowledges that it will 'ensure that such consent will be forthcoming before considering any application'. However, the Catholic Education Service notes that 'the availability of strong academy sponsors is central to driving up performance in a school-led system', so it is unlikely that suitable sponsor applicants will be refused.

If a sponsored Catholic academy underperforms and requires urgent remedial action, the relevant RSC will engage with the Diocesan Schools Commissioner to agree alternative support arrangements through re-brokerage.

Church of England schools

There are 4,500 CofE primary schools and over 200 CofE secondary schools. However, the governance arrangements of the maintained CofE school will have an impact on the academisation routes open to it.

Unlike Catholic schools, the majority of CofE schools have no requirement for children to attend church or come from a family of practising Christians. CofE schools are inclusive and established primarily for the communities where they are located irrespective of the faith of pupils or their families.

Nevertheless, the DfE confirms its commitment 'to securing the religious character of every church school and to preserving diocesan families of schools'.

Each individual Diocese has a Diocesan Board of Education (DBE) with a Diocesan Director of Education (DDE).

Any school wishing to convert to academy status must seek the prior consent of the DBE as well as any other Church trust or diocesan body that may be connected with the school, such as by owning the land on which it is sited. The DfE 'respects the statutory right and requirement for the consent' but it does 'expect the DBE's final consent to be quickly forthcoming'.

CofE schools wishing to join or establish a MAT must ensure that the articles of association reflect the appropriate Church representation in the governance of the MAT. A Voluntary Controlled school has diocesan or foundation governors in the minority, whereas in a Voluntary Aided school they are in the majority – this must generally be reflected in the MAT model following conversion. This means that MATs with foundation governors in the minority have 25% of members and trustees which is increased to 75% for the majority foundation governor model. However, many DDEs take a pragmatic approach to academisation and in exceptional circumstances may approve an arrangement where a VA school joins a MAT with a Church minority or a Church school joins an existing MAT without

Church governance. In such cases, it is essential that the religious character and ethos of the school is preserved and safeguarded:

'Apart from normal clauses required in the associated Supplemental Funding Agreement the Secretary of State recognises that special changes to the articles including a reference to schemes of delegation to local governing bodies or equivalent and a Members' Agreement in models agreed with the National Society will be required.'

CofE schools wishing to become sponsors must 'seek and secure the support of their DBE before applying, and . . . the application [must] confirm:

i. The school's commitment to taking on and helping underperforming schools to improve;
ii. That the MAT will be set up in accordance with the Church of England minority or majority model articles as appropriate and will be conducted in accordance with a Members' Agreement in the model agreed between the Secretary of State and the National Society.'

Any maintained Church schools which are identified as inadequate will be expected to be sponsored as an academy and:

'The Secretary of State and the National Society both expect a diocesan or strong church school-led MAT will be the outcome in the vast majority of cases'.

This will also be the case for underperforming Church academies and any academy where the distinctive Christian character is at risk. The RSC will engage with the DBE at the earliest opportunity to secure an appropriate re-brokerage of the academy into a different MAT.

Umbrella trust

The umbrella trust has fallen out of favour with the DfE and it looks unlikely that any new arrangements will be approved. In this collaborative arrangement, the over-arching body, or umbrella, is a charitable trust in its own right with its own board. Each of the individual schools is a single academy trust. An umbrella trust also allows schools of different status such as community, VC and VA to work together in a formal structure without having to alter their governance structure or change the representation by a faith or other foundation body.

There is a lot of flexibility in the model to decide on the level of collaboration and joint working. The umbrella often has the power to appoint members or trustees to the individual academy schools providing a governance link. A close structure could be set up whereby the umbrella enables collaboration and shared governance which could include central services, employment of umbrella staff and a shared vision and strategy. A much looser arrangement may be preferred where the single academies wish to remain relatively independent.

Unfortunately, umbrella trusts have not produced the level of governance and collaboration required in a self-supporting system. Consequently, we are unlikely to see the model continued long term and the DfE is now clear that it prefers the more formalised approach provided by the MAT model.

Free schools

Free schools were set up by the Coalition government following the general election in 2010. They were influenced by similar models in Sweden and New Zealand and the Charter movement in the US and Canada.

They are state-funded schools, independent of LA control. Academically non-selective free schools are nevertheless subject to the School Admissions Code of Practice (with the exception that they are allowed to give priority to founders' children). Free schools are charitable companies limited by guarantee in just the same way as academies. In other words, free schools are a type of academy. This has been recognised by the Labour shadow cabinet who plan to rebrand them 'Parent-led academies' if, and when, it gets into power.

Free schools can be set up by 'proposer groups' of parents, teachers, charities or other groups. Free schools can be mainstream, special, alternative provision or 16- to 19-year-old schools which have demonstrated evidence of demand in the area. The group applying to set up a free school will generally adopt complete responsibility for the management of the school on an ongoing basis. Alternatively, it may be possible for the group to either hand over day-to-day running of the school or transfer complete control to an external education provider. Many of the existing free schools have been set up by existing providers and academy chains. At present, free schools cannot be set up or be taken over by for-profit companies. The proposer group must use the pre-opening period to identify appropriate trustees. The DfE will provide guidance in designing governance structures and reporting arrangements to drive school improvement.

Independent schools

Independent schools can convert to academy status but they do so via the free school route.

Studio schools

Studio schools were also introduced by the Coalition government in 2010. Intended as innovative institutions offering project-based practical learning as well as mainstream academic qualifications, they are schools for 14- to 19-year-olds which are set up with the backing of local businesses and employers. Studio schools are small with around 300 students. They follow workplace opening hours with a 9 to 5 working day and year-round timetable.

Studio schools offer core academic qualifications together with more vocational qualifications, all of which are taught following a practical and project-based approach. Study is combined with paid work placements. Studio schools endeavour to provide students with the skills that are required by employers including punctuality, good communication, reliability and team-working, whilst ensuring a strong grounding in English, maths and science.

The DfE states that there is a benefit to being part of a strong partnership with successful secondary schools and therefore there is a 'presumption that any future studio schools will be established as part of a multi-academy trust (MAT) alongside other highly performing secondary schools'. Although the single academy structure is not ruled out, it would require significant evidence of how the 'educational and financial benefits offered by MATs will be secured in alternative ways'.

Studio schools are a type of academy, and a model funding agreement and annexes are available.

University technical colleges (UTCs)

UTCs are technical academies for 14- to 19-year-olds and are sponsored by universities and employers; UTCs are all-ability and co-educational. Typically, further education colleges and other educational institutions such as established academies work in partnership with a UTC. The UTC programme is sponsored by the Baker Dearing Trust, an educational trust established by Lord Kenneth Baker, former Secretary of State for Education.

Typically with around 500–800 students drawn from a catchment area that can extend across a number of local authorities, UTCs offer technically orientated courses of study which are taught alongside core GCSEs. There is a focus on disciplines that require modern, highly specialised equipment such as engineering, manufacturing and construction, which are taught alongside general business and ICT skills. UTCs prepare students for a range of careers and continuing education at 19.

UTCs are generally for pupils aged from 14–19 years of age on the basis that university and employer sponsors regard this as the right age for a young person to choose to follow a more specialised technical route. However, the DfE has acknowledged that it may be challenging to recruit pupils at an age when they do not normally change schools. A UTC can apply to start at an earlier age if it can show that it would 'improve pupil recruitment and be of benefit to the educational landscape locally'.

UTCs are a form of academy, and a model funding agreement and annexes are available.

Nominees of the employer and university sponsors must together form the majority on the board of trustees.

3 Becoming an academy

There are various routes to becoming an academy which will largely depend on whether it is a new or existing school and, if it is an existing school, whether it is deemed to be a good/outstanding school or has issues which put in doubt its ability to improve itself. However, once set up, all academies have the same legal structure, although the details of the individual constitution will differ from academy to academy depending on the funding agreement and articles.

Free schools

It is possible to set up a new free school for mainstream, 16 to 19, alternative provision, special and studio schools.

Independent schools can also convert to academy status by going through the free school process. The DfE states that an independent school is unlikely to be approved to become a free school unless it is possible to prove that it will 'provide good value for money and will be successful in the state sector'.

It is important to establish evidence of need in the area in which the school will be situated showing that children and young people would attend. However, there is no longer a requirement to conduct a parental demand survey. Occasionally a local authority will identify the need to set up a new school and, in this case, a competition is launched to choose a group to run the new school. Local authorities retain the responsibility to ensure that there are sufficient school places and this is the route they must use to fulfil that responsibility.

Outline of the free school application process:

- Apply within the twice-yearly application timeframes.
- The DfE assess against their criteria but the application must cover:
  - suitability of the applicant with a 'strong educational track record'
  - the vision and rationale for the free school
  - an education plan that will achieve the vision
  - evidence of need in the area
  - financial plans that are consistent with the application and demonstrate financial viability
  - any potential sites for the school.

- Suitable applications may be invited to attend an interview where the DfE will question applicants about the proposal.
- The application is approved or rejected on the basis of the application and performance at interview.

Once the application has been approved, the project enters its 'pre-opening' phase. A designated contact in the DfE's Free Schools Group (FSG) will be assigned to work with the group through to opening.

Established MATs and approved sponsors may have already discussed their capacity and capability with their RSC and agreed, in principle, how many free schools their trust had the expertise and time available to open. This information will be used by the DfE to assess capacity.

Free advice and guidance can be obtained from the New Schools Network, an independent charity set up to support free school applicants. The Studio Schools Trust is another independent charity that developed the studio school model which can provide support and advice to applicants.

University technical colleges (UTCs)

The UTC programme is sponsored by the Baker Dearing Educational Trust (BDT), which was founded by Lord Baker and Lord Dearing specifically with the aim of developing and promoting the concept of UTCs. The advisory team of BDT provides guidance and supports applications to open new UTCs.

UTC academy trusts are required to sign a licence agreement with BDT which prescribes the terms for use of the UTC brand and must pay an annual subscription providing access to BDT's services and support.

When considering applications to set up a new UTC, there is a presumption by the DfE that any future UTCs will be established with strong, preferably formalised, partnership arrangements such as a MAT, working closely with a MAT or being part of another educational partnership arrangement with good or outstanding schools. MATs can apply to set up a UTC. There must also be strong evidence of need for the UTC in the location. The DfE have committed to one UTC within the reach of every city and believes that UTCs have a better chance of succeeding and attracting pupils if they are located in areas where:

- there is a large population of primary and secondary aged children and 16–19-year-old pupils within the catchment area to ensure current and future viability;
- there is no other similar technical provision within reasonable travelling distance of the proposed site;
- public transport links are good; and
- existing secondary schools are at capacity and/or underperforming.

Applications must be submitted within the appropriate window and will be assessed against the DfE's criteria and against other UTC applications, taking into account a range of contextual factors including value for money, how the proposed UTC will make use of academy freedoms to improve standards in the local area and relevant developments in area-based reviews of post-16 provision. Particular emphasis is put on the capacity and capability of the proposer group, especially:

- being part of a strong partnership including successful secondary schools;
- relevant secondary education expertise;
- the track record and level of commitment of those in the proposer group who run existing education provision;
- expertise in school finances; and
- employer and university expertise in the chosen specialism(s) which are linked to local, regional and/or national skills gaps/needs.

Forced academisation

All schools deemed to be failing or 'coasting' will be required to become academies. This sets the bar much lower than previous equivalent levels for maintained schools, where an Interim Executive Board (IEB) would be appointed for a school put into special measures. The requirement will apply to those failing schools but also to 'coasting schools' which is much more widely defined.

Schools will be deemed to be 'coasting' if, for a period of three years, they have 'failed to push every pupil to reach their potential'. A 'floor standard' is set below which a school should not fall without immediate intervention and/or scrutiny being required. The coasting levels are proposed to be set at a higher level on the same measure. Schools will only be deemed to be coasting if they fall below this level in three successive years. Data for coasting schools shows that pupil performance is below a reasonable level for attainment as well as progress. The measures mean that schools with challenging intakes who are providing sufficient challenge as reflected in progress data will not be caught by the data. By contrast, those schools which have achieved good results but had strong cohorts which could have made more progress will!

The White Paper, Educational Excellence Everywhere, published in March 2016, promised to make every state-funded school an academy by 2022. Following an outcry, the Rt Hon Nicky Morgan MP, Secretary of State for Education, announced that schools would not be forced to academise if they did not wish. However, schools will be required to become academies if:

- they are found to be underperforming or coasting;
- the local authority fails to meet a 'minimum performance threshold' across its schools; or
- a 'critical mass' has been reached indicating that the local authority can no longer viably support the remaining schools.

It seems likely, therefore, that all schools in time will be forced to academise. The timescales are unclear but the majority of schools are expected to have converted before the original 2022 deadline. There is an inevitability to complete academisation: more schools converting and less local authorities offering services and support means that there is less reason or incentive to remain a maintained school.

Those schools that are deemed to be underperforming or coasting may find that their route to academisation is mapped out for them, joining a MAT which promises to make the improvement necessary.

However, all schools should undertake their own research and consider the arrangements that could provide the support necessary. Schools have an opportunity to control their own destiny in a real way.

Sponsorship

Historically, the very first academies were recipients of sponsorship funding and support. Failing schools were transformed physically with shiny new buildings and facilities. Significant amounts of money helped to transform them into the academies for the future.

Sadly though, this type of sponsorship arrangement has largely disappeared. However, there are now opportunities for sponsorship arrangements negotiated on an individual basis depending on the particular circumstances and the schools concerned. Sponsors can be another educational establishment or from any other type of organisation or industry: the success of the UTC relies on sponsorship arrangements with industry and universities. Schools looking to convert, even 'Good' or 'Outstanding' schools, should look at possible sponsorship arrangements that will benefit their pupils.

COMMENT

Kirsty Watt, Head of Academy Ambassadors at the New Schools Network, highlights the importance of having the right board in place to ensure that sponsorship arrangements are successful:

'Sponsorship often means turnaround

- Do the board understand turnaround?
- Have they the experience?
- Would they be able to lead at pace?
- Do they do culture change?
- Who is there to support the CEO in the hard decisions?'

The DfE will sometimes provide some funding to trusts sponsoring a failing school. However, there are no guarantees and it is essential to negotiate a deal which could include writing off historical deficits, and the DfE will usually pay a restructuring grant to cover the cost of staff redundancies or similar costs.

A good sponsorship arrangement, though, is more than simply a one-way support mechanism and it offers the sponsor opportunities for growth and development.

COMMENT

Wellington College Academy Trust is a MAT based in Tidworth, Wiltshire, which is sponsored by leading independent school, Wellington College. Executive Principal, Dr Mike Milner:

'Sponsorship relationships imply that there is an inequality of organisational strength as many come about from failed providers needing rapid improvement. Although sponsorship therefore implies one direction of support – from sponsor to academy – these relationships need to be of mutual benefit if they are going to work in the long term. Sponsors will gain from the experience of supporting another school, for example by learning about other contexts and working with a larger staff pool. The potential benefits to the academy being sponsored are obvious, although it is dependent on careful planning: the magic of the sponsor does not imply rub off. Crucially, successful school improvement also needs the sponsored academy to develop its own capacity to improve alongside whatever additional help it receives from the sponsor. There is no point thinking that lasting success will be dependent on long-term intensive support. Therefore, it is important to think about what the relationship will be like in both the short and long term.

On a practical level, sponsored academies benefit from staffing and expertise across the whole range of school operations: from teaching to premises management. Financial support, given the current economic climate that schools face, is desirable and can be used to accelerate improvement or maintain standards. Recruitment and retention of the best staff will be enhanced in schools that struggle in this area if the sponsorship is successful and staff are valued. Students themselves may benefit from working with children from another context.'

Converting to a single academy trust

Multi-academy trusts (MATs) arrived quite late to the party. The early converter academies were single academy trusts (SATs) (see Chapter 2) and retained their independence as individual educational institutions. This was a realistic possibility for the large secondary schools with the resources to support academisation. However, the situation is now very different and the DfE states that 'not all schools are able to convert as single academies'.

To be able to convert as a SAT, a school must have:

- 'outstanding' or 'good' Ofsted grading
- above national average pupil attainment and progress
- healthy finances.

Schools will, however, be under pressure to convert as a MAT. At the very least, they will be required to indicate what school/s they will support and great care should be taken in identifying such schools as the SAT could well find itself becoming part of a MAT with that school in due course.

Converting to a multi-academy trust

The DfE have made quite clear that:

> 'we expect that most schools will form or join multi-academy trusts as they become academies'

The process for a school joining an established MAT is simpler as the structures and governance arrangements are already in place. However, schools must undertake robust due diligence and be absolutely clear that they are happy with what is on offer and that it aligns with their own vision and ethos.

The terminology is confusing – the schools in the MAT are known as 'academies' but are not academy trusts in their own right. All academies in a MAT are governed by a single trust and a single board of trustees. The trustees can establish a separate governing body for each of their academies and can maximise economies of scale in procurement and sharing of staff and resources. However, it must be remembered that the trustees can decide at a later date to change the internal governance arrangements and level of delegation to the local governing bodies or individual academies.

To set up a new MAT, each school in the proposed trust needs to submit a separate application and each governing body must pass a resolution to convert to become an academy. Evidence must be provided of how the stronger schools in the proposed MAT will help the weaker schools to improve.

If a school is in an existing federation they will be in an arrangement where two or more schools work together under one governing body. In this case, the school must comply with the School Governance (Federations) (England) Regulations 2012 (as amended) which requires that the support of at least 50% of its 'prescribed governors' must be obtained before applying to convert. 'Prescribed governors' are the head teacher, parent governors, staff governors and foundation governors.

Stone King outlines the key advantages and disadvantages of MATs:

Table 3.1: Key advantages and disadvantages of MATs

Advantages	Disadvantages
■ Possibility of cohesive strategic leadership through MAT structure ■ Increased flexibility and operational efficiencies – less duplication of effort than two single academy trusts ■ Increased value for money and buying power through economies of scale ■ Top-down approach to driving school improvement allows academies to achieve strong collaboration and to use this collaboration and accountability to drive up school standards ■ Sharing best practice and staff and leadership development opportunities ■ Possibility of broader range of opportunities and benefits for students and staff ■ One single employer – allowing greater flexibility for employer over staff teams ■ Any future schools can easily be brought within the MAT family.	■ Possibility of becoming a 'mini-LA' without LA equivalent economies of scale ■ No 'firewall' – risk of financial or educational failure for a single school affects all other schools ■ Academy budgets may be top sliced to support the central organisation ■ No clear exit route for an academy which wishes to leave the MAT.

Outline of the academy conversion process

It is sensible for any school to undertake detailed research before embarking on the academy conversion process, irrespective of the route to conversion.

The process as set out by the DfE:

Pre-application

■ Submit a registration of interest form to the DfE who will then contact the school and allocate a project lead to work with the school through the conversion process.

■ Read the *Academies Financial Handbook* to understand the financial responsibilities of an academy (see Chapter 12).

- Consider the different types of academy structures (see Chapter 2).
- Obtain consent of:
  - ☐ governing body
  - ☐ the MAT (for schools wishing to join an established MAT)
  - ☐ the trust or foundation (for foundation schools and voluntary schools with a foundation)
  - ☐ the religious body (for church and faith schools).
- Prepare the application including the names and experience of the people that will be part of the academy's governance structure.
- Schools with a PFI contract will need to complete additional steps.
- Start informal discussions with staff about the Transfer of Undertakings (Protection of Employment) Regulations 2006 (TUPE) process.

Start of the conversion process

- Appoint a legal adviser.
- Get an actuarial assessment on pension contributions.
- Compile a list of all contracts held by the school/local authority.
- Complete the academy conversion application form and submit to the DfE.
- Notify the local authority of the decision to convert.

Set up or join an academy trust

- The academy order will be granted between two and six weeks after successful submission of the application form.
- A support grant of £25,000 will be paid into the school's existing bank account within 14 working days.
- Ask the project lead about eligibility for primary academy chain development grant or small school supplement grant.
- Formally appoint a solicitor.
- Statutory consultation with staff, parents, pupils and the wider community.
- Apply to open the academy's bank account.
- Solicitor completes and returns the land questionnaire.
- Solicitor submits draft memorandum and articles of association, and funding agreement based on the relevant model documentation.
- Register with Companies House when the memorandum and articles of association have been approved by the DfE.
- Appoint trustees if setting up as an academy or MAT.

Transfer responsibilities to the academy

- Solicitor makes arrangements for land to be transferred to the academy school and local authority sign the commercial transfer agreement (CTA) which records all local authority contracts and staff transferring to the academy.

- Staff are transferred to the academy through the TUPE process which follows the rules set out by the TUPE (as amended).
- Agree use of shared facilities.
- Agree changes to contracts for unfinished building works.
- Review contracts with external providers and agree novation if appropriate.

Prepare to open as an academy

- Finalise consultation.
- Sign the funding agreement which is then counter-signed and dated by the Secretary of State.
- Open the academy bank account and send the details to the EFA by the middle of the month in which the academy will open.
- Appoint the accounting officer, chief financial officer and external auditors (see Chapter 12).
- Register with the Information Commissioner's Office and appoint a data protection officer (see Chapter 17).
- Finalise insurance arrangements (see Chapter 15).
- Contact Edubase so that the academy's new unique reference number (URN) is issued.
- Secondary schools must notify the National Centre Number Register of the change to academy status and any change of name, though the same exam centre number can continue to be used.

Following opening

- A welcome letter and information pack outlining the steps that must be completed in the first few months of opening is received from the EFA.
- The first payment will be received direct from the EFA.
- The academy financial support grant expenditure certificate is completed by the chair of governors confirming how the grant has been spent and whether any will be carried over into the academy's budget.
- The funding agreement must be published on the academy's website.
- The land and buildings valuation form must be completed within six weeks of conversion.

TUPE

When a school converts to become an academy, the staff will be transferred over to the new legal entity and the academy becomes the employer of the staff. The Transfer of Undertakings (Protection of Employment) Regulations 2006 (TUPE) as amended by Collective Redundancies and Transfer of Undertakings (Protection of Employment) (Amendment) Regulations 2014 will protect the terms and conditions of such transferring staff so that they transfer on identical contractual terms. This means that the school staff (who will have been employed by the local authority or school governing body) automatically become employees of the academy on the date of conversion.

TUPE will also apply if a school joins an existing MAT or, if at a later date, it is removed from one academy chain and joins another.

Once the academy order has been granted, the employer (local authority/ school board of governors) must begin the TUPE process.

There are specific TUPE obligations in relation to notification to, and consultation with, unions and employee representatives. The employer must inform and consult with employees through 'appropriate' elected representatives – these could be trade union representatives or, in the absence of a recognised trade union, formally elected employee representatives. Since 2014 it has not been necessary to elect representatives to inform and consult where there are no existing recognised trade unions or elected employee representatives if there are fewer than 10 employees overall. This is extremely unlikely in the case of a school, but, in such a case, the board of governors would need to inform and consult directly with each individual employee regarding the transfer.

Employees must be given information in writing about the transfer which includes:

- the fact that the transfer is going to take place, approximately when and why
- any social, legal or economic implications for the affected employees
- any measures that the outgoing and incoming employers expect to take in respect of their own employees (even if this is nothing)
- the number of agency workers employed, the departments they are working in and the type of work they are doing
- any measures which the incoming employer is considering taking in respect of affected employees.

The employer must provide the academy with employee liability information.

A trust cannot change an employee's terms and conditions unless the reason is an 'economic, technical or organisational reason' (ETO) involving changes in the workforce or workplace and is not related to the transfer. The employee must agree to any change. Trusts can, of course, decide to improve employees' terms and conditions or they can decide to consult with employees to make changes.

Pensions

Teachers working in an academy are still subject to the Teachers' Pension Regulations 2010 and belong to the Teachers' Pension Scheme (TPS). The TPS is a defined benefit scheme with index-linked pensions. Contributions are made by both the employer (i.e. the academy) and the scheme member (i.e. the member of teaching staff). The TPS is a national scheme, but the academy will be responsible for all administrative matters in connection with it and will need to pay for an audit which is likely to be required annually. Liability for the TPS is long term and funded through contributions; the deficit represents a gap calculated under certain assumptions made by the actuary which is likely to represent an inflationary pressure on future funding in order to reduce the deficit.

MATs should give careful consideration and, if necessary, take advice regarding the eligibility of any executive head to join the TPS. Whilst head teachers will fall within the scheme where they are the academic head and responsible for the teaching and learning function, an executive head who occupies a mainly financial or administrative role would not. Eligibility is determined by the MAT on an individual basis and will depend on the particular circumstances of the case.

Non-teaching staff will be eligible for membership of the Local Government Pension Scheme (LGPS) although not all support staff choose to become members. The LGPS is a 'defined contribution' scheme so only the amount paid in by the staff member and employer is set. Therefore, an independent actuarial assessment is made which will take into account the age profile of the staff involved. The assessment is used to determine the academy's contributions. The LGPS is locally administered; the academy will become an 'admitted body' of the scheme in its local area. Annual reports from the LGPS actuary may be required at an additional cost to the academy.

The presence of the LGPS valuation does cause an issue in accounting terms, albeit theoretical. Often the pension fund will be found to be managing a deficit which transfers from the LA to the academy at conversion. This liability will impact on the bottom line of the accounts so that it appears that the academy is insolvent as liabilities are greater than assets. The Charity Commission has advised that this will not be indicative of insolvency because the deficit is being reduced by the contribution made. Nevertheless, it is good practice to provide a full explanation in the notes to the accounts.

Stakeholder management

There is a statutory consultation requirement for both new academies and converters. For existing schools, the consultation should be carried out with existing parents of pupils, staff, pupils and the wider community. There are specific additional requirements in respect of TUPE consultations for staff (see above). New free schools or other new academy structures should consult with stakeholders, the local community and anyone else appropriate.

The process should be embraced by schools and proposer groups. It gives an ideal opportunity to address concerns and allay fears raised by the changes proposed as well as giving useful feedback and suggestions. It can also form a central element in a wider marketing strategy which helps to raise awareness of the new academy and could help to increase pupil numbers.

The consultation process is normally run for a minimum of six weeks. It must be done before the funding agreement is signed. However, it is important that the process is advanced enough to give meaningful information to those interested.

It is a good idea to use various different media to reach as many people as possible and popular channels include use of a website, mailshots, leaflets, open meetings and media announcements. It is also sensible to consider translating consultation materials if the school is in an area with a diverse population.

All responses should be considered so that any necessary changes or additions can be made. A report of the key findings should be drawn up and published to any interested parties as well as provided to the DfE if required.

Marketing

Having a marketing strategy is absolutely vital for new schools to attract sufficient pupils to make the project viable. However, marketing should be considered by all schools looking to become academies and should become an element in every school development plan going forward.

Key to successful marketing is knowing the audience and feedback from statutory consultations is a useful way to gain an insight into their worries and motivation. Regular targeted updates are generally more effective than one major campaign – keep in touch using a variety of channels. Make sure information is up to date so that the website is continuously developed, newsletters are issued regularly and emails or telephone calls are answered quickly.

Advertising is usually expensive and can have limited results. It is possible to achieve publicity on local radio or television by suggesting creative ideas for programme content or inviting along a reporter to events that may be of interest. They may also be interested to hear from a spokesperson for topical on-air debates or phone-in programmes. Always send a press release to the local papers or invite them in to take photos – but make sure that any pupils selected have appropriate permission to be photographed!

It is sensible to have a single individual with the responsibility for marketing/advertising and for ensuring a consistent profile. Any spokesperson, generally the principal/principal designate, will wish to develop that profile further.

Build up contacts in the media – there will be a better response to a press release or email sent to an individual who has already had dealings with the academy than one that is just sent to an anonymous news@ email address.

Social media is also a very powerful tool but needs to be in the hands of someone who knows how to use it! A social media message can very quickly become something that was not intended.

Events can give an opportunity for prospective parents and the wider community to hear the message that the academy is giving and to visit the school site to see for themselves what is going on and to meet staff. Open days, mock lessons or enrichment days are a popular way to entice families into the academy.

Land transfer

Land transfer can be a complicated aspect of the conversion process. The appointed solicitor must complete the land questionnaire giving details about the ownership of the land on which the school is based, legal arrangements for the use of land including any restrictions, shared usage, current or planned building works, as well as whether there are any leisure facilities, nurseries or children's centres on the land and how these are operated.

The solicitor will also have conducted title searches to ascertain the ownership of land if it is registered. The transfer will depend on the ownership. However, generally the position after conversion will replicate the situation beforehand, i.e. the academy will have no greater claim over the land than they did before.

Due to the complexities in this area, specialist legal advice is recommended.

Land owned by local authority:
Community schools enter into a long-term lease of 125 years with the local authority. Whilst this will transfer a beneficial interest giving exclusive possession of the school site to the academy, the freehold remains the property of the local authority. There is a model long-term lease which should be used.

Land owned by a foundation or trust, or the school's governing body:
If the freehold of the school site is to be transferred to the academy, the model directions relating to the particular type of academy are used.

Land held by a trust or foundation that is not a diocese:
A trust modification order is used based on the model relevant to the type of academy. This is likely to be required for schools which are:

- voluntary controlled
- voluntary aided
- foundation.

Church schools
Church schools are often sited on land that is a mixture of privately and publicly owned land. Generally the diocese owns the church buildings and the local authority owns the playing fields, although other more complicated arrangements may be in place where there are also trusts. This means that the solicitor will need to:

- negotiate the long-term lease from the local authority;
- complete the land supplemental agreement to transfer the use of buildings from the school to the academy trust; and
- agree a trust modification order.

COMMENT

Howard Dellar of Lee Bolton Monier-Williams outlines the extra due diligence needed for Church schools:

'Church schools, and particularly Church of England schools, many of which date back to at least the nineteenth century, tend to throw up a large number of issues which relate to the land and trusts of the school site. Commonly, the land will be unregistered or there will be discrepancies with the registration, and often title and trust deeds will have been lost or be incomplete. It may be necessary to look behind what is registered at the Land Registry. A Church school site registered to the local authority will be subject to an outstanding obligation on the part of the local authority (under the School Standards and Frameworks Act 1998) to carry out a transfer of the land to the trustees of the school. Such a transfer must take place prior to the conversion of the school, as otherwise the obligation on the local authority to make the transfer will fall away. What is part of the "school site" as opposed to playing fields can be the cause of disagreement.'

PFI schools

Academisation can be less straightforward for a school which is part of a private finance initiative (PFI) construction scheme. There is extra complexity and additional documentation is needed to protect all parties' interests.

COMMENT

Matthew Wolton, Partner at Clark Holt Commercial Solicitors:

'Being a PFI school is not an absolute barrier to a school converting to academy status, but there are enough difficulties and complications involved that the implications must be considered carefully before deciding to proceed.

Unlike the early heady days of the academy explosion in 2010, when the DfE "bought" schools out of their PFI contracts, the current approach is that PFI schools must remain part of the PFI arrangement when they convert to an academy. This means there is a significant amount more legal work needed to achieve conversion. In simple terms the local authority will still have all its obligations to the PFI contractor (e.g. allowing it access to the school and enabling it to do its job), but they will no longer have active control of the school to allow them to meet these obligations. This means the academy will have to enter into an agreement which obliges it to meet the local authority's obligations. There will also be an agreement in favour of the local authority whereby the DfE effectively underwrites the academy's performance.

Although detailed and lengthy, the conversion of a PFI school is a tested procedure and will generally not cause problems. What is more important to understand is the practical consequences of an academy being part of a PFI contract. One of the fundamental attractions of being an academy is the freedom to make its own decisions – these freedoms can be significantly curtailed when the PFI contract sets out when the school opens, what use can be made of the premises outside "school hours", what the cost of electricity is etc. Of even more relevance is the financial contribution the academy will need to make to cover the costs of "the PFI membership". If the academy is to be part of a MAT, then serious consideration will need to be given as to how the school will avoid being isolated and how it can be helped to feel "part of the family". This is because the MAT is likely to put various things into place for the rest of its schools that the PFI school won't be able to take part in, whether that's a catering contract, new ICT provision etc.

In theory there is no problem in an academy seeking to vary the terms of the relevant PFI contract to its benefit, but in practice there are two major complications:

1. The academy cannot negotiate directly with the PFI contractor, it would have to be done through the local authority; and

2. In many cases the original PFI contractor will have passed its interests on to a syndicate of banks. Rather than negotiate a variation with one entity, the academy would have to get the approval of all the relevant parties which might mean multiple banks, all of whom are risk-averse and would want their full legal costs reimbursed as a starting point.'

▓ Role of the local authority

The local authority is involved in the academisation process as legal responsibility for operating the school is passed to the trust board. However, the local authority retains certain obligations despite academisation.

COMMENT

Charlotte Christie, Academies and Collaborations Co-ordinator at Oxfordshire County Council, explained:

'In Oxfordshire the LA has a small academies team (2.4 fte) which co-ordinates the work of the various teams within the county, such as property and HR, and instructs the county solicitors. The Team maintains a website providing information on the process and produces guides for school and officers on the tasks involved in the conversion process.

Where the LA owns the site the 125-year lease is negotiated using a standard template. The difficulties occur when there are third party users or the LA requires continued use of any parts of the site; for example for a library or Adult Education facility. The terms for use need to be formally documented in order to be transferred to the academy usually through a sub-lease.

The authority retains its responsibility for individual children in the looked-after system and as a champion for all children. In this capacity it monitors the data of academies though reference to what is in the public domain, e.g. Ofsted reports, and standards data provided by the academies and raises any concern with the academy and, if necessary, the RSC. The LA has produced a protocol which is issued to all academies.'

Mergers and acquisitions

In June 2016, National Schools Commissioner Sir David Carter told the Commons Education Committee that 119 academies had been removed from their sponsors and placed in new trusts. Clearly, Regional Schools Commissioners are now acting to 'rebroker' academies where performance is not acceptable. There are no formal guidelines regarding when the circumstances requiring rebrokerage will be deemed to have been met but it will be when the academy's performance is unacceptable and the MAT does not have the capacity to ensure improvement. There have already been a significant number of academies removed from one MAT to join another.

It is extremely likely that the movement of academies between MATs will continue and further develop. There are also likely to be structural changes to MATs both in terms of MATs joining together and splitting up to become separate legal entities. It is hoped that in time further guidance will be produced to set out the circumstances when rebrokerage is required and the way in which academies can be transferred from one MAT to another.

4 MATs and due diligence

The DfE's preferred model for academies in the future is the multi-academy trust (MAT). The MAT is a single legal entity run by a board of trustees. However, the MAT is still relatively immature and is likely to develop in complexity and structures in due course.

Likewise, individual MATs develop as they grow in size. This will be reflected in the need to develop the board to deal with the demands of the MAT.

COMMENT

Kirsty Watt, Head of Academy Ambassadors at the New Schools Network, explained that a 'good board is not a board for life' and will need to be adapted as they develop:

'At 1–3 schools the trust is a start-up and needs board members who understand what it is to grow an SME while holding onto the outcomes for the children.

At around 6 schools the group becomes more financially viable but there are other challenges as the Executive Principal grows into a CEO and expectations of the trust "adding value" grow so the CEO needs a board that can go with them on this step of the journey.

At 8–11 the group reaches "critical mass" and the financial risks lessen. Holding the vision true over a larger organisation can become harder – the board needs people who have experience of organisational design at scale and can balance systematisation and autonomy.

At 20 plus and beyond does the board bring sufficient expertise at scale? Can they rethink structures and systems to be fit for purpose? The board is likely to need people to lead substantial reorganisation and the trust needs board leadership to hold the vision across a large organisation.

The role of the board is crucial to how the trust fares through these critical growth stages, but the power of the board needs to be consciously developed and deployed.'

Academy Ambassadors has undertaken research on why so many trusts are looking to business and the professions to help with growth. Key findings were as follows:

- Widespread recognition that running a successful growing, medium, or large MAT is very different to running an individual school/small MAT.
- Good governance changes/evolves as chains grow in size.
- A lot of the boards we have been speaking to wished they had given more consideration to board structure, size and composition while smaller, to better prepare for growth.
- Realisation that the skills of a good individual school governor and those of a MAT non-executive director are different, especially in larger MATs; this is a limitation to promoting from within.

Centralised services

One of the advantages of the MAT structure that is often cited is the ability to centralise core services to reduce overheads in individual academies and ensure a consistent approach which takes advantage of economies of scale. Many MATs centralise services such as finance, HR, payroll and general administration, etc. Costs are financed through a contribution from each of the academies which is often known as 'top slicing', i.e. a percentage of the academy's General Annual Grant (GAG) is passed to the trust. This sum will also cover the costs of the chief executive/executive head, finance director and any other trust staff.

> **COMMENT**
>
> John Banbrook MA FCMI FNASBM, Business and Finance Director at the Faringdon Academy of Schools and elected Council Representative for the South East for ASCL:
>
> 'There is criticism of MATs "deskilling" head teachers; they had autonomy to do what they wanted as a maintained school. But head teachers often don't have the business management skills required and have little training in HR, finance, etc.'

Most academy trusts top-slice 3–5% from their academies which compares very favourably with the average 8–12% charged by local authorities. The amount charged is decided by the trust board. However, whilst a particular level may be agreed, it is open to the trust board to raise or lower the level of top-slicing at any time in the future.

It is also difficult for schools joining an established MAT to make comparisons between top-slicing of different MATs. Whilst the levels of top-slicing can differ hugely, so can the level of support and central services provided. A higher top-slice might work out cheaper for an academy than having to pay for various services.

Some MATs use a variable contribution rate which is calculated according to need. For example, a school rated inadequate or requiring improvement will be charged relatively more than an academy rated good or outstanding. This is a clear reflection of the increased need in some academies for greater support and involvement of the trust.

However, we may be moving away from the concept of top-slicing. MATs are now able to pool their academies' GAG and then allocate it to academies according to whatever methodology it feels appropriate. Commentators have said this approach enables shared reserves and flattens out financial risk.

COMMENT

John Banbrook:

'When other schools visit us, the first question they ask is how much is the contribution to central services. This really misses the point and does not consider what is included such as insurance or audit fees.

At FAoS we put together a central budget including anything that will add value. This is considered by the MAT Leadership Team who will identify anything that should not to be paid centrally. Once that sum is approved it is entered into the budget. We multiply the pupil number in the funding allocation by the AWPU amount for the school to produce a total which is then used to calculate a percentage of that total sum for central services. The charge is based on the size of the academy and weighted according to AWPU; our independent Audit Committee has confirmed that it is a fair and equitable way to deal with charges.

All schools in the MAT are currently converter academies and all bar one are good or outstanding. Consideration may be required to a different way of allocating charges if a school in RI or special measures joined the MAT requiring support calling on more central services.'

Church schools

Church schools have particular restrictions depending on their governance structure and the policy of their Church and Diocese (see Chapter 2).

The Catholic Bishops' Conference of England and Wales decided that Catholic schools can only convert in MATs with other Catholic schools. Any

Catholic schools wishing to convert to academies must obtain the prior consent of the Diocesan Bishop.

Church of England schools have greater options available to them. Many Diocesan Directors of Education take a pragmatic approach to academisation which takes account of the circumstances of the particular case and make decisions based on what is regarded to offer the best option for the pupils.

COMMENT

Canon Joy Tubbs, Director of Education of the Church of England's Diocese of Salisbury:

'Our vision is to facilitate a landscape of multi-academy trusts across the diocese that stands the test of time: preserving, protecting and enhancing Church school distinctiveness and effectiveness.

The Salisbury Diocesan Board of Education (SDBE) actively supports Church schools to explore Multi Academy Trust (MAT) status which may include schools from a range of designations: Voluntary Aided, Voluntary Controlled, standalone academies and community schools. Our commitment is to work with schools and their local communities to build a Multi Academy Trust landscape across the diocese that is logical, that meets the needs of all children and which utterly protects Church school status and Christian character.

To ensure the Church school effectiveness and distinctiveness, governance is structured to maintain representation of any former VA or VC school, at member, director and local governor level.

The SDBE as a Corporate Member provides a continual link between the SDBE, schools and the MAT board and appoints a person to represent them, being known as "SDBE Corporate Member"; this person is usually nominated by the MAT.

Our expectation is for each MAT to deliver the highest outcomes for all pupils. Church school academies within "mixed" status MATs should be beacons of Church school distinctiveness and effectiveness, at the same time working with community schools within a MAT ethos that totally supports the individual school's values.

The SDBE has established its own MAT, the Diocese of Salisbury Academy Trust (DSAT), offering an innovative local hub model and high quality central services. DSAT offers a stimulating and exciting home to Church and non-Church schools across the Diocese, living out its vision of going "beyond expectations for all of God's children", walking alongside them during and beyond conversion.'

Performance tables

Performance tables (sometimes known as league tables) are published by the government showing data for schools relating to:

- exam and test results
- financial information
- Ofsted reports.

It is possible to search and view performance data by trust group to consider comparative data.

Due diligence

The term 'due diligence' is generally used in a commercial and legal context to describe the process that investors undertake when evaluating whether they should invest in a company or not. At its heart it is a financial process to establish whether the company is a good investment and a safe place to put your money. However, due diligence in a wider context should be employed where a merger-type relationship is envisaged as it is only by effectively fusing the two organisations that true success can be achieved.

Due diligence is essential in the context of academisation for an individual school looking to join an existing MAT or create its own MAT with other schools as well as for an existing MAT considering a new academy.

COMMENT

Liz Holmes, Vice Chair of the Faringdon Academy of Schools, explains the importance of due diligence:

'I think there are a couple of things which are key to a successful MAT: It is absolutely essential that as a school joining a MAT you really must have a clear understanding of how the MAT is structured and what it is going to mean to be part of that MAT, what will continue to be delegated to you and what local governance is going to have to look like going forward. From the MAT's standpoint having a well-thought-out and effectively communicated scheme of delegation is an absolute necessity.'

Any school considering joining an existing MAT or joining together with other schools to create a new MAT must undertake thorough due diligence. Where there is an existing MAT, schools must undertake their own research to establish the governance structures employed within the MAT and whether the values and ethos of the MAT align with those of the school.

Joining a MAT should be approached with gravity; those involved should undertake as much research as possible. As some have said, joining a MAT is like getting married without the option for divorce; joining a MAT means that the individual school legally becomes part of the same organisation.

COMMENT

When asked what advice we should give to heads and governors about becoming an academy or joining a MAT, Laura McInerney, Editor of Schools Week, said:

'The same advice you would give kids about sex. Be safe, be sure, be legal and don't do it hurriedly just because everyone else is.'

Some of the well-known MATs are recognised for a fairly aggressive approach to re-branding schools when they join the MAT. They take over failing schools, change the uniform and the policies, take a notoriously robust approach to staff appraisal and create a new academy on a trusted model. It is an approach that has an immediate impact and a proven track record of success. But it is not popular. For governors of schools looking to convert, consideration should be given to the approach of the MAT they are considering joining and how this fits with their own vision and approach.

COMMENT

Allan Hickie BSc FCA, Partner of UHY Hacker Young Chartered Accountants:

'There are two sides to due diligence: the MAT taking on or sponsoring an academy needs to understand the financial position and performance of the joining academy, but it should not be overlooked that it is also advisable for the joining academy to carry out its own due diligence.

The joining academy should ensure it fully understands the strength of the MAT it is proposing to join, taking into account:

- The financial strength and recent financial performance of the MAT. The joining school should pay close attention to the level of reserves across the MAT as a whole, and how these are spread across the constituent academies; do any of these academies appear to have a financial weakness which could require intervention?
- What is the MATs approach to top slicing, and is it clear what services will be provided centrally for the contribution being made? There should always be a service-level agreement in place to clarify the central services.

- Governance; how the MAT is structured, and its approach to delegation of authorities from the central trust and board of trustees down to the local governing bodies and local leadership teams will have a huge impact. Is the MAT going through a rapid period of growth which may cause instability, or is the MAT well established with a central team which has been through the process of taking in an academy several times?'

Specific areas to consider in a full due diligence process include the following:

- Values and ethos
  Do these align with those of the school?

- Governance structure
  How is the MAT organised and what level of freedom, support and independence is delegated to each academy?
  What is the composition of the board and members and how are they appointed?

- Financial management
  Consider the financial position and management of the MAT and the financial policies and procedures in place.
  Does the MAT have any obvious financial deficiencies?
  How will any surpluses be dealt with – will they remain with the school or potentially be redistributed amongst the MAT?

- Top slice
  What are the payment arrangements for central services?

- Central services
  What support is provided to academies? Are finance, HR, payroll, etc centralised and, if so, are there potential redundancies of academy staff? What is covered by the top slice sum and what services are additional?

COMMENT

Chris Powell, Director of Finance and Services at Didcot Academy of Schools:

'Any school considering joining a MAT should also carry out their own due diligence of the MAT. Most importantly they should look at the most recent audited accounts of the MAT to make sure the accounts had no significant auditor qualifications. Have a close look at the MAT's balance sheet to check that it is healthy and make sure that you ask for copies of the most recent external auditor management letters in order to find out what recommendations the auditors have made.'

COMMENT

Bob Wintringham, Chair of the Board at Faringdon Academy of Schools, a MAT consisting of eight schools which were previously community and Church of England VC schools:

'Our plans to create more efficiency through developing effective central services have proved largely successful, and all our schools now benefit from a much greater degree of common process. It has provided much needed headroom to grow services like a strong school improvement team, which we believe is essential in any academy chain.

But the overwhelming concern has been the unrelenting and unpredicted financial pressures applied by Government which has seen the initial Educational Services grant – previously called the LACSEG – all but eradicated since our conversion. This means that the academy has to find in excess of £600K in savings year on year to stand still, and our early financial model is no longer sustainable. These kinds of pressures will undoubtedly force MATs to grow, and because of the greater financial clout of larger secondary schools, they will be an essential part of both growth and long-term stability. Smaller primaries will find it impossible to thrive alone, particularly as the LAs finally run out of steam, and even grouping smaller primaries without making substantial and deep economies may prove unviable.

The challenge is then to face these business concerns whilst not forsaking the very principles that we built the academy on.'

- Geographic location
  Are all academies within a defined geographical area? If it is a widely distributed MAT, are they geographical clusters to enable efficient governance and communication?

- Size of MAT
  How many academies are there within the MAT? Does this align with the vision of the governing body?
  A joining school is likely to have a greater influence in a smaller MAT.

- Identity of academies
  Do all of the academies have a similar background, e.g. all formerly community schools? Is it a mixed MAT, e.g. formerly community, VC schools, etc. and what are the implications?

- Staffing
  What are the arrangements for staff? Do pay and conditions for MAT staff

follow national pay and conditions? Are staff redeployed across the MAT? What opportunities are there for CPD and career development?

Due diligence for MATs

MATs must also undertake thorough due diligence whenever considering the admission of a new academy.

COMMENT

Allan Hickie BSc FCA, Partner of UHY Hacker Young Chartered Accountants:

'The MAT should ensure it fully understands issues such as:

- The recent historical financial performance of the joining school, and whether there are exceptional items within these results, or alternatively costs that could potentially be saved following a restructure or by utilising MAT resources.
- The accuracy of financial reports.
- Short- and medium-term forecast results, which may reveal future financial problems.
- The strength of the joining academy's balance sheet, and specifically how cash rich the school is: a weak cash position could result in a fairly immediate drain on the MAT's central resources. This and many of the points above are particularly important if the academy is joining the MAT in a "forced" sponsorship.
- Existing contracts and commitments in place, how long these will run and the costs of an early exit.
- The pension scheme liabilities which will be inherited. Some local authorities are being aggressive and attempting to negotiate the repayment of Local Government Pension deficits through annual lump sum payments in addition to the standard monthly contributions. MATs need to understand the ongoing level of contributions they will inherit.

Of course these are only the financial due diligence considerations, and there are many other aspects. Legal due diligence should always be carried out, and naturally educational due diligence will be necessary too. Although each academy in a MAT retains its own identity it is important that there is a blending of cultures, values and priorities for the relationship to be successful. Unless these are consistent there are likely to be problems.'

COMMENT

Chris Powell, Director of Finance and Services at Didcot Academy of Schools, agrees:

'Carrying out due diligence when considering admitting schools to your MAT is critical in order to ensure that trustees have a full knowledge of the financial position of the school concerned, and the assets and liabilities that it will bring to the trust, prior to any legal transfer taking place. Ensuring that there are "no surprises" after the school has joined the MAT should be one of the aims of the due diligence work.

Make sure that you have clearly identified the levels of reserves a school holds (both capital and revenue) and the degree to which there are commitments against them, the latest financial forecasts (both in the year concerned and into the future), cash and bank balances, contractual commitments, including leases, pension liabilities, any outstanding claims against the school and the condition of the school assets. If there is a need to invest in the premises or technology it is important you know about it. Don't forget to check staff terms and conditions either. Staff will transfer into the MAT by TUPE transfer so it is important to know in advance whether there are any significant differences in pay and conditions from your current staff.

Don't just focus on the finances in your due diligence work either. If the standards of teaching and learning are poor the MAT will have to tackle these so get a full understanding of the educational strengths and weaknesses of the school and the drive within the school for improvement.'

Existing MATs must put together a clear due diligence process prior to expansion which aligns with the board's vision and strategy.

COMMENT

John Banbrook MA FCMI FNASBM is Business and Finance Director at the Faringdon Academy of Schools and elected Council Representative for the South East for ASCL. FAoS is a MAT in Oxfordshire consisting of one secondary school (the Community College), five primary, one junior and one infant school. He explained:

'We are now looking at expansion of the MAT, possibly to grow to two to three secondary schools each with a cluster of primaries. Last time, we relied on the local authority due diligence process though we would have accepted the schools anyway as there were educational benefits for the partnership. There is now a clear vision for the MAT which is closely aligned to sustainability. We would look to make sure that there was a much more thorough due diligence process in future and possibly even an organisational review conducted during the TUPE process.'

Great care should be taken not to expand too quickly so that a MAT exceeds its 'span of control'. There is a limit to the number of direct reports that can be effectively supervised by one individual or entity: this applies equally to academies. If the span of control is going to be exceeded, alternative internal governance arrangements will be required to ensure that appropriate and effective measures are put in place.

COMMENT

Martin Matthews, Chair of Governors at Hodge Clough Primary School, Oldham and NLG:

'The expansion of Multi Academy Trusts (MATs) should be driven by the desire to enhance the educational opportunities of the students.

It shouldn't be driven by economics, expediency or ego.

Once a MAT expands beyond the "starter" size, issues can stress the whole organisation. Trustees need to understand the potential impact before changes are made.

During expansion the core issues are scalability, accountability and identity.

Scalability has well-known pitfalls and can place undue strain on the trust if it is not carefully planned and managed. It often involves the whole organisational structure becoming more similar to facilitate effective management.

Accountability to trustees should be organised in a business-like manner to ensure all schools are equally scrutinised. The aim of the board should not waiver from delivering the very best education to every child.

Schools in an expanding MAT need to be clear that part of what makes them unique will change as the trust grows. The ethos of the trust should percolate through the strategy of every school.

Plan expansion carefully, manage it well and children will benefit. Get it wrong and the whole trust could fail.'

In June 2016, National Schools Commissioner Sir David Carter told the Commons Education Select Committee that he was introducing a 'health check' for MATs. This would be required for any MATs wishing to take on more schools and would require the trust to demonstrate a 'track record' of school improvement. This is hoped to prevent the over-rapid expansion of MATs. There have been concerns over some of the larger chains which have grown exponentially and many fear their inability to ensure sustained school improvement across their ever growing number of academies. E-ACT and Academies Enterprise Trust, two larger trusts, had already been told that they could not continue to expand.

COMMENT

Matthew Wolton, Partner at Clark Holt Commercial Solicitors:

'One of the early issues some MATs experienced was that the desire to expand was greater than the desire to ensure the right fit between the MAT and new joiners. This resulted in chains of schools that were not a good fit, MATs finding nasty surprises coming out of the woodwork after schools had joined them, and schools not getting the support they were expecting from the MAT.

Having learned the right lessons, well-run MATs now place a huge amount of importance on the due diligence process involved in looking carefully at schools before they join the MAT to ensure they are suitable. It is important to note this is a two-way process – although joining a MAT is not necessarily for life, the procedure for leaving is not straightforward and so the school should also be carrying out its own due diligence to make sure it is joining the right MAT for that school.

The due diligence process should involve a number of different areas, and these may be looked at all together, in order, or at a high level first followed by a more detailed consideration. Timing is also crucial as some degree of compatibility should be understood before an academy order is applied for, however it would not be appropriate to do too much before the order is granted. Examples of the sort of areas that should be considered are:

- the management of the MAT and the school need to have the same vision for the future and there must be a genuine shared culture;
- the educationalists need to agree that they have the same ethos for the best way to teach and improve outcomes for children;
- the MAT finance director needs to be sure that taking on the school will not be an unacceptable financial risk to the MAT – what is the deficit position, what are the ongoing liabilities etc.;

- the MAT HR team need to understand the employment position – will changes be necessary, are there employment liabilities which will become MAT responsibilities etc.;
- the MAT estates manager needs to ensure the school buildings are fit for purpose and any capital funding requirements are understood.

Possible new-joiners can be rejected if they "fail" in any of these areas. It should be noted that uncovering something "unpleasant" does not necessarily mean rejection though – the important point is that a final decision should be taken when both the MAT and the school are in possession of all the facts and information. At that point they can make an informed choice.

It is often the case that a MAT takes on a school knowing that it will be a "net taker" from the MAT for a period of time, but if this is the case the MAT must be confident that within a set period of time the school will become a "net giver" thereby enabling the MAT to improve the other schools within the chain.

Sometimes the old clichés are the most appropriate: "Marry in haste, repent at leisure"!'

The board of trustees must set a clear vision and strategy around expansion plans. There should be an agreed plan which details the schools that could potentially join, due diligence processes and future governance structures. What fits a MAT with just three academies may well be different to that required where there are 15 academies – or more.

COMMENT

John Banbrook MA FCMI FNASBM is Business and Finance Director at the Faringdon Academy of Schools and elected Council Representative for the South East for ASCL. FAoS is a MAT in Oxfordshire consisting of one secondary school (the Community College), five primary, one junior and one infant school. He explained:

'As the MAT grows, it may be useful to evolve hubs structured on a geographical basis. There would be leadership structures for the hubs which allowed for a safety net of experience at the top enabling risk to be taken lower down. It would be an effective way to deliver leadership whilst making savings.'

▓ Expansion and staff

Care must be taken when expanding a MAT and incorporating new schools. The terms and conditions of existing staff of joining schools are protected as a result of The Transfer of Undertakings (Protection of Employment) Regulations 2006 (TUPE) (see Chapter 3). This means that the MAT cannot change the employees' terms and conditions to align with existing staff as this would be as a result of the transfer. Changes can only be made if the reason is an 'economic, technical or organisational reason' (ETO) involving changes in the workforce or workplace and, in any case, the employee needs to agree to the change.

Trusts can, of course, decide to improve employees' terms and conditions to make them the same for everyone – and it is hard to imagine an employee refusing to agree!

Any changes will be subject to the requirement for proper consultation.

COMMENT

John Banbrook MA FCMI FNASBM, Business and Finance Director at the Faringdon Academy of Schools and elected Council Representative for the South East for ASCL:

'It is not a safe assumption that because schools are in the same local authority that there will be consistency across schools in the way that they pay their staff. We found that, although they were in the same local authority, people in different schools were on very different grades despite doing the same jobs. As a single company, the MAT needed consistency and an organisational review was conducted of office and support staff.

It was emotive and divisive and had an impact on morale.

We followed the local authority process and engaged with the Unions which were pleased that we had done it. There is now a more consistent and coherent approach across the MAT. HR processes have been central-ised and there are standard job templates, gradings, etc. All appointments, including internal vacancies, are advertised so that none are made by word of mouth.'

5 Funding agreement

The funding agreement is effectively the contract by which the academy trust agrees to provide educational services in exchange for funding provided by the Department for Education (DfE). There are model versions of the funding agreement but these have been updated over time to reflect changes in policy and legislation.

The DfE does not expect schools to deviate from the model documents unless there are exceptional circumstances, although some variation may be agreed where the rationale can be satisfactorily justified. As a result, it is essential to refer directly to the trust's funding agreement to verify the particular requirements applicable.

Schools looking to convert must use the latest version of the funding agreement which incorporates the Memorandum and Articles of Association as appendices. Trusts on older versions of the funding agreement can change to the latest version should they wish to do so.

COMMENT

Nick MacKenzie, Partner at Browne Jacobson:

'The funding agreement is the key contract between the Secretary of State and the academy trust. It governs the basis on which the academy trust will receive funding from central government. The academy trust is bound to conduct the academy in accordance with the terms of the funding agreement and it is therefore essential that the directors and senior management team have a comprehensive understanding of their obligations under the agreement.

The DfE updates its model funding agreement relatively regularly, for example to reflect changes in policy and to make clarificatory amendments. The DfE will sometimes contact existing academies asking them to agree to vary their existing funding agreement to adopt the latest model or a particular new clause. It is important that academies carefully consider the position before agreeing to vary their existing funding agreement. Ideally, legal advice should be sought on any proposed deed of variation issued by the DfE or EFA. There may be benefits to adopting a newer version of the funding agreement, but equally there may be less favourable implications.'

General obligations

The trust must ensure that the academy 'is at the heart of its community, promoting community cohesion and sharing facilities with other schools and the wider community' so far as this is compatible with the charitable purpose of advancing education.

Governance

The trust will be governed by trustees who must have regard to any guidance published by the Secretary of State for Education. The names of trustees and members must be provided to the Secretary of State for Education within 14 days of their appointment.

The Articles of Association may not be amended by the members without prior approval of the Secretary of State to the proposed amendment or removal.

Running of the academy

Length of school day and year

The trust can determine the duration of the school day, term dates and year. The provisions in respect of school sessions required for maintained schools do not apply and there are no other obligations in respect of the number of days or length of a school day.

Disclosure and Barring Service checks

Enhanced Disclosure and Barring Service (DBS) checks and any necessary further checks will be made for members of staff, supply staff and trustees. A copy of an enhanced DBS certificate must be provided to the Secretary of State for Education on request.

COMMENT

Katie Michelon, Solicitor at Browne Jacobson:

'In terms of safe recruitment and vetting, academies are bound by the legislation that applies to independent schools, not maintained schools. This is made clear in the funding agreement which confirms that the academy trust must comply with the requirements of the Education (Independent

School Standards) Regulations in relation to carrying out disclosure and barring service checks on all staff and governors. Importantly, these Regulations require an academy to carry out enhanced DBS checks on all its governors, which is different to the position for maintained schools.'

Designated teacher for looked-after children

The trust will act in accordance with, and be bound by, all relevant statutory and regulatory provisions, guidance and codes of practice in the same way as they apply to a maintained school.

Teachers and other staff

Under the terms of the latest model funding agreement documents, a mainstream trust can employ 'anyone it believes is suitably qualified or is otherwise eligible to plan and prepare lessons and courses for pupils, teach pupils, and assess and report on pupils' development, progress and attainment' as a teacher. Only a SEN coordinator and a designated teacher for looked-after children must hold qualified teacher status.

All staff must be given access to the relevant pension scheme: TPS for teachers and LGPS for all other employees.

If a teacher applies for a teaching post in another publicly funded organisation, the trust must advise in writing whether there have been any formal capability hearings over the past two years and details of any proceedings.

Pupils

The planned capacity of the trust is detailed, including the age range and whether there is a sixth form or nursery unit.

COMMENT

Katie Michelon, Solicitor at Browne Jacobson:

'The funding agreement sets out the academy's size, including the number of nursery and sixth-form places if applicable, and its age range. If any changes are made to these characteristics these will therefore need to be reflected in the funding agreement. The Secretary of State's agreement will be required as they will need to be party to the Deed of Variation that will legally amend the funding agreement. Remember though that it is the academy's capacity figure that should be included in the funding agreement, not its Published Admission Number (PAN), so a change to PAN will not necessarily trigger the need to amend the funding agreement.'

The Funding Agreement specifically states that the trust 'must ensure that the academy meets the needs of individual pupils, including pupils with SEN and disabilities'.

School meals

School lunches should be provided when they are requested by or on behalf of any pupil. A school lunch must be provided free of charge to any pupil entitled to free school lunches including any pupil in KS1 under Universal Infant Free School Meal provision.

The trust must comply with school food standards legislation in the same way as maintained schools.

Pupil premium

The pupil premium is additional funding given to publicly funded schools in England to raise the attainment of disadvantaged pupils and close the gap between them and their peers.

Pupil premium funding is available to both mainstream and non-mainstream schools, such as special schools and pupil referral units. It is paid to schools according to the number of pupils who:

- have been registered as eligible for free school meals at any point in the last six years;
- have been looked after for one day or more; or
- were adopted from care on or after 30 December 2005 or left care under:
  - Special Guardianship Order on or after 30 December 2005
  - Residence Order on or after 14 October 1991.

In addition, there is a 'service child premium' payable at a lower rate for children who have parents in the armed forces.

Information must be published annually in relation to:

- the amount of pupil premium allocation that will be received in that financial year;
- what the pupil premium allocation will be spent on;
- how pupil premium was spent in the previous financial year; and
- the impact on educational attainment resulting from expenditure of pupil premium in the previous financial year.

Charging

A trust is treated in the same way as a maintained school in respect of charging, particularly in relation to the obligation to enter pupils for public examinations, charges, regulations about information about charges and school hours, voluntary contributions, recovery of sums as civil debt and interpretation regarding charges. The terms also place an obligation on a trust to have a charging and remissions policy.

Admissions

A trust is its own 'admission authority' and must act in accordance with the School Admissions Code and School Admission Appeals Code published by the DfE.

Pupils in a school that converted or joined a MAT will automatically transfer to the new trust or MAT on opening.

The trust is also obliged to participate in the local Fair Access Protocol and the co-ordinated admission arrangements operated by the local authority where the academy is situated. Free schools are not required to participate in co-ordination for its first intake of pupils.

Exclusions agreement

The trust can enter into an arrangement with a LA to the effect that payment will flow between the trust and the LA in the same way as it would do were the trust a maintained school.

Curriculum

Academy trusts do not have to follow the national curriculum, but they must provide a 'broad and balanced' curriculum for pupils up to the age of 16, including English, mathematics and science in mainstream academies. Information on the curriculum provision must be published on the trust's website including:

- content of the curriculum;
- approach to the curriculum;
- GCSE options, other Key Stage 4 qualifications or other future qualifications offered;
- names of any phonics or reading schemes in operation for Key Stage 1; and
- how parents (including prospective parents) can obtain further information.

The trust must not allow 'any view or theory to be taught as evidence-based if it is contrary to established scientific or historical evidence and explanations'. This applies to all subjects taught.

In particular, the trust must provide for the 'teaching of evolution as a comprehensive, coherent and extensively evidenced theory'.

The trust must prevent political indoctrination. The promotion of partisan political views in teaching should be forbidden and political issues dealt with by offering a balanced presentation of opposing views. This also applies to any extra-curricular activities offered at the trust. Pupils under 12 should be prevented from taking part in any political activities either in school or elsewhere if it is arranged by a member of staff or someone acting on behalf of the trust.

The trust must make provision for the teaching of religious education and for a daily act of collective worship in both faith and non-faith academies.

Academies designated with a religious character must ensure that provision for religious education and collective worship are in accordance with the tenets and practice of the specific religion or religious denomination. The requirements will be slightly different depending on whether the trust is treated as a voluntary aided school with a religious character, a foundation school with a religious character or a voluntary controlled school.

The trust should have regard to guidance issued by the Secretary of State on sex and relationship education to ensure that pupils are 'protected from inappropriate teaching materials' and 'learn the nature of marriage and its importance for family life and for bringing up children'.

Assessment

The trust must ensure that pupils take part in assessments and in teacher assessments of pupils' performance and reporting will take place in the same way as in maintained schools. The trust will take part in monitoring and moderation of assessment arrangements in respect of all Key Stages.

The academy must upload information in relation to results obtained at Key Stage 2 and Key Stage 4 on its website (see Chapter 17).

The trust must provide such information as required by the Secretary of State for participation in international surveys such as Programme for International Student Assessment (PISA).

Grants funding

The Secretary of State commits to pay grants towards 'recurrent expenditure' to cover the 'establishment, conduct, administration and maintenance of the academy'. Two separate and distinct grants are made: general annual grant (GAG) and earmarked annual grant (EAG).

The trust cannot budget for expenditure in excess of expected income without the Secretary of State's prior agreement. The trust must get prior approval of the Secretary of State for any commitments to spending 'which have substantial implications for future grant'. However, the funding agreement does not clarify what 'substantial implications' might look like.

Capital grant

Grants may also be made towards capital expenditure; however, there is no commitment on behalf of the Secretary of State to do so.

Capital expenditure may include costs for building new premises or for substantially refurbishing existing premises.

The payment of the capital grant is subject to the following conditions:

- such grants are used solely to defray expenditure approved by the Secretary of State
- the trust certifying and providing evidence that all planning and other

consents necessary for the development and all related infrastructure to be completed have been obtained or put in place
- any other conditions that the Secretary of State may specify.

Supporting invoices and certificates must be provided to the Secretary of State in the format specified.

General annual grant

The general annual grant (GAG) will be paid to cover the normal running costs of the trust such as salary and administration costs. The funding is equivalent to that which would be received by a maintained school with similar characteristics, together with an additional element for functions which would be carried out by the LA if the trust were a maintained school.

A larger GAG may be available for the 'start-up period' of a newly opened trust to enable it to operate effectively.

The amount of GAG is determined annually based on the pupil count at the academy and is notified to the trust in a funding letter preceding the trust's financial year. GAG is paid in monthly instalments on or before the twenty-fifth day of each month via BACS; the payment should be available in the trust's nominated bank account on the first working day of each month. A monthly remittance advice is also issued. Each instalment should be used to fund the salaries and other payroll costs for the relevant month of all monthly paid employees and all other costs payable during the following month.

GAG funding may only be used for the educational charitable purpose of advancing for the public benefit education in the United Kingdom, in particular by establishing, maintaining, carrying on, managing and developing a trust offering a broad and balanced curriculum.

Earmarked annual grant

Earmarked annual grant (EAG) may be paid for either recurrent expenditure or capital expenditure for such specific purposes as have been agreed between the Secretary of State and the trust. EAG may only be spent in accordance with the scope, terms and conditions of the grant set out in the relevant funding letter.

To apply for an EAG, the trust must submit a letter outlining its proposals and the reasons for its request to the DfE.

Other relevant funding

The trust's costs in connection with the transfer of employees from a predecessor school that has transferred over may be paid by the Secretary of State. Any such payment will be agreed on a case-by-case basis.

Funding may also be received from a LA in respect of statements of SEN for pupils. The trust must ensure that provision detailed in statements of SEN is provided for such pupils.

Financial and accounting requirements

The trust must apply 'financial and other controls which meet the requirements of regularity, propriety and value for money'. The trust must comply with guidance for charities and charity trustees issued by the Charity Commission, especially the Charity Commission's guidance on 'Protecting Charities from Harm'.

An accounting officer must be appointed who is assigned with the 'responsibilities of the role set out in the *Academies Financial Handbook* and HM Treasury's publication *Managing Public Money'*.

Application of the *Academies Financial Handbook*

The trust must abide by the requirements set out in the *Academies Financial Handbook*.

COMMENT

Nick MacKenzie, Partner at Browne Jacobson:

'It is important that the funding agreement is read in conjunction with the *Academies Financial Handbook*. The funding agreement specifically states that the academy trust must abide by the requirements of the *Handbook* and there are various clauses within the funding agreement which refer back to the detail set out within the *Handbook*. For example, if an academy wishes to write off a debt or make a compensation payment, it will need to refer to the limits set out in the *Handbook* to check whether the value of the transaction is such that it needs Secretary of State consent to do so.'

Budgeting for funds

The formal budget plan must be approved by the trust each financial year. The budget must balance for each financial year although the trust may:

- carry a surplus from one financial year to the next
- carry forward from previous financial years sufficient cumulative surpluses on grants from the Secretary of State to meet an in-year deficit on such grants in a subsequent financial year
- incur an in-year deficit on funds from sources other than grants from the Secretary of State in any financial year provided that it does not affect the trust's responsibility to balance its overall budget from each financial year to the next.

Trusts can spend or accumulate any funds from other sources and identify such funds separately in the trust's accounts.

The budget must be approved each financial year by the board of trustees and submitted to the Secretary of State.

Carrying forward of funds

The trust may carry forward surpluses (subject to any limitation set out in the *Academies Financial Handbook* or as notified by the Secretary of State).

Annual accounts and audit

Audited accounts must be prepared and filed with Companies House and the Secretary of State for Education.

The annual reports and accounts, current memorandum of association, articles and funding agreement and the names of trustees and members must be published on the trust website.

Financial records

Proper accounting records including statements of income and expenditure, statements of cash flow and balance sheets must be produced and made available to officials of the DfE, the National Audit Office and their agents for inspection.

Acquiring or disposing of publicly funded assets

The Secretary of State's consent is required where a trust wishes, in relation to publicly funded assets, to:

- acquire or dispose of freehold land;
- take up or grant a lease of land; and
- dispose of any other class of capital asset.

A trust must give 30 days' written notice to the Secretary of State where it wishes to take such action. The *Academies Financial Handbook* sets out the classes of asset that require specific consent prior to disposal, in particular publicly funded land and buildings. Proceeds of sale of any asset funded by a capital grant from the Secretary of State may need to be repaid in whole or part.

COMMENT

Nick MacKenzie, Partner at Browne Jacobson:

'Where an academy trust is contemplating acquiring or disposing of land, such as entering into a lease or tenancy agreement or selling land, it will need to refer back to the terms of its funding agreement as Secretary of State consent to the arrangement may be required. The terms in the funding agreement are supplemented by the provisions of the *Academies Financial Handbook* which set out further detail as to when Secretary of State consent is required and how to obtain this.'

Transactions outside the usual planned range

Thirty days' prior notice must be given to the Secretary of State of any intention to:

- give any guarantees, indemnities or letters of comfort;
- write off any debts or liabilities owed to it; and
- offer to make any ex gratia payments.

The prior written consent of the Secretary of State must be obtained where such actions relate to publicly funded assets or property or exceed the thresholds set out in the *Academies Financial Handbook*.

Insurance must be procured in respect of the leasehold/freehold interest of the site upon which the trust is situated.

Borrowing powers

The trust cannot borrow against publicly funded assets or so as to put publicly funded assets at risk without the specific approval of the Secretary of State which will only be granted in limited circumstances.

Land clauses

The land clauses set out the trust's obligations in respect of the academy site and with 'protecting the public investment in the land used for the academy' and will be tailored to reflect the particular land ownership relevant to the trust.

Complaints

Complaints which arose prior to conversion and were investigated by the Local Government Ombudsman will continue to apply to the trust as if it were a maintained school. The Secretary of State will also have the power to investigate the matter as if it had taken place after conversion and the trust will be bound by any recommendation.

The Secretary of State can give an order and/or a direction in respect of any matters occurring within the 12 months immediately prior to conversion.

The trust must investigate any complaint made relating to matters arising in whole or in part during the 12 months prior to the opening of the trust.

Termination

Either party may give at least seven financial years' written notice to terminate the Agreement, such notice to expire on 31 August.

Termination warning notice

The Secretary of State can issue a written notice of their intention to terminate the funding agreement where they consider that:

- the trust has breached the provisions of the funding agreement;
- the standards of performance of pupils are unacceptably low;
- there has been a serious breakdown in the way the trust is managed or governed;
- the safety of pupils or staff is threatened, including by a breakdown of discipline; or
- the academy is coasting.

The termination warning notice will specify:

- reasons for the termination warning notice;
- the remedial measures required; and
- the date by which the trust must respond to the termination warning notice.

Notice of intention to terminate

Written notice of the Secretary of State's intention to terminate the funding agreement can be given where the chief inspector has found either that:

- special measures are required to be taken in relation to the trust; or
- the trust requires significant improvement.

The notice will state the time frame in which the trust can respond.

Termination

The funding agreement can be terminated by the Secretary of State to take effect on the date of the notice where the trust has significant financial issues or is insolvent.

The trust must notify the Secretary of State as soon as possible after receiving any petition which may result in an order for the winding up or administration of the trust.

In the case of a free school that has not yet opened, if the total number of prospective pupils who have accepted offers of places to attend the academy has not reached a stated level, the Secretary of State may serve a Termination Notice or require the academy not to open until sufficient numbers have accepted offers.

Free schools or new provision academies may be served with a Termination Warning Notice or a Termination Notice if they are not regarded as 'financially viable because of low pupil numbers'.

The Funding Agreement also contains various provisions enabling the Secretary of State to serve a Termination Notice or to require the trust to resolve the issues identified prior to opening.

Change of control

The Secretary of State may terminate the funding agreement if there is a change in control of the trust (i.e. an organisation or individual who is able to appoint and remove a majority of the board and is thereby able to control the way that the trust acts). This could potentially occur where there is a change in the identity of the sponsor, although the Secretary of State can choose not to terminate if satisfied that the organisation assuming control is acceptable.

COMMENT

Katie Michelon, Solicitor at Browne Jacobson:

'Like any contract, the funding agreement can be terminated. A common myth is that the funding agreement is only a seven-year contract. In fact, the funding agreement does not have a set "expiry date"; the seven-year period stems from the fact that either the academy trust or the Secretary of State can choose to bring the funding agreement to an end by providing seven years' written notice. In practice, it is difficult to envisage a situation where the ability to terminate with seven years' notice would be exercised by either party. A funding agreement is more likely to be brought to an end due to circumstances requiring more urgent attention, such as slipping standards or financial difficulties. The funding agreement includes terms which enable the Secretary of State to step in and ultimately terminate the funding agreement in situations such as these. For example, if the Secretary of State considers that there has been a breakdown in the way the school is governed, there is a process through which the Secretary of State can issue a Termination Warning Notice and ultimately may terminate the funding agreement, in a similar way to how a local authority can issue a warning notice to a maintained school.'

Effect of termination

If the funding agreement is terminated, the school shall cease to be a trust. Provisions set out any indemnity to be provided by the Secretary of State and the treatment of any capital assets held by the trust at the date of termination.

Other contractual arrangements

Information

The Secretary of State has the right to call for information which the trust shall make available. The Secretary of State shall provide such information as is reasonably required for the running of the trust.

Access by Secretary of State's officers

The trust shall allow access to DfE officials at any reasonable time to its premises and make available all records, files and reports relating to the running of the trust. In advance of such a visit, the trust shall provide papers prepared for board and member meetings. Two DfE officials shall be entitled to attend and to speak at any board meetings or other meetings of trustees. Such officials will withdraw from any discussion of the academy's/trust's relationship with the Secretary of State or any discussion of bids for funding.

The trust must make available for inspection by any interested party:

- the agenda for every meeting of the board or any committee with delegated authority;
- the draft minutes of every such meeting, if they have been approved by the person acting as chairman of that meeting;
- the signed minutes of every such meeting; and
- any report, document or other paper considered at any such meeting.

This documentation must also be sent to the Secretary of State upon request.

Any confidential information or references to named staff or pupils can be excluded or redacted.

Notices

Notices or communications should be sent to the address inserted into the agreement and must be in writing (i.e. not by e-mail) and in English.

Any notice or other communication must be either:

- delivered by hand;
- sent by pre-paid first-class post; or
- sent by another next working day delivery service.

It will be considered to have been received if delivered by hand on signature of a delivery receipt or at the time the notice is left at the address or at 9.00am on the second business day after posting.

The provisions do not apply to the service of any proceedings or other documents in any legal action.

Additional or alternative clauses

Further clauses will be added to the funding agreement depending on the particular circumstances:

- former voluntary controlled or foundation schools where the trust has a religious designation with foundation governors defined in the articles
- where freehold or leasehold land will be held by the trust
- a wholly selective academy
- academies with private finance initiative arrangements
- sponsored academies
- academies with special educational needs units/provision reserved for pupils with special educational needs
- academies with 16 to 19 provision.

Annexes to the funding agreement

Various documents form the appendices to the funding agreement:

Annex A – Memorandum and articles of the trust

This is the constitution of the trust and sets out the rules by which it must be governed (see Chapter 6).

Annex B – Admissions requirements

A trust is its own admissions authority and responsible for managing its own admissions process. Academies are required to comply with the Admissions Code and must follow the procedures set out if they wish to change admission arrangements. A converter trust retains the admission criteria relevant to it as a maintained school (e.g. a selective school can continue to use selective criteria).

Alternative arrangements are sometimes agreed for new free schools, studio schools and UTCs to aid establishment and ensure fair access.

Annex C – Arrangements for pupils with SEN and disabilities

This annex provides specific details relating to admission and support for SEN pupils.

Academies have equivalent SEN obligations to those placed upon the governing bodies of maintained schools by reason of the Education Act 1996 and subsequent regulations.

Annex D – Wholly selective school to remove selective admissions arrangements

This sets out the process to remove selection for a designated grammar school that has become an academy.

▪ MATs

In a MAT, the trust enters into a master funding agreement, the terms of which apply to all of the academies operated as part of the MAT and which include provisions along the same lines as the single model funding agreement already discussed.

The trust is required to ensure that it 'engages with the relevant Local Governing Body (if any) or representatives of each academy' and it must put in place arrangements so that matters relating to each academy can be brought to the attention of the trustees.

Each of the individual academies within the MAT also enters into a supplemental funding agreement with the Secretary of State for Education which sets out the specific requirements in respect of that academy. If the academy is designated with a religious character, the diocese or foundation faith body will be included as the 'relevant religious authority'. An academy that was formerly a grammar school or had partially selective admissions may continue to 'select its intake by reference to ability' on the same basis and in the same proportions as prior to academisation.

COMMENT

Nick MacKenzie, Partner at Browne Jacobson:

'In a multi-academy trust (MAT) structure, termination clauses will be set out in each supplemental funding agreement meaning that one academy's supplemental funding agreement can be terminated without the master funding agreement or other supplemental funding agreements being affected. For example, if one academy within a MAT went into special measures, under the terms of the current model funding agreement, the Secretary of State could give notice of their intention to terminate that supplemental funding agreement without the other funding agreements being impacted. Of course, notwithstanding that the other funding agreement would remain in force, where Ofsted and the Secretary of State have deemed one academy operated by that academy trust to be inadequate, there is likely to be a reputational impact across the group.

In a multi-academy trust, the terms of the master funding agreement are likely to require that the academy trust establishes an "Advisory Body" for each of the academies in its group. The funding agreement may also set out requirements for the constitution of the Advisory Body – most commonly that it must include two parent governors. Where MATs are looking to retain a substantial amount of control centrally, they must have in mind, therefore, that it is still a term of their funding agreement to establish an Advisory Body or Local Governing Body for each academy. If the academy trust believes this extent of local governance is not appropriate, it could look to explore agreeing an amendment to this requirement with the EFA.'

6 Memorandum and Articles of Association

Appended to the funding agreement are the Memorandum and Articles of Association which are the constitution of the company and set out the rules by which the company must operate.

Memorandum of Association

The Memorandum of Association is a simple document setting out the name of the academy trust and providing details of the three 'subscribers' who wish to form the academy trust and become its members under the Companies Act 2006.

Articles of Association

The Articles of Association prescribe the internal management, decision making and running of the academy trust and its liability.

The Department for Education (DfE) has model documentation which schools are expected to adopt. This has changed over time and additional models introduced for use with new governance structures. The following commentary generally refers to the version for use by mainstream, special, 16 to 19, alternative provision academies and free schools, as well as by studio schools. The same version has alternative sections for use by multi-academy trusts (MATs) incorporating such academies.

The DfE does not generally expect schools to make changes to the model Memorandum and Articles of Association. However, in some instances, academies have negotiated and had amendments cleared by the DfE.

The DfE has indicated its willingness to consider granting approval to academies who wish to change their Articles to the latest version.

Given the differences between the various versions of the Articles, it is essential to refer to the particular details contained in the version adopted by the academy trust.

Objects

This standard clause states the purpose and range of activities that the academy trust is set up to carry on. The primary object contained within the current model

Articles is to 'advance for the public benefit education in the United Kingdom'. This can be 'by establishing, maintaining, carrying on, managing and developing' school/s (depending whether it is a SAT or MAT) offering the type/s of provision appropriate to that type of academy whether mainstream, alternative provision, 16 to 19 or special academy.

The clause goes on to set out the various powers that may be exercised in furtherance of its object such as 'to raise funds', 'to acquire, alter, improve and… to charge or otherwise dispose of property', 'to employ such staff, as are necessary' and 'to pay out of funds of the academy trust the costs, charges and expenses of and incidental to the formation and registration of the academy trust', as well as numerous other powers that enable an academy trust to operate.

COMMENT

Julia Green, Partner at Browne Jacobson:

'The academy trust as a limited company has to record its purpose. In company law this is known as the "objects" and they are recorded in the Articles of Association. The Articles of Association are the corporate record of how the academy trust governs itself. The objects of an academy trust are prescribed by the Secretary of State and specifically require the company directors and members of the academy trust to establish, maintain, carry on, manage and develop education through a broad and balanced curriculum for the benefit of the children attending the named school or schools, in the case of a multi-academy trust.

When considering whether a proposed action by the academy trust is appropriate (e.g. offering the use of sporting facilities to the wider community), it is vital that the directors first look at their objects and decide whether the activity would fall within the objects or not. If it does not, then the academy trust needs to consider an alternative approach which could include amending the Articles to reflect the proposed activity. Such an approach would require the members of the trust to vote and agree the amendment.'

The Objects clause specifically states:

'The income and property of the academy trust shall be applied solely towards the promotion of the Objects.'

Members

Sets out details regarding the appointment of members and the removal or termination of their membership (see Chapter 8). The Articles also contain specific restrictions regarding the benefit that may be received by a Member from the academy trust.

Every Member 'undertakes to contribute such amount as may be required (not exceeding £10) to the academy trust's assets if it should be wound up while he or she is a Member or within one year after he or she ceases to be a Member'. This sum is supposedly due to be paid towards any debts or liabilities incurred whilst the individual was a Member or towards the 'costs, charges and expenses of winding up'. However, although it is merely the nominal sum of £10, it is hoped that the Secretary of State will have stepped in long before any such payments are due!

COMMENT

Julia Green, Partner at Browne Jacobson:

'The academy trust is a company. In order for the company to be formed it has to be created by a number of individuals known as founding members. These are the signatories of the Memorandum that brings the company into existence. In an academy trust there must be a minimum of three members but there can be more, either at the outset or subsequently if agreed by the existing members. The Department for Education's preferred number is 5, an odd number, but a mixed faith MAT, where there is a Diocesan requirement for 25% representation, can end up as 4. The members then go on to appoint directors up to the number set out in the Articles of Association.

Governors of maintained schools converting to academy status often find the concept of members difficult. Common questions are around their role and whether they are more important than directors or trustees. The role of the member is to act as a "guardian" of the company, ensuring that it is operating in accordance with the rules (the Articles of Association) and that it is financially healthy. It is the members that sign off the accounts each year and who have a financial liability if the company fails; usually £10 per person. Whilst the figure is deliberately not burdensome in order that volunteers are not put off taking on the role, it underlines the significance of the responsibility that the members have in keeping an overview of the performance of the company. Since the Trojan Horse situation where there was found to be too much overlap between the members and the board, the Department for Education are keen to ensure that there are different people in each (accepting the chair of trustees) to encourage accountability.'

General meetings (members' meetings)

The provisions relating to calling of general meetings and notice thereof, proceedings at meetings, voting by members and the appointment of proxies are detailed (see Chapter 8).

Trustees

The model Articles set out the number of trustees and the terms of their appointment including co-option, term of office, resignation and removal and disqualification. The provisions cover the appointment of the chair and vice-chair of the trustees, the powers of the trustees and conflicts of interest (see Chapter 9).

The model Articles of Association set out the requirements regarding the constitution of the board.

A SAT should have a minimum of two parent trustees. These will generally be elected by parents and other individuals exercising parental responsibility of registered pupils at the academy. However, there may be circumstances where parent trustees will be appointed by the board.

If there is no requirement for specifically appointed/elected parent trustees, parents are not prohibited from involvement in the board or LGB but will not be appointed AS parents.

A MAT may have parent trustees on the board. However, there is no obligation to have parent trustees on the board if there are at least two parent governors on each LGB. This does not necessarily mean that there will be no parents on the board, but they are not elected or appointed AS parents.

The model Articles also provide for the chief executive officer/principal to be appointed as a trustee if they agree 'so to act'. However, consideration should be given to the appropriateness of this appointment. The board appoints the chief executive officer/principal and holds him/her to account; it is hard to see how the separation of the roles of the board and the executive can be truly achieved when the chief executive officer/principal sits on the board!

The remainder of the board will be appointed in accordance with the specific Articles. This may include a number of appointments by the members, the Foundation or sponsor, as well as co-opted trustees.

There is no maximum number of trustees, but care should be taken to ensure that the board has the necessary skills and expertise to carry out its functions.

Trustees are appointed for a term of four years, apart from any ex officio post. Reappointment or re-election may be possible.

COMMENT

Julia Green, Partner at Browne Jacobson:

'Directors are arguably the most important constitutional element of the academy trust. The directors are responsible for the strategic running of the trust. This is separate from the day-to-day running of the school which is the responsibility of the head teacher and the Senior Leadership Team. A simple way to identify the different roles is to regard the members as the guardians with the directors and Senior Leadership Team being responsible for strategy and operational management respectively.

The directors are also governors and trustees. The "director" label depicts the responsibilities that they have under company law, the "trustee" label depicts the role that they have under charity law and the "governor" label depicts the role that they have under education law. These differences often confuse governors looking to change and it is common for schools to query the relationship between the different designations for some time after conversion. They are the same person but wearing three different hats. To add to the layering, it is also possible (particularly in academies established some time ago) that the members of the company are also governors, trustees and directors.

The maximum number of directors will be set out in the Articles of Association and can be appointed a number of different ways although the majority are likely to be appointed by members.'

Clerk/secretary to the trustees

The trustees can appoint a clerk/secretary 'at such remuneration and upon such conditions as they may think fit'. This person need not be the company secretary although there is a certain overlap between the roles (see Chapter 14).

The clerk cannot be either a trustee or principal. However, the board may appoint a trustee to act as clerk for the purposes of any meeting where the clerk fails to attend.

COMMENT

Julia Green, Partner at Browne Jacobson:

'The role of the company secretary is to submit the annual report to Companies House and input to Companies House any changes in the make-up of the trust, including resignations and appointments. They should maintain statutory books and registers and advise the trust in respect of their governance responsibilities.

The role of the clerk to the governing body is to assist the chair of governors in running the board of the academy trust, convening meetings in accordance with the provisions of the Articles, minute keeping, record keeping and acting as correspondent for the governors.

There is overlap between these two roles in that the purpose of both is to enable the academy trust to function smoothly and efficiently.

"Academy trusts" appoint the two roles in different ways; for some both roles are carried out by the same person (usually the original clerk to governors) and sometimes the role of company secretary is taken by the business manager. Alternatively, the role of company secretary can be outsourced. All options are perfectly acceptable and will depend on the confidence and capacity of the individual staff members.'

Chairman and vice-chairman of the trustees

The trustees must elect a chairman and vice-chairman of the board each year who are not employed by the academy trust. Generally, they hold office until a successor has been elected, but will cease to hold office if they:

- cease to be a trustee;
- are employed by the academy trust; or
- are removed from office.

The vice-chairman will also cease to hold their office if they are elected as chairman.

The trustees may agree to remove the chairman or vice-chairman, but

- the removal must be confirmed by a resolution passed at a second meeting of the trustees held not less than 14 days after the first meeting; and
- the matter is specified as an item of business on the agenda for both meetings.

Power of trustees

The Articles state that:

'the business of the academy trust shall be managed by the trustees who may exercise all the powers of the academy trust'.

It is not possible to make changes to the Articles that will retrospectively invalidate the actions of the trustees.

Conflicts of interest

Any trustee with a 'direct or indirect duty or personal interest' that conflicts or could conflict with his/her role as a trustee should disclose it as soon as he/she becomes aware of it. This will include any employment or remuneration received from the academy trust.

The minutes

The clerk must draw up minutes of board meetings which should be kept in a book kept for the purpose. Once approved by the board, the minutes shall be signed by the person acting as chair at the same or next meeting.

Committees

The board can establish any committee and determine the constitution, membership and proceedings that will apply. The establishment, terms of reference, constitution and membership of any committee must be reviewed annually. Persons who are not trustees can be appointed to a committee as long as the majority of members are trustees. They can also be given voting rights as long as the majority of members of the committee present for any vote are trustees.

In a MAT, the trustees may appoint separate committees known as local governing bodies (LGBs) for each separate academy or in respect of a group of academies. The requirements in respect of trustees making up the majority of a committee do not apply in the case of LGBs. The functions and proceedings of LGBs are subject to regulations made by the trustees from time to time.

Delegation

The board can delegate any power or function to an individual trustee, committee, the chief executive officer/principal or any other holder of an executive office. That person must report to the board when that delegated authority has been exercised and any action taken or decision made. The delegation can be made subject to conditions imposed by the trustees and may be revoked or altered.

Any such delegation 'shall be made in writing' and it is sensible to formalise it in a Scheme of Delegation (see Chapter 2).

Any power or function may be sub-delegated to another person but the original person to whom it was delegated 'must inform the trustees as soon as reasonably practicable which powers and functions have been further delegated and to whom'. The trustees are at liberty to impose any conditions on the sub-delegation or to revoke or alter it.

COMMENT

Julia Green, Partner at Browne Jacobson:

'The directors are responsible for the strategic direction of the academy trust. In order to have sufficient resources to implement the strategy and to understand the intricacies of what is in commercial terms a sophisticated business entity, the directors can choose to set up committees which will report back to the main board. Most governors are used to this principle and have varying ways of dividing the different aspects of running a school. Most usually, committees are made up of a teaching and learning or curriculum committee; a finance committee; a personnel committee and a sites and buildings committee. Each committee will have directors who have a particular interest or strength in that area of activity. The committee will have written terms of reference which clearly set out what the purpose of the committee is and what it is responsible for.

A particular issue may be considered by the committee and a recommendation taken back to the main board for a decision and vote. The main board is entitled to rely on the recommendation of the committee but is not automatically expected to accept it favourably, allowing for an additional layer of scrutiny. It appears to be a growing trend that, with a smaller board, committees are being dispensed with in favour of Full Governing Body Meetings instead. The advantage of this is that those in the committees do not sit through the same information twice and further it helps every board member to be fully immersed in every element of the decision making affecting the academy. There is, however, no right or wrong and it is up to the Board to decide what is in the best interests of the academy.

Multi-academy trusts have resulted in a further development of governance and management. The Articles allow for committees to be set up and anticipate that there will be a "Local Governing Body" for each school within a MAT. Given that the emphasis is to make the board of governors "lean" and "effective", not every member of an existing governing body can sit on the board when they join a MAT as this would result in too many numbers of directors and become unmanageable. A significant number will remain at LGB level. The name is slightly confusing as the LGB has no legal status and is essentially a committee with delegated powers. For a MAT there will be a "Scheme of Delegation" setting out the extent of the authority that has been passed on to them. Where a MAT has schools of different abilities, the delegated authority may vary and can operate on a "sliding scale". The remit of the LGB is in the gift of the board and is not prescribed by the Department of Education through any model documents that need to be approved. The board might want a "mini governing body" covering all aspects of governance or it might want the LGB to focus on a particular area such as teaching and learning. The LGB is ultimately responsible for the performance of the local school and where the school is a faith school, upholding the religious ethos. The Diocese may have a % requirement of representation on the LGB although there is no prescribed minimum or maximum number of members overall.'

Chief executive officer/principal

The trustees appoint the principal and/or CEO in a MAT, to whom they delegate powers and functions necessary 'for the internal organisation, management and control' of the academies/academy.

Meetings of trustees

The Articles set out the requirements for board meetings (see Chapter 10).

The trustees must hold at least three meetings in every school year. The quorum for any meeting and any vote is 'three trustees, or where greater, any one third (rounded up to a whole number) of the total number of trustees holding office at the date of the meeting'.

Patrons and honorary officers

The trustees can appoint someone as a 'patron' or to hold an honorary office without the need to appoint them as a member or trustee. They can agree the period of office that will apply.

The seal

The Articles provide that a seal can be used if authorised by the trustees. Historically, a company or common seal was used to stamp an impression on melted wax signifying that the document was the act and deed of the company. However, since 1989, there is no requirement for a seal provided documents are signed by a director/trustee and secretary or two directors/trustees.

Although not legally required, seals may sometimes still be used which create a raised impression on the paper. Often this is combined with a stick-on wafer which imitates a wax seal and also shows up better on photocopies.

The Articles provide that where the seal is used, it shall also be signed by a trustee and the clerk or by two trustees, or whoever the trustees shall determine.

Annual report and accounts

Accounts should be prepared in accordance with the relevant SORP and filed with the DfE by 31 December each year (see Chapter 13).

Annual return/Confirmation Statement

The trustees are responsible for preparation of an annual return (now replaced by the Confirmation Statement) to be filed at Companies House (see Chapter 7).

Notices

Any notice, apart from a notice calling a meeting of the trustees, should be in writing or given using electronic communications to an address notified to the person giving the notice. Notice given by the academy to a member may be given:

- personally;
- by post in a prepaid envelope addressed to the member at his/her registered address;
- by hand delivery to their registered address; or
- via electronic communications to an address notified to the academy.

A member based outside the United Kingdom may only receive notices either electronically or to an address within the United Kingdom.

Indemnity

Any trustee, officer or auditor of the academy is entitled to be indemnified against any liability incurred whilst in that role in connection with any court action. This means that as long as the individual is acting within their capacity, they will be recompensed for any loss.

COMMENT

Julia Green, Partner at Browne Jacobson:

'As a limited company the academy trust is the legal entity that has liability when something goes wrong, rather than the individuals that make up the members and directors. The Articles of Association specifically provide that the governors are entitled to be indemnified by the academy trust if they incur any costs as a result of successfully defending any proceedings. However, like maintained schools, governors will be held liable where they have acted beyond their remit and been negligent. In a situation where a governor has acted recklessly or wilfully against advice and the decision to do so has resulted in a loss, the individual will be held to be personally liable and any indemnity will not apply.

Governors of maintained schools converting to academy status and becoming a director often get concerned over the possibility of action against them but equally often do not realise that they are in this position already as a governor. There is also often confusion about the difference between making a wrong decision and making a bad decision. A decision made following appropriate advice and after consideration which turns out to have been the wrong decision is unlikely to lead to personal liability. A decision that has been made recklessly without seeking proper guidance or one that has been made wilfully ignoring advice or guidance is one that could lead to personal liability. In these circumstances, an indemnity may not be relied upon. In short, acting professionally and responsibly will make it very unlikely that there will be personal liability and the indemnity from the academy trust will provide protection from expenses.'

Rules

The trustees are entitled to make 'such rules or bye laws as they may deem necessary or expedient or convenient for the proper conduct and management of the academy' in connection with matters that are 'commonly the subject matter of company rules' such as in connection with meetings or members.

Avoiding influenced company status

The Articles contain strict limits on the number of 'Local Authority Associated Persons' (LAAPs) that can be involved in the management of the academy trust.

This is to avoid 'influenced company status' (i.e. where the LA has significant influence or power in the running of the company). This, therefore, is closely regulated.

A person is a LAAP if:

- they are a member of the LA;
- they are an officer (i.e. direct employee) of the LA;
- they are both an employee and either a director/trustee, manager, secretary or other similar officer of a company which is under the control of the LA; or
- at any time within the preceding four years they have been a member of the LA.

Any person who is an elected councillor will, therefore, be regarded as a LAAP along with anyone who has been a member within the past four years. An officer will be any person who is employed by the LA. This could be someone who is directly employed by the LA as a council officer, administrator, cleaner, etc. It will also apply to any staff employed by a maintained school.

A LA can be:

- a county council;
- a district council (including metropolitan boroughs, non-metropolitan districts/ boroughs and unitary authorities);
- a London borough council;
- a parish council; and
- a community council.

The number of votes exercisable by LAAPs must not exceed 19.9% of the total number of votes exercisable by members. The votes of the other members will be increased on a *pro rata* basis to avoid this situation.

LAAPs must make up less than 20% of the total number of trustees.

A LAAP must have their appointment as trustee authorised by the LA with which they are associated.

If a member or trustee subsequently becomes a LAAP, they will be 'deemed to have immediately resigned his membership and/or resigned from his office'.

The Articles make reference to s. 69 Local Government and Housing Act 1989 (LGHA 1989), which defines 'companies subject to local authority influence'. However, the effect of the drafting in the Articles makes them much more stringent than the requirements of LGHA.

Interestingly, under LGHA 1989, the relevant percentage limits are only effective where there is a business relationship with the LA. This requirement will be fulfilled where an academy continues to occupy their land and buildings as a tenant of the LA under a 125-year lease.

The limitation does pose logistical difficulties, particularly for academies situated in large conurbations where there may be several LAs relatively closely situated.

COMMENT

Judith Barnes, Partner and Head of Local Government at
DAC Beachcroft LLP:

'The DfE introduced a set of "model" Articles for academies. They contain strict limits on the number of "Local Authority Associated Persons" (LAAPs) that can be involved on the board of the academy, in order to avoid it being a local authority "influenced company" under the Local Government and Housing Act 1989 and the Local Authorities Companies (England) Order 1995.
   A person is a LAAP if:

1. He/she is a member (councillor) of the LA, or
2. He/she is an officer (i.e. direct employee) of the LA, or
3. He/she is both an employee and either a director, manager, secretary or other similar officer of a company which is under the control of the LA, or
4. At any time within the preceding four years he/she has been a member of the LA.

It is worth noting that local authority interests, where there is involvement by more than one, including the LAAP, are amalgamated, even where those personnel are unconnected.

   In order to be an influenced company there needs to be both a LAAP of between 20% and 50% and a business relationship with a local authority (or more than one). Business relationships can include the occupation of premises from a LA at less than the best consideration reasonably obtainable.

   To avoid LA influence, where LAAP involvement is equal to 20% or more there is a mechanism in the model articles to reduce decision-making and involvement of the LAAP to 19.9%.

   Originally the legislation was intended to ensure that where local authorities controlled or had decisive influence over companies it was treated for financial purposes as the expenditure of the local authority, but this was dropped when the new prudential financial regime was adopted in 2004. The only controls that remain are "propriety controls" which require various steps to be taken such as noting on letterhead when a company is controlled or influenced; expenses being limited to no more than members' allowances; no party political publicity; avoiding LA appointees who would be disqualified from being local authority members; and the provision of information to LAs and their auditors.

   The provisions in the model Articles are outdated and no longer necessary, in the context of controls on academies.

The effect of compliance is that it may not always be possible to appoint otherwise good candidates for the role of director (e.g. an individual who has been nominated and voted for in a ballot by the parent body may not be eligible for appointment due to their LA association). This will be the case whether they are associated with the LA in which the academy is situated or not and even if they are employed by the LA in a role which has no educational connection and with no potential for entering into any business relationship with the academy. The model Articles may therefore have the unintended consequence of reducing effective community involvement.'

Changes to the Articles

Changes can, in theory, be made to the Articles of Association to alter the existing organisational arrangements. However, a formal application must be made to the Secretary of State via the Education Funding Agency (EFA) setting out a business case for the proposed change and seeking approval.

Since 28 January 2014, fast-track significant changes relating to expansions, age-range changes (by up to three years), adding boarding provision and amending admissions arrangements in old-style funding agreements will no longer require a formal business case. Formal approval from the Secretary of State is still required, but requests are likely to be approved where there has been adequate local consultation, financial arrangements are sound and appropriate planning permissions have been secured.

7 Statutory registers and Companies House

Trusts are required by law to keep specific records which collectively are known as statutory registers or the statutory books. The registers record information relating to the trust's operations and structure such as the current trustees. Records should be kept up to date to reflect any changes that take place.

The registers should be held at the company's registered office and are the official records of the trust (Companies House records are effectively copies).

Statutory registers are generally held in a loose-leaf binder, although it is possible for them to be written, printed or in machine-readable form (i.e. a version held on computer would be acceptable).

If a company fails to maintain the statutory registers, an offence is committed by the company and every officer of the company who is in default may be punishable by a fine.

The statutory registers should be maintained and preserved for the life of the trust.

Register of members

A register of members must be kept which should contain (ss. 113–128 CA 2006):

- the names and addresses of the members;
- the date on which each person was registered as a member; and
- the date at which any person ceased to be a member.

The register is evidence that the relevant appointments have been made as members are not registered as such at Companies House (see Appendix 1 for example registers).

Register of secretaries

Where a secretary has been formally appointed, details are kept in a register (s. 275 CA 2006) (see Appendix 1).

Register of directors/trustees

A register of directors/trustees must be kept (ss. 162–166 CA 2006) recording the required information for every trustee. Each trustee must provide:

- forename and surname and any former name;
- a service address;
- the country or state (or part of the United Kingdom) in which they are usually resident;
- nationality;
- business occupation (if any); and
- date of birth.

Where a trustee is a corporate body, the following is required:

- the name of the corporate body or firm;
- the registered office address;
- for companies registered within the European Economic Area (EEA) the country/state where the company is registered and its registration number; and
- for non-EEA companies, the legal form of the company or firm, the law by which it is governed and, if applicable, the country/state in which it is registered and its registration number.

The register should also record the date of termination or resignation (see Appendix 1).

The Companies Act allows directors to use a service address so that their private home address is not included in the public records. Generally, the service address will be the registered office of the trust which is often the academy site. Although trustees can opt not to disclose their private address publicly, it must be declared to the trust and to Companies House.

The register of directors/trustees must be open to inspection by any member of the company without charge. It must be made available to any other person under the provisions of the Freedom of Information Act and on payment of any fee required (see Chapter 17).

Register of directors'/trustees' residential addresses

A register of the trustees' residential addresses is also required (s. 165 CA 2006). However, this is a confidential register that is not available for public inspection (see Appendix 1).

Register of directors'/trustees' interests

There is no longer a statutory requirement to maintain a register of directors' interests as was the case under previous legislation. However, the *Academies Financial Handbook* contains the provision that:

'The academy trust's register of interests **must** capture relevant business and pecuniary interests of members, trustees, local governors of academies within a multi-academy trust and senior employees.'

This means that all SATs and MATs must maintain a register which extends to cover key members of staff who may have delegated authority to act on behalf of the trust and enter into contracts on its behalf.

Trustees and key staff should be asked to complete a declaration on appointment which should be updated annually. The individual should provide details of any interests that could possibly conflict with those of the trust. These details should be used to produce the Register which should also be updated annually or on appointment of any new persons.

Declarations should be made in relation to 'any material interests arising from close family relationships between the academy trust's members, trustees or local governors. [Declarations] **must** also identify relevant material interests arising from close family relationships between those individuals and employees.'

The *Academies Financial Handbook* defines connected persons as:

- a relative of the member or trustee – a close member of the family, member of the same household who may be expected to influence or be influenced by the person;
- an individual or organisation carrying on business in partnership with the member, trustee or one of their relatives;
- a company in which the member, trustee or their relative holds more than 20% of the share capital or is entitled to exercise more than 20% of the voting power at any general meeting – this will apply if the holding is taken separately or together; and
- an organisation controlled by a member, trustee or their relative (acting separately or together).

Trusts must also publish relevant business and pecuniary interests of members, trustees, local governors and accounting officers on their website. There is discretion over the publication of other connected individuals.

Single alternative inspection location (SAIL)

A trust can arrange for a professional firm to provide company secretarial services and maintain all records and registers. In this case, the registers would be kept at a place other than the registered office and it is necessary to formally disclose their location to Companies House (which can be searched by any member of the public).

The location where the company records and registers are kept is known as the single alternative inspection location (SAIL).

A SAIL address is notified to Companies House via WebFiling or on form

AD02 and form AD04 is used to notify of company records moving from the SAIL address back to the registered office.

Inspection of the registers

Every trust must keep the statutory registers and provide access to them. They must be kept at the registered office or the SAIL notified to Companies House.

The register of interests must be published on the trust website showing relevant business and pecuniary interests of members, trustees and local governors.

The register of members must be available for inspection without payment to any member and to any other person under the provisions of the Freedom of Information Act and on payment of any appropriate fee required (see Chapter 17).

A request must be made to inspect the register or to seek copies which must contain:

- the name and address of the individual making the request;
- the name and address of any individual who is making a request on behalf of an organisation and the name of that organisation;
- the purpose for which the information is to be used; and
- whether the information will be disclosed to any other person, and if so who they are and the purpose for which the information is to be used by that person.

The trust must comply within five working days of receipt of such a request or apply to the court if the request was not made for a 'proper purpose'. Failure to comply is an offence and the trust and any employee in default may be subject to a fine.

In reality, there are rarely requests to view statutory registers. Much of the information they contain is, in any event, also recorded at Companies House and is easily obtainable electronically and by post for a small fee.

Register of gifts, hospitality and entertainments

Trustees and key staff should declare any instances where they receive gifts, hospitality or entertainment from any third party (Bribery Act 2010).

It is possible to include the information within the register of directors'/trustees' interests rather than maintaining an additional register.

All members, trustees and staff must be seen to act with complete honesty and integrity. Formal declarations ensure transparency and avoid conflicts of interest which could potentially arise through the acceptance of gifts or hospitality compromising the impartiality of decision making.

A clear gifts, hospitality and entertainments policy should be agreed which will set *de minimis* levels below which declarations need not be made.

Any individual who is found to be involved in bribery, either by offering or accepting a bribe, will be guilty of an offence. However, a trust could also be found to have committed an offence if it, as a corporate body, or an individual acting on its behalf, is involved in bribery. It will be a defence for the trust to show that it has adequate procedures to prevent bribery, so it is extremely important that appropriate procedures, including a register, are put into operation (see Appendix 1).

Register of People with Significant Control

All UK companies, including academy trusts, must keep a register of persons who have significant control over them (PSCs). The relevant details must be kept up to date and be filed annually with Companies House as part of the new Annual Confirmation Statement (which replaces the Annual Return).

For trusts, this means formally identifying any persons who:

- hold more than 25% of voting rights at general meetings;
- hold the right to appoint a majority of the board of trustees;
- actually exercise or have the right to exercise significant influence or control; or
- actually exercise or have the right to exercise significant influence or control over any trust or firm, which is not a legal entity, which has significant control over the company.

The PSC register must include details of any person who qualifies as a PSC. The register will be open to public inspection although the residential address and date of birth will be suppressed for individuals.

A PSC is defined as an individual. Any other legal entity will only be registrable if it is a relevant legal entity (an RLE) where:

- it keeps its own PSC register;
- it is subject to Chapter 5 of the Financial Conduct Authority's Disclosure and Transparency Rules; and
- it has voting shares admitted to trading on a regulated market in the UK or EEA or on specified markets in Switzerland, the USA, Japan and Israel.

For any SAT or MAT with fewer than four members, all members will need to be listed as they will each hold more than 25%. Many of the early converters used model articles with three members and so will be affected. More generally now there will be four or more members so that each individual will hold no more than 25%. In this case there will be no PSC.

The following details must be included in the PSC register:

- Name
- Date of birth
- Nationality
- County, state or part of the UK where the PSC usually lives

- Service address
- Usual residential address
- Date the individual became a PSC in relation to the trust (this will be 6 April 2016 for existing trusts completing a PSC register for the first time)
- Which of the five conditions for being a PSC the individual meets – the official wording must be used
- Any restrictions on disclosing the PSC's information that are in place – the official wording must be used.

The trust must confirm the information about a PSC. If this has not been done, it must be noted on the register with the wording:

'The company had identified a registrable person in relation to the company but all the required particulars of that person have not been confirmed.'

A PSC Register must be kept whether there is a PSC or not. Specific wording must be included where there is no registrable person:

'The company knows or has reasonable cause to believe that there is no registrable relevant legal entity in relation to the company'.

If a trust has sought information from a PSC but they have not responded, the register must state:

'The company has given a notice under section 709D of the Act which has not been complied with.'

A PSC's failure to comply with the rules could see their interest in the trust frozen and will leave them open to prosecution for committing a criminal offence.

A separate PSC register must be maintained for any trading subsidiary companies. However, if the trading subsidiary is wholly owned by the trust, then the PSC register will only disclose details of the parent charity.

Company registers and Companies House

Trusts can now opt to keep certain information on the public register instead of holding statutory registers in respect of:

- members;
- directors/trustees;
- secretaries;
- directors'/trustees' residential addresses; and
- people with significant control (PSCs).

However, a trust can continue to hold its own registers. This may be preferable as information such as members' addresses or trustees' date of birth will be protected when registers are held by the trust. If registers are held at Companies House they become part of the public record and available for inspection by anyone via the Companies House website.

Companies House

All limited companies, including trusts, must be registered at Companies House.

Companies House is an Executive Agency of the Department for Business, Innovation and Skills (BIS) and is the government body tasked with maintaining a register of information on every company. Information must be provided to Companies House which examines and stores it and makes it available to the public.

Basic information must be delivered including details of the trustees and company secretary, annual report and accounts and an annual return. Documents may be filed with Companies House either in hard copy form or online via WebFiling.

The main company registry for companies registered in England and Wales is in Cardiff and there is a satellite office in Bloomsbury Street, London. Search, inspection and copying facilities are available at both locations.

The public record

Generally, information filed with Companies House can be inspected by any member of the public. There are some exceptions (s. 1087 CA 2006), most notably:

- directors'/trustees' residential addresses; and
- documents supporting a proposal to use certain words or expressions in the company name.

Certain administrative correspondence is not put on the public record.

The following basic information about the company is available free of charge:

- name
- registered number
- registered office address
- names and service addresses of directors/trustees
- accounting reference date
- date last accounts were made up to and when next accounts are due
- date last returns were made up to and when next return is due.

Other information, as well as copies of specific forms and documents that have been filed, is also available subject to a small fee.

Records can be checked online using the WebCHeck facility on the Companies House website. Searches can be carried out on a company using either its name or its company registration number.

Some of the information, including certain free information such as the current appointments report showing the most recent details of trustees and secretary registered, is available but must be 'ordered'. This requires users to register with Companies House and, where necessary, make payment by means of credit or debit card or PayPal. Where a large number of chargeable filings are made, the trust can apply for a credit account so that a monthly invoice is generated.

All documents are delivered electronically and can be downloaded. It is possible to monitor a specific company, receiving e-mail alerts whenever new documents are filed at Companies House.

Companies House now offers a mobile app which is available to download free. No chargeable information is contained so there is no need to register. The app provides easy access to basic company details as well as information on filing history and details of appointments of officers (which needs to be ordered online). Alternatively, copies of forms and documents filed can be obtained by visiting Companies House in person, or can be ordered by phone for postal delivery.

Filing hard copies

Originally, all filing was done by filling in the relevant forms or providing appropriate documentation which was physically lodged or sent to Companies House. There is a move by Companies House towards electronic filing, but it is not mandatory and certain filings must still be done in hard copy.

Forms can be downloaded free from the Companies House website or purchased from legal stationers.

Certain changes such as amendments to the Articles of Association and the audited annual report and accounts must be filed in hard copy even if the company is registered for WebFiling. In any event, a company can choose for hard copy documentation to be sent by post or delivered by hand. It is worth bearing in mind that documents can be posted into Companies House post boxes right up until midnight (beyond normal office hours) to be regarded as being filed on that day. The Companies House website should be checked to confirm hand delivery options.

A receipt can be obtained for documents sent by post or courier, if a copy of the covering letter is enclosed with a pre-paid addressed return envelope. Companies House will barcode the copy letter with the date of receipt and return it in the envelope provided.

All documents should state the registered name and number of the trust and should be printed on plain white, A4 size paper with a matt finish. The text should be black, clear, legible and of uniform density. Companies House states that failure to follow the following guidelines is likely to result in the document being rejected:

- use black ink or black type
- use bold lettering (some elegant thin typefaces and pens give poor quality copies)
- do not send a carbon copy
- do not use a dot matrix printer
- photocopies can result in a grey shade that will not scan well
- use A4 size paper with a good margin
- supply in portrait format (i.e. with the shorter edge across the top)
- include the company name and number.

The original form or document should be submitted and should generally be signed by an authorised person (i.e. a trustee or the company secretary).

Most forms contain a checklist of information that should be included.

WebFiling

Whilst it is possible for all filing to be done in hard copy, increasingly use is made of Companies House WebFiling service which can be used for filing:

- the confirmation statement; and
- changes of trustees, secretary, company address or name.

A full list of the forms that can be filed by means of the WebFiling service can be found on the Companies House website.

Filing online will generally be quicker and almost immediate confirmation of filing is received in the form of an automatic e-mail acknowledgement. WebFiling is also cost-effective and charges, such as the fee for filing a confirmation statement, are actually significantly cheaper. Payment of any applicable fee must be made prior to the submission of any form or documentation.

Trusts must register with Companies House in order to use WebFiling. However, no specific software is necessary to make use of the service. When registering, the user sets up a password which is linked to the particular e-mail address used to log in. An authentication code comprising six alpha-numeric characters is generated by Companies House and sent by letter to the registered office address. Filing can only be done by a user who has a registered e-mail address, a registered password and an authentication code.

When documentation has been filed, an e-mail confirmation is automatically sent to the user's e-mail address; a further e-mail is sent when the document has been accepted or rejected.

Companies registered for WebFiling can sign up to an 'eReminders' service which will send e-mail reminders to up to four addresses that the accounts and the annual return are due. This is a particularly useful service given the increasingly strict approach to the appropriate time limits and may well help to avoid any resultant fines!

PROOF

Companies can choose to take advantage of the PROOF (PROtected Online Filing) service, whereby they commit to filing all documents electronically. Companies House will generally reject any attempt to lodge paper filings of:

■ change of registered office address;
■ appointment or termination of trustee or company secretary;
■ changes in trustee's or secretary's details; and
■ the annual return.

However, it may be possible to file in hard copy if an accompanying form PR03 is completed with the trust's authentication code.

This gives some protection against fraudulent attempts to change company information or corporate identity theft. This is a huge issue with reportedly around 50–100 cases of corporate identity threat identified by Companies House every month.

Companies must choose to opt into PROOF and agree to the terms and conditions of the scheme. However, it is possible to opt out at any time and the company can then deliver in either electronic or paper formats that will be accepted by Companies House.

Monitor

Companies House also offers the Monitor service which is accessed via WebCHeck. By signing up, registered users are notified by e-mail whenever documents are filed at Companies House. The request is valid for a 12-month period and can be renewed or cancelled. Documents can be downloaded for a small additional fee.

As well as the opportunity to see what other trusts are up to, the service can be used to monitor your own trust so that any illegitimate filings will immediately be identified.

Confirmation Statement Every trust must file a completed confirmation statement at Companies House each year (CA 2006, Part 24). This must be lodged within 14 days of 'the end of each review period'.

A review period is either:

(a) the period of 12 months beginning with the day of the company's incorporation
(b) each period of 12 months beginning with the day after the end of the previous review period.

Care should be taken as the date of incorporation may not be the same as the date that the trust converted or commenced 'trading'.

Companies House will send reminder e-mails for trusts registered for WebFiling and requesting the eReminder service. Alternatively, a letter will be sent to the registered office.

A fee is payable in respect of the confirmation statement. There is a continuing duty to notify a relevant event such as a change in the registered address or change in trustees. The confirmation statement can be updated. However, there will only be one fee charged each year irrespective of how many times the record is updated.

Filing may be done by means of WebFiling. Alternatively, a CS01 form can be completed in hard copy which can be posted or hand delivered to Companies House. There is a significantly higher fee payable to file a confirmation statement on paper. Companies House explain:

> 'Whilst 99% of Annual Returns are electronically filed (and we anticipate the same for Confirmation Statements) a paper provision has been made in the form of a CS01.

> This document is a little large as it covers all scenarios. It really is a very electronic process and is much quicker and easier to file in this way.'

The confirmation statement reviews and confirms that company information is correct in respect of:

- the name of the trust;
- its registered number;
- the date to which the confirmation statement is made up;
- the SIC code;
- the principal business activities of the company;
- the type of company (i.e. private);
- the registered office address;
- the address (single alternate inspection location – SAIL) where the company keeps certain company records if not at the registered office, and the records held there;
- company secretary (corporate or individual), where applicable; and
- the company's trustees (corporate or individual).

In addition, the first confirmation statement must also include the information contained in the register of people with significant control (PSC).

The confirmation statement must reflect the information that is held at Companies House at the relevant time. There will be the opportunity to amend data in relation to SIC codes and PSCs. All other information should be updated through the year as changes happen. If any amendments are required prior to 'confirming', the applicable filing should be made first.

A confirmation statement which does not include the required information will be rejected. However, Companies House can accept a completed annual return but mark it as inconsistent with the public register if the records do not match what is already held there.

Each confirmation statement must include a five-digit 'standard industrial classification' ('SIC' code), which can be used to identify a company's business.

A list of the various codes is available, although most trusts will fall under one or more of the following:

- 85100 Pre-primary education
- 85200 Primary education
- 85310 General secondary education
- 85320 Technical and vocational secondary education.

Many MATs will have more than one SIC code relating to the nature of their business (e.g. a MAT with both primary and secondary schools may have both 85200 Primary education and 85310 General secondary education). However, as more complex multi-academy structures develop, it is possible that further classifications will be created so the SIC code should always be checked.

The confirmation statement must be signed by a trustee or the secretary.

The trustees and secretary (where applicable) are responsible for ensuring that the confirmation statement is filed on time. Failure to do this is a criminal offence and, as a consequence, Companies House may prosecute the company and its officers.

Annual report and accounts

Under the CA 2006, the annual report and accounts must be filed with Companies House each year (see Chapter 13).

The deadlines for filing are initially set by the incorporation date of the company; this may not correlate with either the date of conversion, or the date when the trust commenced operations. For the first period, accounts may be prepared for a period of more than 12 months. These must be delivered to Companies House either:

- within 21 months of the date of incorporation; or
- three months from the accounting reference date, whichever is longer.

In subsequent years, trusts must submit accounts to the registrar of companies within nine months of the date to which the accounts are made up. The accounting reference date (ARD) for all trusts is 31 August, meaning that accounts must be submitted by 31 May each year (although the accounts must be submitted to the EFA by 31 December). Filing may be done through the Companies House e-filing service or through submission of a paper filing.

Filing deadlines are calculated to the exact day and cannot be extended except in exceptional circumstances. Failure to submit the annual accounts on time will trigger an automatic late filing penalty.

With respect to signatories when filing, the copies of the accounts must ensure the following:

- the copy of the balance sheet must be signed by a trustee

- the copy of the balance sheet must show the printed name of the trustee who signed it on behalf of the board even if the signature is legible
- the copy of the trustees' report must include the printed name of the trustee or company secretary who signed the report on behalf of the board
- the auditor's report must state the auditor's name. Where the auditor is a firm, the report must state the name of the auditor and the name of the person who signed it as senior statutory auditor on behalf of the firm.

Change to the accounting reference date

When a new company is incorporated or set up, the first accounting reference date (ARD) will automatically default to the anniversary of the last day of the month in which it was incorporated (e.g. a company incorporated on 17 April 2016 will have a first ARD of 30 April 2017). Subsequent ARDs automatically fall on the anniversary each year.

Trusts, however, are required to have an ARD of 31 August which brings the financial year into line with the academic year. This means that after conversion, the records at Companies House must be amended; no resolution by the trustees is necessary to facilitate this. In any event, the change of ARD must be made before the filing deadline of the accounts.

The change may be made via WebFiling or using Form AA01 'Change of Accounting Reference Date'. There is no charge for making the change.

The following must be provided:

- company number
- company name
- current date of accounting reference period
- the new end date for the accounting period, either:
  – extending the accounting reference period, or
  – shortening the accounting reference period.

The change to the ARD should be made immediately after the trust goes live.

It is not possible to extend the accounting reference period so that it lasts more than 18 months from the start date of the accounting period. Trusts should note that this is calculated including the date of incorporation as the first day of the accounting period. For many trusts, the date of incorporation will, in fact, pre-date the date of conversion, so advice should be sought from a relevant professional.

Change of registered office address

The registered office address can be changed. The registered office is the official address of the trust and need not be in an academy location (e.g. this might happen in a MAT where the central services move out from a school base and into separate offices). It may also be possible for the trust's registered office to be that of a firm of solicitors or accountants which provides ongoing professional support and is the address for service.

The change may be made via WebFiling or using Form AD01 'Change of Registered Office Address'. The new registered office will not take effect until it has been formally registered by Companies House. There is no charge for making the change.

The following must be provided:

- Company number
- Company name
- New registered office address (including postcode).

The Post Office address database is used to verify addresses.

Appointing a director/trustee

When a new trustee has been appointed, by whatever means, the change must be notified to Companies House within 14 days (see Chapter 9).

The change may be made via WebFiling or using Form AP01 'Appointment of Director' or Form AP02 'Appointment of Corporate Director'. There is no charge for making the change.

The following must be provided when an individual is appointed as trustee:

- company number
- company name
- date of trustee's appointment
- new trustee's details including any former names
- new trustee's service address
- new trustee's usual residential address.

If the trustee is a corporate body such as a company or charitable organisation, the following must be provided:

- company number
- company name
- date of corporate trustee's appointment
- new corporate trustee's details
- registration details for EEA companies
- details for non-EEA companies.

Trustees will generally use the trust's registered office address as their service address instead of their private home address.

The trust must agree a statement that the person has consented to act as a trustee in both paper and electronic forms. Companies House writes to all newly appointed trustees to make them aware that their appointment has been filed on the public register and make them aware of their general legal duties.

Appointment of a company secretary

Trusts do not need to formally appoint a company secretary (see Chapter 14). However, when one has been appointed, the change must be notified to Companies House within 14 days via WebFiling or using Form AP03 'Appointment of Secretary' or Form AP04 'Appointment of Corporate Secretary'. There is no charge for making the change.

The following must be provided:

- company number
- company name
- date of secretary's appointment
- new secretary's details
- the service address of the new secretary.

Further details in respect of EEA companies or non-EEA companies must be given if the appointment is a corporate secretary.

When filing, the trust must agree a statement that the person has consented to act as a secretary in both paper and electronic forms.

Change of trustee's or secretary's details

Changes can be made to the information registered via WebFiling or by submission of Form CH01 in respect of a change of trustee's details, CH02 for a corporate trustee, CH03 for the secretary and CH04 for a corporate secretary. There is no charge for making the change which must be made within 14 days.

The following must be provided:

- company number
- company name
- current details
- date of change of details
- details of change:
  - name
  - service address
  - usual residential address
  - other change.

Termination of appointment of trustee or secretary

Generally, appointments are made to the board for a fixed period of time, usually four years. However, appointments filed at Companies House are not time-limited and there is no automatic expiration at the end of the relevant term of office. This means that it is necessary to manually terminate the appointment via WebFiling or by submission of Form TM01 'Termination of Appointment of

Director' or TM02 'Termination of Appointment of Secretary' within 14 days. There is no charge for making the change.

The following must be provided:

- company number
- company name
- current details
- termination date.

Notification of single alternative inspection location (SAIL)

Every trust must maintain company records and registers (see Chapter 7) and trustees must disclose where these are held. A trust can arrange for a firm of solicitors or accountants or other professional firm to keep and maintain all such records and registers. In this case, the SAIL is the location where the company records and registers are kept. A company may only have one SAIL so that it is not possible for certain records to be kept in different locations.

For initial notification of a SAIL, either WebFiling or use of Form AD02 'Notification of Single Alternative Inspection Location' is required and the following must be provided:

- company number
- company name
- address of the SAIL.

Notification that relevant documents have relocated to the SAIL address are made on Form AD03 or, where they have moved back to the registered office, on Form AD04.

The SAIL must be included in the annual return together with a full list of the records kept there.

Removal of auditor

An auditor can be removed at any time during their term of office (see Chapter 13). Within 14 days of the resolution being passed at a general meeting of members, Form AA03 'Notice of Resolution Removing Auditors from Office' must be filed at Companies House.

The following must be provided:

- company number
- company name
- date of resolution
- auditor's details
- date of removal.

The following filings must be made, free of charge, within 14 days by WebFiling or lodging the relevant form:

Change to accounting reference date	Form AA0 'Change of accounting reference date'	ARD must be 31 August. Change as soon as possible and, in any event, before the filing deadline of the accounts.
Change of registered office address	Form AD01 'Change of registered office address'	The new registered office will not take effect until it has been formally registered.
Appointment of director	Form AP01 'Appointment of Director' Form AP02 'Appointment of corporate director'	Directors generally use the academy's registered office address as their service address.
Appointment of company secretary	Form AP03 'Appointment of Secretary' Form AP04 'Appointment of Corporate Secretary'	
Change of director's or secretary's details	Form CH01 'Change of Director's details' Form CH02 'Change of Corporate Director's Details' Form CH03 'Change of Secretary's Details' Form CH04 'Change of Corporate Secretary's Details'	
Termination of appointment of director or secretary	Form TM01 'Termination of Appointment of Director' TM02 'Termination of Appointment of Secretary'	Appointments do not automatically expire.
Notification of single alternative inspection location (SAIL)	Form AD02 'Notification of Single Alternative Inspection Location' Form AD03 to notify that documents have relocated to SAIL Form AD04 where documents have moved back to Registered Office	
Removal of auditor	Form AA03 'Notice of Resolution Removing Auditors from Office'	

Special resolutions

Any special resolutions passed by the members, whether in general meeting or by means of a written resolution which amend the constitution, must be filed with Companies House within 15 days. This means that any appointment of a new member made by a special resolution should be notified to Companies House.

COMMENT

Nick MacKenzie, Partner at Browne Jacobson:

'Sections 29–30 Companies Act 2006 state that any special resolution must be filed with the Registrar within 15 days.

Article 16 of the latest DfE models for both single and multi-academy trusts stipulate that a Member must be appointed by special resolution. Strictly speaking, the trust must then satisfy the filing requirements and a failure to do so is an offence by the trust and every officer in default (s. 30(2) CA 2006) with a potential level 3 penalty fine.

It is important to note, however, that the DfE model articles have changed over time and, additionally, they can be varied. So there is every chance that academies may have an altered Article 16 which does not stipulate a "special resolution" but, perhaps, "unanimous agreement" which is different and does not invoke the filing requirements.'

Subject to the prior approval of the Secretary of State, members may pass a special resolution to amend the Articles and change the trust's constitution (see Chapter 6). If so, the trust must file a copy of the amended Articles within 15 days of the amendment taking place (s. 26 CA 2006).

The following must be filed with Companies House:

- the amended Articles, clearly stating that they are 'amended' on the front page and showing all amendments made
- the resolution signed by a trustee or company secretary.

MEMBERS' SPECIAL RESOLUTION

Company number: 7990029

Company name: Presdales School Academy Trust

SPECIAL RESOLUTION

At the Annual General Meeting of the Members of the above-named company duly convened and held on Tuesday 4 October 2016 at the registered office of the company, Hoe Lane, Ware SG12 9NX, the following resolution was duly passed: In accordance with the provisions of the Companies Act 2006, that the requirement to hold an Annual General Meeting of the Members is removed from the Articles of Association and that Article 19 be deleted and Articles 21, 40 and 41 be amended accordingly.

(Signed)   *Katie Paxton-Doggett*
            Company Secretary

(Date)   3 October 2016

Powers and duties of Companies House

Forms and documents lodged at Companies House are examined to ensure that they meet the requirements relating to form, manner of delivery and authentication of documents (CA 2006, Part 35). Companies House has set out clear guidance about what is expected irrespective of whether documents are submitted in hard copy or electronically. Failure to comply with these requirements will mean that the document or form is not 'properly delivered' and will be rejected. Companies House will notify the trust of the rejection and what needs to be done to correct it.

Where a submitted document is either incomplete or has inconsistencies within it, Companies House can request that it is corrected. However, although Companies House does have some powers to remove 'unnecessary material' or resolve inconsistencies, correcting information may be difficult to do – best to get it right first time!

Late filing

Failure to file information within the specified time limits is an offence, potentially resulting in prosecution and fines. Any 'officer' of the company will commit such an offence if she/he 'authorises or permits, participates in, or fails to take all reasonable steps to prevent, the contravention'. An 'officer' can be any trustee, shadow or *de facto* director, manager or secretary (s. 112 CA 2006).

If the annual accounts are not filed by the deadline, Companies House will automatically issue a late filing penalty notice levying a fine. The penalty reflects the importance that is attributed to making the information available for the public record. The deadline cannot be extended or waived even by a day except in 'exceptional circumstances'. If there is a special reason why the accounts might be filed late, an application to extend the period for filing can be made prior to the deadline. Companies House will usually only extend the period if the reasons really are 'exceptional'.

Trusts must file their audited accounts within nine months of the end of the accounting period (i.e. no later than 31 May (s. 442(2a) CA 2006). The first accounts following incorporation, if made up for a period of more than 12 months, must be filed within 21 months of incorporation, or within three months of the end of the accounting period, whichever is later (s. 442(3) CA 2006). Again, care must be taken as the date of incorporation may not correlate with the date of conversion to academy status.

Accounts should, as far as possible, be delivered in advance of the last date for delivery. If accounts are delivered within the deadline, but are subsequently returned due to omissions or errors which require amendment, the corrected accounts must be delivered within the relevant period to avoid a late filing penalty.

As the accounts are audited in accordance with the requirements of the EFA in the Funding Agreement, they must be submitted in hard copy and cannot be submitted online or via WebFiling.

If the deadline is missed, the initial fine will be £150 with penalties on a rising scale if the accounts continue to be late. Penalties will be doubled if a company files accounts late in two successive financial years.

Filing reminders in respect of the annual accounts are sent to the registered office address and it is flagged whenever WebFiling is accessed in the period up to the deadline.

There are no filing penalties for other company documents, although it is obviously good practice for them to be filed as soon as possible and certainly within any relevant period (usually 14 days).

Trustees are responsible for filing of annual accounts. Any failure to do so is a criminal offence and the trustees may find themselves personally liable. There is no late filing penalty for annual returns but, again, trustees could potentially find themselves liable.

8 Members

The academy trust is set up as a charitable company limited by guarantee. Consequently, it has a two-tier management and governance structure. The members are responsible for strategic oversight with the trustees responsible for the day-to-day management of the company.

Figure 8.1: Two-tier management system

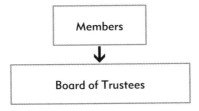

The members are akin to the 'shareholders' in a company limited by shares. However, the members in a trust do not have shareholdings but offer a guarantee which is limited to £10. The amount of the guarantee is fixed when the trust was incorporated and cannot subsequently be increased. The members will only be liable for the maximum amount they have guaranteed (i.e. £10) if the company goes into insolvent liquidation or is wound up leaving debts or the costs and expenses of winding up to be covered. The guarantee is only payable during the time that a person is a member or for one year after s/he ceases to be a member. In practical terms, this is unlikely ever to happen as the DfE will have stepped in long before the £10 becomes payable!

Multi-academy trusts (MATs)

In a MAT there is only one body of members irrespective of the number of individual academies. Generally, they will be responsible for the appointment of the majority of trustees to the board.

Figure 8.2: MAT with three-tier management system

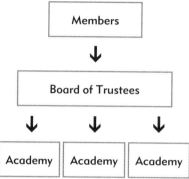

Appointment of members

Upon incorporation, the Memorandum is signed by the 'subscribers' who confirm that they wish to form a company and have agreed to become the first members. Subsequently, the number of members can be increased and members are appointed when their name is entered into the company's register of members.

It is possible to be both a member and a trustee and many of the early single academy converters had a flat governance structure where all trustees were also appointed as members. This was not feasible with Mark 1 sponsored academies or the umbrella structures. The flat governance structure is no longer considered an acceptable model by the DfE. The latest model Articles of Association specifically exclude any employees of the trust from being a member of that trust.

Whilst there is only a requirement for a minimum of three members, it is generally thought better to have five. One of the reasons for this is that a member cannot resign unless 'after such resignation the number of members is not less than three' which can lead to a tricky situation if one member wishes to leave immediately.

> 'The Department recommends that trusts should ideally have at least five members, though they may choose to have more or less than five. A minimum of five members helps to ensure that, to the extent members are available to attend meetings, the trust has enough members to take decisions via special resolution (75% of members agree) without requiring unanimity, while minimizing circumstances in which a split membership prevents decisions being taken by ordinary resolution (at least 51% of the members are in favour).'

In Church of England VC and non-church school MATs, there are generally four members, so that church representation amongst the members is never more than 25%. The same proportion of 25%/75% must be applied if (by exception) the number of members is greater than four.

Members can be either natural persons (i.e. humans!) or corporate bodies. As the academy trust is a charitable company, members are not eligible to participate in any profit of the company. This is particularly relevant for companies or other for-profit organisations appointed as members as they should not profit from that involvement.

Reference should be made to the specific requirements of the Articles to ascertain who the members are.

The original subscribers are the first members.

A Foundation or sponsor body will often be a signatory to the Memorandum. However, the Foundation or sponsor will generally have the power to appoint a number of the members; sponsors will generally have the right to appoint the majority of members.

In a Church of England VC and non-church school MAT, the Diocesan Board of Education is a signatory to the Memorandum which acts 'corporately by hand of its director'.

In addition, the members themselves may appoint additional members by passing a special resolution either by means of a vote achieving a 75% majority in a meeting or by means of a written resolution. Any such appointment should be 'in the interests of the academy trust'.

For non-sponsored trusts that have developed from a collaborative approach, it is often the trustees who identify and recommend suitable candidates to be appointed.

Older versions of the Articles can see other arrangements such as automatic appointment of the chair of the board.

A person nominated to be a new member either signs a written consent to become a member or signs the register of members which signifies consent.

COMMENT

Graham Burns, Partner with Stone King:

Appointment of members

'The starting point to determine who appoints the members is to check the academy trust's Articles of Association. The Department for Education's model articles provide the basic outline of the appointment procedure. The current model articles provide it is the existing members' role to appoint (and remove) members, provided that such appointment or removal is in the interests of the academy trust.

Depending on the individual requirements of the academy trust, the Articles may be amended to provide for appointment rights to organisations or third parties (such as a foundation, religious group or Diocese). In cases where the academy trust has a corporate member, an individual of the corporate member's choice will be nominated to attend members' meetings.'

Responsibilities, rights and remedies

Members' responsibilities

One of the most important functions of the members is the appointment of the majority of the trustees.

In addition, the Articles permit the members to remove any trustees that they have appointed. In order to do so, members pass a special resolution and then give written notice to the clerk that the trustee is thereby removed. This simple provision means that a considerable amount of control is retained by the members.

Although the members theoretically have strategic oversight of the trust, in most cases the general power to manage the trust is vested in the trustees. The level to which the vision and strategic direction is set by the members will depend very much on the organisational structure and will be greater in sponsored trusts.

However, ultimately, only the members (subject to approval by the Secretary of State) have the power to amend the Articles and change the trust's constitution. In order to do this, the members must pass a special resolution in accordance with s. 21(1) CA 2006 (see Chapter 6).

Members' rights

Company law gives members certain rights:

- to receive a copy of the Memorandum and Articles of Association
- to receive notices of meeting, proposed written resolutions and audited accounts and annual report
- to attend, speak and vote at general meetings
- to require the trustees to call a general meeting
- to remove a trustee from office
- to remove an auditor
- to appoint proxies to vote at general meetings
- to inspect the register of members on reasonable notice during normal office hours.

Restrictions

The Articles of Association prevent members from benefiting from the trust except in certain defined circumstances. A member who is not also a trustee may:

- benefit as a beneficiary;
- be paid reasonable and proper remuneration for any goods and services supplied;
- be paid rent for premises let if the amount of the rent and other terms of the letting are reasonable and proper; and
- be paid interest on money lent to the trust at a reasonable and proper rate (subject to a maximum of 2% below base lending rate of a UK clearing bank or 0.5%, whichever is the higher).

Any sums paid must be 'reasonable in all the circumstances' and 'in the interests of the academy trust to contract with that member rather than with someone who is not a member'. The trustees must explicitly consider and make the decision which should be minuted appropriately.

Protection against 'unfair prejudice'

A member may petition the court for a remedy where the company's affairs are being, have been or are likely to be 'conducted in a manner that is unfairly prejudicial to the interests of members generally or of some part of its members (including at least him/herself)' (s. 994 CA 2006). The member would have to show that:

- *The prejudice was unfair.* An objective approach is taken so that it is not necessary to show that the prejudice was intentional or that anyone acted in bad faith, but that a hypothetical reasonable bystander would regard it as unfair.
- *The rights/interests of the member have been prejudiced.* This relates to rights or interests of the member in his/her capacity as member and not arising as a consequence of any other relationship that he/she has with the trust such as trustee or employee. However, the courts have interpreted this widely so consideration is likely to be given to legitimate expectations that the member may have but which are not included in the Articles of Association.

Occasions when recourse to this protection will be made are likely to be extremely rare. However, this is powerful protection for members. Examples might be:

- being excluded from the management of the trust where there is a legitimate expectation of participation; and
- abuses of power and breaches of the Articles such as delaying accounts and depriving members of the right to know the state of the trust's affairs.

If a petition is successful, the court can make any order it thinks fit and this will often be to require the trust to do, or to refrain from doing, the act complained of (s. 996 CA 2006).

Derivative claims

Members are also able to bring an action on behalf of the trust against a trustee, former trustee or shadow director. A derivative claim can be brought in respect of a cause of action arising from an actual or proposed act or omission by a director involving:

- negligence;
- default – the failure to perform a legally obligated act;
- breach of duty – including 'general duties' (see Chapter 9) or any other duty; and
- breach of trust.

Negligence is ratifiable, so that if a negligent action is subsequently confirmed or sanctioned by the trust any derivative claim would be barred.

It remains to be seen how derivative claims might arise in the context of academies; in a wider context the number of derivative claims made remains low with the majority refused permission to continue to full trial. Possible situations might be financial mismanagement, acting outside the company's powers and applying trust money to an object not in the trust's Articles. The courts have adopted a strict application of the tests which need to be satisfied to grant a derivative claim, so any such course of action will need careful consideration and preparation.

CASE STUDY

In June 2016, Greg Wallace, Executive Principal of Best Start Federation in East London, was banned from teaching indefinitely. He was found to have awarded an IT contract worth over £1 million to the company of his 'close friend' and former boyfriend. He admitted that he had not obtained trustees' approval prior to the contract.

However, if Mr Wallace had been a trustee of the trust and the contract, awarded otherwise than on the basis of the merits of the supplier, had caused the trust a loss because of his acting in a conflict of interest, that could well have been grounds for a derivative claim.

Of course, a derivative claim allows members to sue individual trustees on behalf of the trust. This means that any resultant award is due to the trust rather than the member themselves. Further, bringing a claim is a time-consuming and expensive process and members must be convinced that the trustee against whom action is to be taken is able to fund any potential award.

Ceasing to be a member

Termination of membership

Membership will terminate automatically if a member:

- in the case of a corporate entity, ceases to exist and is not replaced by a successor institution;
- in the case of an individual, dies or becomes incapable by reason of illness or injury of managing and administering their own affairs; or
- becomes insolvent or makes any arrangement or composition with that member's creditors generally.

Removal of a member

Those who are entitled to appoint members, such as a sponsor or foundation body, can remove any member appointed by them by delivering written notice to the trust's registered office.

The subscribers to the Memorandum can be removed where the remaining members 'agree unanimously in writing' to remove them. Additional members appointed by the members, other than the Foundation/sponsor body or anyone appointed by them, may be removed if the members pass a special resolution. The member concerned is not entitled to vote on the resolution to remove them.

All such removals must be 'in the interests of the academy trust'.

Resignation

Any member may resign provided that three members remain in office. Resignation is effected by lodging a notice in writing signed by the person or persons entitled to remove him/her and a member ceases to be one 'immediately on the receipt by the academy trust' of the notice.

General meetings

Meetings of the members are known as general meetings. Apart from any specific requirement to call an Annual General Meeting, the Articles contain no specific obligations with regard to holding general meetings. This means that it is feasible for long periods of time to pass without any meetings being held since all resolutions may be passed using the written resolution method!

Members' meetings are closely regulated and the Companies Act 2006 has a whole chapter (Part 13, Chapter 3) dedicated to the requirements. This can be contrasted with board meetings which have very little in the way of formal requirements.

It is extremely important that members' meetings and board meetings are kept separate both in terms of managing the work and in preparing minutes. This is particularly an issue where there is a flat governance structure and all trustees are also members, or when the members are a sub-section of the board. In these circumstances, there may be a temptation for a member's decision to be taken in the course of the board meeting. This is not legally permitted. If a decision is required before the board meeting can continue, then the meeting must be adjourned, the members' meeting held (on short notice if necessary) and the board meeting subsequently reconvened.

Extract of board minutes:

21/16	Governance	
	i.	Governor terms of office
		It was noted that the terms of office of PD, MD, EG and BR were coming to an end.
		BR did not wish to stand again. Governors thanked him for his hard work and efforts on behalf of the school.
		Governors felt that there was a need for continuity on the board and PD, MD and ED confirmed their willingness to stand for a further term of office.
6.30pm The meeting was adjourned PD, MD and EG left the room A Members' General Meeting was held. 6.33pm The meeting was reconvened PD, MD and EG returned to the meeting		

Trustees, who are not also a member, are entitled to attend and speak at any general meeting, although they will not have a vote.

When general meetings are held, it is important that all procedural requirements are met in order that resolutions passed are legally valid.

Convening a general meeting

Members' meetings will generally be called by the trustees. However, the trustees must call a general meeting if it is requested by members holding at least 5% of the total voting rights of all the members able to vote at general meetings.

Members must state the general nature of the business to be conducted when they make the request and can provide any resolution which they wish to be considered. A request may be made in hard copy or electronic form, and must be authenticated by the member/s making it.

Where a request is properly made, the trustees must, within 21 days, call a meeting for a date not more than 28 days after the date of the notice calling the meeting. Where a request included the text of a proposed resolution, this must be included in the notice signifying whether it is a special resolution. Any such resolution will become part of the business that can be conducted at the meeting.

If the trustees do not comply with a valid request to convene a general meeting, members representing over half of the members' total voting rights may call a general meeting within three months of the date on which the trustees became subject to the requirement to call a meeting. Such a meeting should be called in a similar manner to that in which it would have been had the trustees called it.

Notice

The model articles provide that the notice of members' meetings must be given with 14 clear days' notice. This period of notice is dictated by s. 307(1) CA 2006 and cannot be shortened (although a longer period could be specified in the articles if desired).

Giving notice is more than simply notifying members that a meeting is taking place – there is a legal requirement for a formal notice containing details of the business to be circulated. It is a technicality, but it does need to be recognised so that there can be no future challenge to any decisions taken at the meeting.

When calculating the correct day on which, or before which, the notice should be provided, the period is calculated excluding the day on which the notice is given and the day of the meeting. Therefore, notice must be given on Monday of week one for a meeting on Tuesday of week three (to comply with a requirement for 14 *clear* days' notice).

It is possible to call a meeting on short notice if a majority of the members holding at least 90% of the voting rights agree.

The notice must be sent to every:

- member;
- trustee; and
- auditor.

It must be given either:

- in hard copy form;
- in electronic form;
- by means of a website; or
- partly by one such means and partly by another.

The articles do, however, provide that the process will not be invalidated where any individual entitled to receive notice has not done so 'due to accidental omission or non-receipt'.

The notice must state:

- date;
- time;
- place;
- the general nature of business to be dealt with; and
- that members are entitled to appoint a proxy.

Where practicable, the details of any special resolution intended to be passed should be contained within the notice.

On a practical level, it is often more straightforward to include the agenda with, or within, the formal notice.

Quorum

The quorum is the minimum number of persons required to validly conduct business at a meeting. For a general meeting, only individual members or a representative of a corporate member (such as the sponsor or foundation body) count towards the quorum. Any other persons present, such as observers or advisors, even if they are there legitimately, will not count. The exception to this is where there are validly appointed proxies.

The model articles provide that the quorum for general meetings will be two members.

If there are insufficient members present, the meeting is inquorate and any business transacted will be invalid. If the meeting is not quorate within half an hour of the notified start time, or if a member or members leave the meeting, causing it to be inquorate, the meeting will be adjourned. It will be automatically rescheduled to the same day in the next week at the same time and place or to such time and place as the trustees decide.

Chair

The chair of the board will generally chair general meetings of members. In the absence of the chair, the trustees may nominate another member of the board.

If neither the chair nor any other trustee nominated and willing to act as chair are present at the general meeting within 15 minutes of its notified start time, then trustees present will elect one of them to be the chair. If there is no trustee present or willing to act as chair, the members can vote to choose one of the members to be chair.

Adjournment

If a majority of members at a quorate meeting agree, the chair may adjourn the meeting to a later time and place. No business other than that included in the agenda for the original meeting may be transacted at the adjourned meeting.

If the meeting is adjourned for 14 days or more, a fresh notice must be sent out giving at least seven clear days' notice.

▨ Decision making at general meetings

Resolutions

A resolution is a formal decision taken by a meeting. When a resolution is passed, the trust and members are bound by it irrespective of whether they personally voted in favour of it.

Great care should be taken in the drafting of resolutions and reference should be made to Companies House for guidance. If in doubt, always seek professional help when framing the wording to ensure that the resolution achieves the desired aim. The effective date of any resolution should be made clear so that rather than simply approving a resolution, it could state:

IT WAS RESOLVED THAT the name of the academy *be and they are hereby* changed from AN ACADEMY to ANOTHER ACADEMY.

The inclusion of the word 'hereby' indicates that the change is to take place with immediate effect. Alternatively:

IT WAS RESOLVED THAT the name of the academy be changed from AN ACADEMY to ANOTHER ACADEMY on 1 September 2016.

This will be more appropriate where the change is to take place on a stated future date or on the occurrence of a stated event.

SPECIAL RESOLUTION ON CHANGE OF NAME
Company number: 123456789

Existing company name:

At an Annual General Meeting*/General meeting* of the members of the above named company, duly convened and held at:_____

On the _____ day of _____ 20 _____ .

That the name of the company be changed to:

New name: _____

Signed: _____

*Trustee/secretary on behalf of the company.

(*delete as appropriate)

Voting

Most resolutions, known as ordinary resolutions, require a simple majority (i.e. at least 50% plus one of the votes cast).

Special resolutions require a 75% majority. Special resolutions relate to changes to the constitution or more important decisions affecting the future of the trust:

- changes to the Articles
- change of name of the trust
- any resolution required by the Articles to be a special resolution
- the appointment of members.

In addition, changes to the Articles will require approval by the Secretary of State for Education.

If the Articles do not specify that an item should be passed by a special resolution, then only an ordinary resolution is necessary. Where the Companies Act specifies that a special resolution is required (e.g. when changing the name of the trust) this cannot be overridden by changing the Articles.

Each member will have one vote, whether a decision is taken on a show of hands or by poll. No member can vote at any general meeting if they owe any money to the trust.

Voting will be decided on a show of hands and the chair will declare that the resolution is carried in order to pass it. The number of votes for and against and abstentions need not be counted and should not be included in the minutes. The entry in the minutes that a resolution has been passed will be conclusive evidence of the fact without the proportion or number of votes cast.

However, a poll can be demanded by:

- the chair;
- at least two members having the right to vote at the meeting; and
- a member or members representing not less than one-tenth of the total voting rights of all the members having the right to vote at the meeting.

A poll is simply a written vote. In a trust, there is no difference in voting power for individual members between a vote on a show of hands and a poll; each member has one vote.

A poll can be demanded before a vote or on the declaration of the result of the show of hands. However, withdrawal of a demand for a poll may only be done with the consent of the chair. Any result of a show of hands previously declared will still be valid.

The chair shall determine the time, date and place for declaring the results of a poll which will, nevertheless, be regarded as a resolution taken at the general meeting where it was demanded. Any poll on the election of chair or on a question of adjournment must be taken immediately. A poll must be taken not more than 30 days after the poll is demanded. Notice does not need to be given of a poll not taken immediately if the time, date and place at which it is to be taken are announced at the meeting. Otherwise, at least seven clear days' notice shall be given specifying the time, date and place at which the poll is to be taken.

Any member who is absent but who has not appointed a proxy will not count in any vote whether on a show of hands or on a poll.

Proxies

Members are entitled to appoint another person to attend the general meeting in their place and exercise their right to speak and vote. The person authorised to act for the member must be appointed by a formal document signed by or on behalf of the member appointing the proxy that is delivered:

- at the office or at such other place within the United Kingdom specified in the notice convening the meeting or in any instrument of proxy sent out, not less than 48 hours before the meeting;
- not less than 24 hours before the time appointed for taking of a poll, where the poll is taken more than 48 hours after it is demanded; or
- at the meeting at which the poll was demanded (to the chair, clerk or any trustee) where the poll is taken not more than 48 hours after it was demanded.

The proxy can either be appointed simply to attend, speak and vote in the member's name and on their behalf (i.e. voting in favour or against resolutions as they wish) or they can be appointed giving specific instruction on how the proxy should act and the votes to cast in respect of resolutions. The specific wording for both forms of appointment is set out in the Articles and should be followed.

Annual general meeting

It is no longer a requirement for private companies to hold an AGM and some versions of the model articles have no specific requirement to do so. However, care should be taken to take note of the provisions of the trust's Articles to see if it is necessary to hold an AGM; in particular, many MATs are required to do so. For the majority of the early converter academies, the members are not a group entirely independent of the board. This means that requirements for an AGM can sometimes seem somewhat superfluous, as every individual has a platform for raising concerns and an opportunity to consider the details provided at an AGM by virtue of their position as trustee.

The annual reports and accounts are prepared and formally approved by the board of trustees. They are also presented to the members (historically this was done at the AGM). Where trusts do not hold an AGM, the accounts must be sent to all members by the time they are due to be filed with the registrar of companies.

It is feasible for the Articles of Association to be amended so that documentation including accounts can be provided to members by means of publication on a website. This is a provision more generally used by large companies with great numbers of members and is likely to be adopted by MATs looking to adopt a paperless approach to meeting administration. In any event, members will retain the right to request paper copies.

Despite the requirements, members are not required to approve the annual report and accounts and do not have any recourse if they do have issues apart from removing members of the board of trustees!

Some trusts regard the AGM as an opportunity to showcase their activities over the previous year and will invite along the wider local community and press.

NOTICE OF AN AGM

This notice is sent to all members, governors and the external auditors as required by the Articles of Association.

Please note that only *members* i.e. the appointed representative of The Schools of King Edward the Sixth in Birmingham (Foundation), the Chairman of the Foundation Board, the Deputy Chairman of the Foundation Board and the Chairman of Governors of King Edward VI Five Ways School need to attend the AGM and that only these members are allowed to vote. Therefore the reference to proxy voting is only relevant to a *member* who is unable to attend.

Other governors may attend the AGM (it will take place during the governing body meeting) if they wish, but do not need to and should be aware that they cannot vote. It is envisaged that the AGM will take approximately 15 minutes.

Notice of an Annual General Meeting
Notice is hereby given that the Annual General Meeting of King Edward VI Five Ways School Academy Trust (Company) will be held at the Foundation Office on 17 December 2016 during the Governing Body meeting (which starts at 5.00pm) for the following purposes:

1. to receive the annual accounts of the Company for the financial period ended 31 August 2016
2. to reappoint Baker Tilly LLP as auditors of the Company and to authorise the directors to agree the remuneration of Baker Tilly LLP.

By order of the Board

Philippa Cole
King Edward VI Five Ways School Scotland Lane
Bartley Green
Birmingham
B32 4BT   3 December 2016

NOTES to the Notice of Annual General Meeting:

1. A member entitled to attend and vote at the meeting convened by the notice set out above is entitled to appoint a proxy to attend and, on a poll, to vote in his/her place. A proxy need not be a member of the company.
2. A form of proxy is enclosed (for members only). To be effective, it must be

deposited at the office of the company's registered office so as to be received not later than 48 hours before the time appointed for holding the annual general meeting. Completion of the proxy does not preclude a member from subsequently attending and voting at the meeting in person if he or she so wishes.

Drafting the minutes of general meetings

Minutes of all general meetings and Annual General Meetings should be prepared and stored. The basic principles relating to preparation of robust board minutes (see Chapter 11) are equally applicable to general meetings.

Heading

Minutes should be headed with the practical details about the meeting:

- Name of the trust.
- Company registered number. Consider use of the trust's usual headed paper which includes the company number.
- Date, time and location.
- Names of members present.
- Names of proxies present and details of the instrument which appointed them including the member that they are replacing.
- Names of those 'in attendance' including trustees.
- Apologies. Names of those not present who have informed the meeting beforehand that they would not be able to attend and the apologies have been accepted.
- Absent. Where apologies are not given or they have not been accepted.
- Identify who is chairing the meeting.
- Confirmation that the meeting was quorate. If a meeting is not quorate, no valid decision making can take place.

It is good practice to note the actual time that the meeting started.

Participants may be identified in the body of the minutes using their full name, title and surname, or by initials which are identified after the individual's full name in the heading. Whichever approach is selected should be used throughout the minutes.

Written resolutions

Members can also make decisions using the written resolution procedure and, for many trusts, this will be the way that most decision making by members will be done in practice.

Written resolutions cannot be used to dismiss a trustee or to remove an auditor before the end of their term of office.

A copy of the proposed resolution must be sent to every member.

The resolution will be passed if the required majority is met as set out in the Companies Act 2006 unless the Articles contain other specific provisions. Ordinary resolutions require a simple majority of those eligible to vote (i.e. half plus one of all appointed trustees with a vote). Special resolutions, such as a change of name or an amendment to the Articles, require at least 75% of those eligible to vote.

Consent to, or acceptance of, the resolution may be by way of several instruments in like form each agreed by one or more members. This means that the resolution could be returned signed or agreed to by each member individually and still be valid.

A member signifies his agreement by providing an 'authenticated document' which can be in hard copy and signed or electronically sent indicating agreement. A member may not revoke their agreement once it has been signified in this way. Copies of any written resolutions must be kept for 10 years from the date of the resolution and must be made available for inspection by members on request.

Irrespective of the regular use of written resolutions, members and trustees still have the power to demand that a meeting be held.

Companies House filing

A copy of any special resolution or any agreement agreed to by all the members which would otherwise have been a special resolution must be filed at Companies House within 15 days of being passed or made. The resolution should be signed by a trustee or the secretary on behalf of the members.

9 Directors, governors and trustees

The management of a trust, whether a SAT or a MAT, is the responsibility of the board of trustees. The members of the board have a tri-partite role as:

- directors of the charitable company for the purposes of company law;
- governors of the academy; and
- trustees for the purposes of charity law.

This is largely a technical distinction which makes little difference to the day-to-day role of the individuals concerned.

However, the language is confusing and an academy should adopt a title and stick with it rather than using the terms interchangeably.

Role of the board

According to the funding agreement, the board is responsible for the 'general control and management of the administration of the academy trust'.

The funding agreement also requires the board to 'have regard to any Guidance on the governance of academy trusts'. This will include any DfE publications such as the *Academies Financial Handbook* or the *Governance Handbook*.

The board has three core functions:

1. Ensuring clarity of vision, ethos and strategic direction
2. Holding the principal/head teacher to account for the educational performance of the academy/ies and its pupils, and the performance management of staff
3. Overseeing the financial performance of the academy/ies and making sure its money is well spent.

COMMENT

Mark Johnson, Solicitor & Chartered Secretary, Elderflower Legal, Independent Audit Committee Member, The Dean Trust MAT, explained:

'The board should continually review and evaluate the strengths, weaknesses, opportunities and threats and consider how best to play to the organisation's strengths, or bolster the required competencies. Board members are not there to provide operational oversight or 'second guess' the executive managers. Nor are they there to represent or advocate for a particular constituency or interest group. The primary consideration must always be what is best for the pupils. The changing landscape and increasing levels of accountability and responsibility will require high-calibre trustees with specific skills and attributes, who are able to step out of their comfort zone to lead school improvement, provide a high level of professional challenge and work as team players on dynamic boards. Running an academy trust is like running a business, albeit one with a social purpose. Board members must understand that they have corporate collective responsibility and can be personally liable in some circumstances in the event of regulatory action or a legal claim (e.g. breach of trust, accounting irregularities, or negligence leading to personal injury).'

Structure

As a company, a trust's corporate structure is dictated by company law. An individual trust's particular structure is dictated by the Articles of Association.

A trust has a two-part governance structure made up of members and trustees. These trustees are the equivalent of governors in a maintained school (and often in a SAT will be called governors).

Multi-academies are more complex corporate structures but the trustees sit on the main board which retains the legal responsibility for running the overall organisation. 'Governors' sitting on local governing bodies of the separate academies are more like committee members.

Directors

The trustees act as directors of the charitable company for the purposes of company law.

Care must be taken to ensure that appointments of trustees/directors are in accordance with the Articles of Association. With effect from October 2016, corporate directors cannot be appointed (although there are limited exceptions). In practice, trustees/directors on a trust board will be 'natural persons' or a real human being.

The board of trustees is responsible for the management of the trust, although they can delegate functions to committees, individual directors or the CEO/principal. The principal/head teacher will be delegated the responsibility to run the trust or individual academy on a day-to-day basis; they must implement the strategic vision and act within the agreed framework though they will report to the board and provide such information, advice and recommendations as required.

However, irrespective of delegation, the board remains ultimately responsible and accountable.

COMMENT

John Swift, the Business Manager at The Knights Templar School, explained:

'Academy status has changed the landscape for school governance significantly. In the absence of local authority support and with the move to company status, governors are being asked to assume greater responsibility and accountability, yet remain unpaid volunteers. We are very lucky to have such supportive governors whose efforts underpin much of our success.'

The size and make-up of the board will be dictated by the Articles of Association. However, it may include:

- appointments by the members;
- appointments by the sponsor/foundation;
- elected parent trustees;
- staff;
- CEO/principal; and
- co-opted trustees.

No more than a third of trustees can be academy staff including the CEO/principal, but there no longer needs to be a local authority (LA) trustee. The DfE has indicated a move away from the stakeholder model whereby the various different parties involved with the organisation have some form of representation at governing body/board level so that the interests of those groups are given due regard. Moving forward, there will be a greater emphasis on making the right appointments to the board rather than that they are drawn from specific sectors of the community.

Irrespective of the way that appointments are made, careful consideration should be given to ensure that the board has a balance of skills and experience and is truly able to provide effective direction and governance.

Any trustees elected from the staff body as well as trustees elected from the parents of current pupils help to ensure that the focus of the board always remains on the pupils themselves and on providing the best possible education.

The trustees are a central part of the leadership of the school, deciding on the strategic direction and overall conduct as well as overseeing policies and finances. They are there to support the CEO/principal and senior leadership team in realising the vision and ethos of the trust/academy. They are also there to provide challenge so that the trust/academy is continually improving. This relationship between the trustees and the trust/academy – the so-called 'critical friend' – is fundamental to good governance. This much has not changed from the position as a maintained school; as the DfE points out, 'the principles of governance are the same in academies as in maintained schools'.

However, trusts are independent of LA control which means that the board of trustees has greater autonomy – but it also has greater responsibility.

The board of trustees works as a team and is a 'corporate entity'. This means that trustees are bound by decisions made by the board and are loyal to them even if they did not vote for them.

COMMENT

Graham Burns, Partner with Stone King:

Appointment of directors

'The DfE's model articles provide that academy trusts must have at least three directors, but there is no prescribed maximum number. In reality most schools will convert with a similar number of governors to that which they had prior to conversion.

There are some prescribed rules regarding the composition of the governors: firstly it is DfE policy for at least two of the governors to be elected parent governors (i.e. parents of pupils attending the academy). Secondly, the total number of governors who are also employed by the academy trust must be less than one third of the total number of governors including the principal. Finally, the principal is not required but is "expected" to be a director of the academy trust.

Provided the requirements regarding the composition of the governing body are satisfied, the exact powers of appointment will depend upon the individual requirements of the academy trust. For instance the articles may provide provision for a foundation or sponsor body to have certain appointment rights.

It will also be likely that the articles will provide a power for the governors to "co-opt" the appointment of further governors. This provides the current governors with the power to appoint governors themselves; this can be useful if particular expertise is required, for example co-opting a governor with a background in construction would be beneficial if the academy trust was proposing to undertake a new building project.'

Eligibility for directorship

Under company law, there are some restrictions on who can be appointed as a director. However, the Articles should be consulted as there may be specific provisions in relation to some of the appointments:

- Trustees/directors must be aged 18 or over at the date of election or appointment. No current pupil of the academy can become a trustee/director.
- A person cannot be a trustee/director during a period of disqualification whether in the UK or in an overseas jurisdiction.
- A person cannot be a trustee/director during any period s/he is an undischarged bankrupt (without the permission of the court).
- The academy's auditor cannot be a trustee/director.

Directors' duties

As directors of a charitable company, there are legal duties and responsibilities for trustees to observe. Directors/trustees have a fiduciary duty to the trust (i.e. they must act with the 'utmost good faith'). They also have a responsibility to ensure that the trust complies with charity law requirements.

The Companies Act 2006 sets out 'general duties' that apply to directors (ss. 170–177 CA 2006). They have a duty to:

- act within powers – acting in accordance with the trust's constitution and only exercising powers for the purposes for which they were conferred;
- promote the success of the trust;
- exercise independent judgement;
- exercise reasonable care, skill and diligence;
- avoid conflicts of interest;
- not accept benefits from third parties; and
- declare an interest in any proposed transaction or arrangement.

Appointment of trustees

The method of appointment will depend on the category of trustee and the terms of the Articles. However, no more than a third of trustees, including the head teacher, can be academy staff. Trustees are generally appointed for a term of four years.

Parent trustees

A SAT will generally be required to have a minimum of two parent trustees. These will usually be elected by parents and other individuals exercising parental responsibility of registered pupils at the academy. However, there may be circumstances where parent trustees will be appointed by the board.

A MAT may have parent trustees on the board. However, there is no obligation to have parent trustees on the board if there are at least two parent governors on each LGB.

Parent trustees must be a parent of a pupil at the academy at the time when they are elected, although they will not be required to terminate their position if they no longer have a pupil at the school. The board is responsible for making all necessary arrangements for an election which should be held by secret ballot if it is contested.

If the election process brings forward insufficient nominees to fill the vacancies, the board can appoint a person who is the parent of a registered pupil at the academy or if this is not reasonably practical, a person who is the parent of a child of compulsory school age.

The DfE has considered removing the requirement for parent trustees, although parents will, of course, still be able to take up positions on the board.

Staff

There is often a requirement for elected staff trustees.

Member appointments

The majority of trustee appointments will generally be made by the members through such process as they may determine. It is wise to set up a selection process by which the skills and experience of suitable individuals can be considered against the current requirements or weaknesses of the board.

Member appointments may be made in a general meeting. The minuted resolution should reflect the requirements of the Articles, for example:

'It was unanimously agreed that Mr J Smith be appointed as a Trustee of the Academy Trust for a term of four years with effect from [date].'

If the appointment is to be made immediately, this would read:

'It was unanimously agreed that Mr J Smith be and hereby is appointed as a Trustee of the Academy Trust for a term of four years.'

Often, however, it is easier for a written resolution to appoint a trustee to avoid the requirement for holding a meeting. This is a mechanism regularly used by Presdales School Academy Trust, a single academy based in Ware, Hertfordshire.

Company number: 7990029

Company name: Presdales School Academy Trust

ORDINARY WRITTEN RESOLUTION

This written resolution is proposed and made under the procedure set out in Chapter 2, Part 13 of the Companies Act 2006. Upon acceptance of this resolution by an ordinary majority of the Company's Members it shall be as valid and effective as if it had been passed at a properly called and constituted general meeting. This ordinary resolution may comprise more than one document in this form, each signed by one or more Member.

IT IS RESOLVED:

That Mr Michael Robinson be appointed as Governor of the Academy Trust for a term of office commencing on 24 March 2016 and expiring on 23 March 2020.

By signing this document I acknowledge that I have accepted and agreed this resolution:

(Print Name)

(Signed)

(Date)

Trustee appointments

The trustees may be able to appoint co-opted trustees. Resolutions passed at a board meeting should follow similar terms to those of member appointments. The Articles also permit trustees to make decisions via the written resolution procedure. Any co-option of an employee of the trust must not exceed the limit on staff trustees of one third of the total number of trustees (including the CEO/principal).

Sponsor/foundation appointments

A certain number of trustee positions may be retained for appointments made by the sponsor or foundation.

Diversity

Efforts should be made to appoint a board made up of highly qualified skilled/experienced trustees from diverse backgrounds which will promote better corporate governance. Diversity criteria should include gender, age, ethnicity and educational and social diversity.

Finding the right trustee

The DfE have indicated a move away from the stakeholder model of representation on the board. This means that, increasingly, academies will have a level of control over who is appointed.

The *Governance Handbook* states:

'The membership of the board should focus on skills, and the primary consideration in the appointment and election of new governors should be acquiring the skills and experience the board needs to be effective. Boards should therefore develop a skills-based set of criteria for governor selection and recruitment which can also be used to inform ongoing self-evaluation and governor training.'

The *Academies Financial Handbook* emphasises this shift:

'The board of trustees should identify the skills and experience that it needs, and address any gaps through recruitment, and/or induction, training and other development activities. The board should also address this for any local governing bodies it has put in place.'

It is good practice to undertake a regular skills audit; the information gathered can be used to identify the right individuals for appointment. Recognition of the gaps in skills or experience on the board will enable a focused search and appointment. Gone are the days of appointing someone just because they were keen and available!

COMMENT

Dave Gardner, Chair of Governors at Royal Wootton Bassett Academy:

'We undertook a skills audit. Subsequently when we sent out the papers for parent governor elections we suggested the types of skills that we were looking for. Surprisingly it seemed to elicit more volunteers than usual. We had seven nominations for three vacancies where previously we would just fill the vacancies.

For community governors, we usually use our own local network and stretch out to where the current governors have links. If we need an HR professional or a lawyer, for example, we can usually find someone. I have been going out to talk to Rotary Clubs and Chambers of Commerce so that we have a wide range of people to tap into for any specific needs.'

Generally, the first port of call for trusts looking for trustees is the connections of those already on the board. However, if particular skills have been identified, it may be possible to contact a relevant professional body, many of whom will be extremely helpful in the search for a new trustee.

Boards can now take advantage of a free online 'match-making' service offered by Inspiring the Future; see website directory.

'The Inspiring the Future database has over 13,500 professionals, from over 4,000 companies who are willing to volunteer their time and expertise in a variety of ways such as chatting to students about their job and careers route or serving as a school governor.'

Certainly, more needs to be done to raise the profile of trustees who play a vital role in the running of trusts and academies! They are required to make a commitment and accept the responsibility and accountability of running a publicly funded organisation despite being volunteers.

The Inspiring Governors Alliance aims to do just this by:

- celebrating the valuable role played by school governors
- increasing the number of governing bodies actively seeking to recruit and developing high-calibre governors with relevant skills and experience
- increasing the number of employers supporting staff to volunteer as governors as well as promoting governance as a key learning and development opportunity for staff.

COMMENT

Rosemary Bolton, Chair of Governors of Presdales School Academy Trust:

'The board of directors of the new academy consists of competent and capable professionals from a wide range of fields. A skills audit taken at the time of conversion revealed a need for certain experts and these were then targeted and invited to join the board. The current process is for new directors to be approached via personal recommendation, contact with the LA Governance team or using the SGOSS (School Governor One Stop Shop) or other professional bodies; they are invited to meet with the chair, vice chair and head teacher and their CVs together with recommendations are put to the full board for a discussion and vote.

A board of 21 directors is often considered large and unwieldy, but all our directors are busy professionals with various other commitments and many are unable to commit as much time to the academy as often as others, but all of their skills are useful at different times. Each director sits on at least one of the committees and has a link within the school, either with a department or a particular role. Teleconferencing facilities are available at meetings if required. There are five committees in addition to the board, Achievement & Curriculum, Finance, Personnel and Premises and also a Strategic Group consisting of the chairs of the other four committees, the chair, vice chair and the head teacher. There is a separate audit committee. All the committees report back to the board every half term. There is also a panel which deals with disciplinary, exclusions and appeals if required.'

Skills audits and analysis of training needs

A review of board skills and experience should be undertaken periodically. As well as identifying any gaps on the board, it will also assist in developing an ongoing programme of training for trustees to expand and update their existing knowledge and skills.

For some useful documents see Appendix 2.

Induction and training

A structured process should be developed to familiarise newly appointed trustees with the trust and their role. The programme should aim to provide a full grounding as often trustees have no previous experience of a corporate environment and/or the educational world. Whilst induction must convey sufficient information and support to enable the trustee to become effective as quickly as

Figure 9.1: The process for recruiting and appointing new community governors

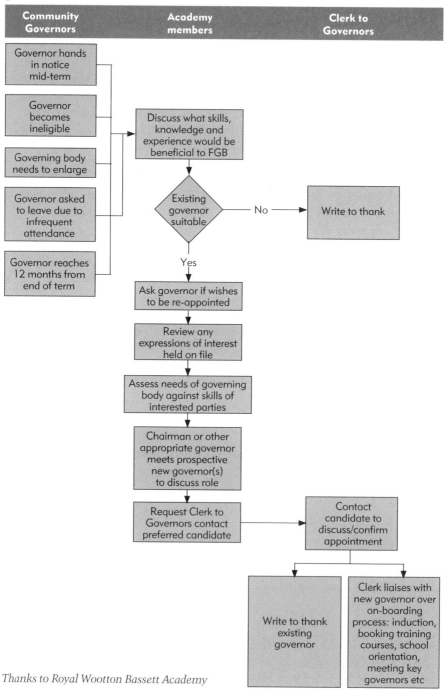

Thanks to Royal Wootton Bassett Academy

possible, it must be remembered that trustees remain volunteers and will generally have other demands on their time which may prevent their attendance.

Despite tight funding, consideration should be given to setting a budget for
governance training and support. The demands on a trustee should not be underestimated and appropriate training and professional development will assist
individuals to feel confident in their role.

Payment of trustees

An academy is an exempt charity and subject to charity law. Generally a trustee,
governor or member is not permitted to make a profit from their role. However,
there are some limited circumstances when trustees can be paid by the trust:

- reimbursement of reasonable expenses properly incurred when acting on
  behalf of the trust (at the discretion of the board)
- payment for services provided outside the role of trustee (subject to strict
  rules)
- payment of salary to staff trustees/governors or the CEO/principal in their
  capacity as an employee and not as a trustee.

Care should be taken by members and trustees when entering into a trading relationship with the trust. The model Articles of Association provide that members
who are not also trustees may be paid reasonable and proper remuneration for any
goods or services supplied to the trust.

A trustee is entitled to enter into a contract for the supply of goods or services
to the trust, other than for acting as a trustee, as long as certain conditions are
fulfilled:

- remuneration or other sums paid to the trustee do not exceed an amount that
  is reasonable in all the circumstances
- the trustee is absent from the part of any meeting discussing such relationship, must not vote on any such matter and is not counted in the quorum
- the other trustees must be satisfied that it is in the interests of the trust to
  employ or to contract with that trustee rather than with someone who is not
  a trustee
- the reason for the trustees' decision is recorded in the minute book
- a majority of trustees then in office have received no such payments or benefit.

However, greater consideration is being given to permitting remuneration,
particularly in relation to the role of the chair, and there have been calls for the
remuneration of the chair of the board to be 'neither mandatory nor banned'.

Termination of office

Generally, trustees are appointed for a fixed term of office, which in the model
articles is set at four years. A trustee may resign by giving written notice to the

clerk at any time, although the articles provide that this will only be valid if there are at least three trustees remaining in office when the notice of resignation is to take effect.

The Companies Act 2006 provides that a 'company may by ordinary resolution at a meeting remove a director before the expiration of his period of office, notwithstanding anything in any agreement between it and him'. This very wide provision is slightly tempered by the model articles which state that trustees can generally be removed from office by the person or persons who appointed them. This means, for example, that where trustees are appointed by the members they can be removed from office, following a member resolution, by written notice to the clerk. Elected trustees cannot be removed in this way.

Disqualification of directors

The Company Directors' Disqualification Act 1986 grants the court the power to make an order disqualifying a person from promoting, forming or taking part in the management of a company without the leave of the court. There are numerous grounds for disqualification and the model articles set out specific instances which will be regarded as disqualification, where a trustee:

- becomes incapable by reason of illness or injury of managing or administering his own affairs;
- is absent without the permission of the trustees from all their meetings held within a period of six months and the trustees resolve that his office be vacated;
- has his estate sequestrated and the sequestration has not been discharged, annulled or reduced; or he is the subject of a bankruptcy restrictions order or an interim order;
- is subject to a disqualification order or a disqualification undertaking under the Company Directors' Disqualification Act 1986 or to an order made under s. 429(2)(b) of the Insolvency Act 1986;
- ceases to be a director by virtue of any provision in the Companies Act 2006 or is disqualified from acting as a trustee by virtue of s. 178 of the Charities Act 2011;
- has been removed from the office of charity trustee or trustee for a charity by an order made by the Charity Commission or the High Court on the grounds of any misconduct or mismanagement in the administration of the charity for which he was responsible or to which he was privy, or which he by his conduct contributed to or facilitated;
- has, at any time, been convicted of any criminal offence, excluding any that have been spent under the Rehabilitation of Offenders Act 1974 as amended, and excluding any offence for which the maximum sentence is a fine or a lesser sentence except where a person has been convicted of any offence which falls under s. 178 Charities Act 2011; and

- has not provided to the chair of the board a disclosure and barring service check at an enhanced disclosure level under s. 113B Police Act 1997. In the event that the certificate discloses any information which would, in the opinion of either the chairman or the principal, confirm their unsuitability to work with children that person shall be disqualified.

Where a person becomes disqualified from holding, or continuing to hold office as a director, the Articles require that he should give written notice of that fact to the clerk. The disqualification provisions also apply to any member of any committee of the trustees even if they are not themselves a trustee.

Shadow and *de facto* directors

The Companies Act 2006 provides that a director 'includes any person occupying the position of director, by whatever name called'.

This is a broad definition which will include all those who have been validly appointed as a director as well as anyone who, although not appointed, may act as a director. This means that boards can no longer appoint an 'associate governor' as any such individual would be regarded as a director irrespective of whether they have been appointed as such. These *de facto* (meaning 'in fact') directors will be subject to the same general duties and other legal responsibilities as a properly appointed director.

A shadow director is 'a person in accordance with whose directions or instructions the directors of the company are accustomed to act' except when advice is given in a professional capacity. Shadow directors are those who have a real influence over an element of the company's business affairs. It is a wide definition and it can be difficult to identify a shadow director. Consequently, case law has identified factors to take into account in ascertaining whether an individual is a shadow director:

- communications were either a 'direction or instruction'
- it is not necessary for a shadow director to give directions or instructions over all areas of the company's activities
- advice of a non-professional nature can constitute a direction or instruction
- it is not necessary to show that the board acted in a subservient manner
- the majority of the board were accustomed to following the directions and instructions and not only a number of individuals
- it must be shown that the directors act on directions or instructions; the mere giving of them is insufficient evidence
- a person can be a shadow director if s/he is involved in the internal management of the company.

A shadow director could be a legal person (i.e. a company, charity or other organisation) which gives directions or instructions that are acted upon by the board.

Although neither *de facto* nor shadow directors are formally appointed to the board and will not be registered as such at Companies House, they may acquire liabilities and, depending on the terms of cover, may not be covered by insurance provision. The general duties contained in the Companies Act 2006 apply to *de facto* and shadow directors against whom a disqualification order could also be made by a court.

The *Academies Financial Handbook* is very clear that trusts '**must** not have *de facto* trustees or shadow directors'.

Liability

Responsibilities also bring potential liabilities, although these should not generally be a threat to a trustee who is acting in good faith. In an extreme situation, a trustee who is found to be acting fraudulently could be charged under criminal law and receive a prison sentence of up to ten years. Trustees could also find themselves disqualified from acting as a director of a UK company for a period of up to 15 years as well as being subject to a fine.

Trustees are responsible for fulfilling the company secretarial requirements of the trust, although they may choose to do so by delegation to an individual. There is an automatic late filing penalty if the Annual Accounts are delivered late which is on an increasing scale. It is also a criminal offence and trustees could find themselves personally liable. The annual return does not have a late filing penalty as such but trustees could also find themselves potentially liable, as well as for failures to file other information at Companies House when necessary.

Members can bring an action on behalf of the academy against a trustee in respect of a cause of action arising from an actual or proposed act or omission by a director involving:

- negligence;
- default – the failure to perform a legally obligated act;
- breach of duty – including the 'general duties' or any other duty; and
- breach of trust.

This means that if a trustee is not fulfilling their duties under company law, they expose themselves to the risk of legal action. It is, nevertheless, possible for the board to ratify or formally approve the trustee's action if it was performed negligently, so that any derivative claim would be barred.

The model articles of association include a specific provision enabling trustees to 'benefit from any indemnity arrangement purchased at the academy's expense or any arrangement so agreed with the Secretary of State to cover the liability'. Therefore, in most cases where a trustee is acting both within powers and in the best interests of the trust, any claim arising as a result of their actions or omissions should be covered by insurance taken out to cover directors' liability. No cover will be provided for:

- any claim arising from any act or omission which the trustees (or any of them) knew to be a breach of trust or breach of duty or which was committed in reckless disregard to whether it was a breach of trust or breach of duty; and
- the costs of any unsuccessful defence to a criminal prosecution brought against any of the trustees in their capacity as directors of the trust.

LAAPs

The Articles contain strict limits on the number of 'Local Authority Associated Persons' (LAAPs) that can be appointed as trustees of the trust (see Chapter 6):

- LAAPs must make up less than 20% of the total number of trustees. On any resolution, the number of number of votes exercisable by LAAPs must not exceed 19.9% of the total number of votes exercisable by trustees. The votes of the other trustees will be increased on a pro-rata basis to avoid this situation
- a LAAP must have their appointment as trustee authorised by the LA with which they are associated
- if a trustee subsequently becomes a LAAP, he/she will be 'deemed to have immediately resigned his membership and/or resigned from his office'.

The limitation poses logistical difficulties particularly for trusts situated in large conurbations where there may be several LAs relatively closely situated. The effect is that it may not always be possible to appoint otherwise good candidates for the role of trustee.

COMMENT

Rosemary Bolton, Chair of the Board of Directors at Presdales School Academy Trust, explains:

'Prior to conversion the governing body had consisted of 21 governors including staff, parent and parent association governors, community and local authority governors; a third of the membership were considered to be LAAPs (Local Authority Associated Persons) according to the DfE guidance, despite the fact that some of them worked in roles unrelated to education and for other local authorities and also included a retired ex-Councillor. At the time the rules were that LAAPs could constitute no more than 19.9% of the board of an academy. Post conversion the board was made up of 21 directors, including community, parent and staff representatives; the LAAP issue has hindered recruitment of experienced and professional people, including democratically elected parents who could not be appointed due to them being regarded as LAAPs.

Presdales is situated in an area where unemployment is very low and, according to census information, one fifth of residents are employed in public services. There is a significant commuter population with many people travelling into London or to other large conurbations.

Directors currently regarded as LAAPs include two who work for London Boroughs which have no relationship with the academy. Both are employed in roles which have no potential for entering into any business relationship with the academy.'

Chair of the board

The model articles require that the board elect a chair and a vice-chair of the board annually. All trustees, with the exception of trust staff, are eligible to stand.

It is a key role in ensuring that robust governance arrangements are in place and that the board is fulfilling its functions.

Governors

Since the Education (No. 2) Act 1986, governing bodies have been responsible for the strategic management of their schools, supervising the budget and appointing the head teacher. This was further expanded in 1988 with many of the administrative and business functions formerly undertaken by local authorities delegated to individual schools. Governors found themselves responsible for the school budget, appointing and dismissing staff, fixing pay, dealing with complaints, maintaining and extending buildings and overseeing catering arrangements.

Governors were already well used to a significant level of responsibility. However, the transition to academy status is another big step and increased responsibility brings with it an increased risk of liability.

As with maintained schools, governors have three key roles of providing strategic management, ensuring accountability and acting as a 'critical friend' by providing support and challenge to the school's leadership team.

School governors make up the single largest group of volunteers in the country. However, 'academisation' has increased the need to professionalise the quality of governors and governance. Being a volunteer does not mean that governors can be amateurs!

In SATs, there is huge overlap between the roles of 'governors' and 'trustees' which cannot really be separated. However, in a MAT, the governance function may be delegated to the LGB where the day-to-day governorship is conducted. Confusingly, members of LGBs are often referred to as 'governors' although legally they are not – and MAT board members must remember that they are governors as well as trustees/directors!

Whilst the role of the trustee is onerous, it is essential that it remains strategic and does not stray into the operational which remains the remit of the executive.

The *Governance Handbook* states:

'It is essential that boards recruit and develop governors with the skills to deliver their core functions effectively. However, it is equally important to emphasise that the skills required are those to oversee the success of the school, not to do the school's job for it. For example, a governor with financial expertise should use their skills to scrutinise the school's accounts, not to help prepare them. If a governor does possess skills that the school wishes to utilise on a pro bono basis, then it is important that this is considered separately from their role in governance, and steps should be taken to minimise conflicts of interest and ensure that this does not blur lines of accountability.'

Link governors

Many schools operate a 'link governor' programme which connects individual governors with a particular department or year group. They can build relationships with key individuals and gain a deeper understanding and insight into a particular area.

A more strategic approach is to set up links to identified priorities within the School Development Plan or Ofsted action areas. Specific links may also be established for safeguarding, SEND, attendance and pupil premium.

A timetable of governor visits should take place which will monitor progress against the SDP or action plan. All visits should be purposeful, focused and recorded.

Governors on LGBs will have a focus specific to the needs of their own academy, but the link arrangement and visits should be made in accordance with a trust-wide policy to ensure consistency and enable monitoring and oversight by the board.

COMMENT

Dave Gardner, Chair of Governors at Royal Wootton Bassett Academy:

'To provide points of contact on specific issues and to ensure all governors have lead roles, we also operate a Link Governor process with links to curriculum subject areas. This facilitates some contact direct with key staff or heads of department that can humanise governors in the eyes of staff (we have nearly 200 staff in a school of our size). I am not keen on governor classroom visits (other than for induction of new governors) as we have a rigorous system of observations undertaken by lead teacher practitioners and peers. On each FGB agenda there is an item: "News from the Links"'.

Trustees

As a charitable company, directors are also trustees for charity law purposes. In essence this means ensuring that the trust is run for the purpose that it was intended, is operated in accordance with its Articles and any applicable laws and that funds are appropriately spent.

However, the terminology is, without doubt, confusing. There is no legal trust in an academy and the pupils are not 'beneficiaries'. Furthermore, particularly in church schools, there will be other trusts relating to the land and buildings with their own trustees!

It is helpful for board members to bear the trustee role in mind when making decisions so that the focus remains on the stated object of the trust (i.e. to advance education).

A person cannot be a trustee if they have an unspent conviction for an offence involving dishonesty or deception, are an undischarged bankrupt subject to bankruptcy restrictions or an interim order, have an individual voluntary arrangement with creditors, have been removed as a trustee by the Charity Commission or High Court due to misconduct or mismanagement or have been disqualified as a director (s. 178 Charities Act 2011).

Just like payment for services to directors, it is generally forbidden to make payments for an individual's service as a trustee except in accordance with the specific circumstances set out in the Articles. The Charity Commission regard the voluntary nature of trusteeship as a strength: 'The concept of unpaid trusteeship has been one of the defining characteristics of the charitable sector, contributing greatly to public confidence in charities.'

In a MAT, where powers are delegated to a local governing body appointed for each academy, the LGB is not a charity. The members of an LGB will typically be known as 'governors' although they will not be directors, governors or trustees of the MAT. Interestingly, this means that the restrictions on payments to trustees do not literally apply. It would still be necessary to consider whether any such payment would be in the best interests of the charity and it will always be best practice that they remain independent and unpaid.

10 Board meetings and trustee decision making

Calling board meetings

Formal meetings of the trustees are known as board meetings.

The trustees are given a certain degree of flexibility in the way that they conduct board meetings as they 'may regulate their proceedings as they think fit' subject to compliance with the rules set out in the Articles of Association.

There must be 'at least three meetings in every school year'. However, the board may decide to meet more frequently to ensure that they are complying with their duties to the company and exercising their duty of care.

Board meetings are called or 'convened' by the clerk who will generally follow the directions of the board. Alternatively, instructions may be given by the chair – or if there is no chair the vice-chair – as long as the direction is not inconsistent with any direction given by the board.

It is also possible for three trustees to requisition a board meeting. This is done by 'notice in writing given to the clerk', who must then convene such a meeting as soon as is reasonably practicable.

On a practical level, it is useful to set dates for meetings prior to the start of the academic year to cover the whole period. Dates should take account of important milestones in the calendar that will require board consideration such as pupil performance data, budget setting or the annual accounts. Ideally, a schedule of dates for local governing bodies (in a MAT) and committees should also be set to ensure that there is sufficient time for detailed consideration of matters by the committee and preparation of minutes to support the report back to the board.

Attendance

There is no legal requirement for trustees to attend board meetings. However, trustees are expected to do so and the annual report that is filed with the accounts is required to set out how many meetings each trustee did, in fact, attend (see Chapter 13). Regular attendance demonstrates that a trustee is diligently fulfilling their role and meeting their statutory duties. Board meetings are central to a robust corporate governance structure. Non-attendance by a trustee for a period of at least six months without the permission of the board can be grounds for removal.

Only the trustees themselves have a right to attend board meetings. There may be other senior staff (e.g. a school business manager) who are accustomed to attending. However, their role is as an advisor to the board and they have no automatic right to attend. Care should be taken to ensure that additional parties who habitually attend remain advisors to the board and do not inadvertently find themselves regarded as a *de facto* director (see Chapter 9).

Notice

In order to be properly convened, a valid notice and agenda of a meeting must be circulated. Without this, decisions may be invalid.

It does not matter whether the trustees were aware of the date and time of the meeting; specific formal notice must be sent prior to each meeting.

The model articles provide for notice of meetings to be called by at least seven clear days' notice, although some versions include the requirement for 14 clear days' notice, so care should be taken to comply with the specific requirements in place. The period is calculated excluding the day on which the notice is given and the day of the meeting. Therefore, notice must be given on Monday of week one for a meeting on Tuesday of week two (where seven days' notice is required) or Tuesday of week three (where 14 days' notice is required).

It is possible to call meetings on short notice (i.e. where it is less than the period required in the Articles) where the chair (or if there is no chair or they are absent, the vice-chair), determines that there are 'matters demanding urgent consideration'.

The notice must specify the date and time of the meeting and where it is to take place. The Articles specify that the notice should be in writing and 'signed by the clerk'.

The notice should be sent to each trustee at the address given by them. On a practical level, notices are now often circulated by e-mail. Even if a trustee has informed the clerk that they will be unable to attend the meeting and given apologies, the notice must still be sent to them. Trustees should read the reports and documentation to keep themselves informed irrespective of whether they can attend every meeting.

There is no required format for the notice which could be along the lines of:

NOTICE OF MEETING

Our Ref: GSGM/4-6
27 February 2017

To: All Governors of King Edward VI Camp Hill School for Girls

Dear Governor
You are requested to attend a Meeting of the Governors of King Edward VI

Camp Hill School for Girls at 6.00pm on Tuesday 7 March 2017 at the School in Vicarage Road.
Yours sincerely

Philippa Cole
Clerk to the School Governors

The notice should be given to each trustee, although the Articles provide that the process will not be invalidated if any individual has not received the notice or agenda. Not only is it good practice to make every effort to ensure that the notice is given to all trustees but it also assists in the efficiency and effectiveness of board meetings which are central to corporate governance.

Agenda

The Articles also require that a copy of the agenda for the meeting is circulated with the notice. The agenda sets out the headings for the matters of business to be discussed at the meeting.

Both the contents and order of the items to be included should be carefully considered and organised. As well as setting out a schedule of the business to be discussed, a good agenda enables all participants to focus on the aims of the meeting.

Whilst it is important that items are self-explanatory, confidential items to be discussed should be described at a high level (e.g. 'Personnel issues' to discuss a staffing reorganisation).

A clear, well-thought-through agenda helps to direct the business and the order will help with the flow of the meeting. Items of greatest importance should be placed near the beginning after the formalities where they will be given maximum focus. However, the agenda is also invaluable to the clerk who is preparing the minutes and gives an easy structure for note-taking!

A typical agenda may include:

- Welcome
- Apologies
- Declarations of interest
- Review of the minutes of the previous meeting
- Any matters arising
- Old business or open issues
- New business such as specific points to be discussed
- Reports from:
  - head teacher/principal
  - chair
  - committees
- Governor visits and training
- Any other business as notified to the chair prior to the meeting
- Items for next meeting.

The agenda to accompany the notice provided previously:

AGENDA

BUSINESS

1. Welcome to Mr M Clark, newly elected Parent Governor, congratulations to Mrs H Singleton on her reappointment as a Foundation Governor and farewell to Mrs P Raghuram, Foundation Co-opted Parent Governor
2. Appointment of Clerk
3. Apologies
4. Minutes*
5. Matters Arising from the Minutes
6. Head's Report*
7. King Edward's Consortium (Initial Teacher Training – presentation by Ms F Child)
8. Widening Accessibility*
9. Composition of Committees*
10. Terms of Reference: Budget Committee*
11. Business Interests
12. Recommending Body included in Head's Report
13. School Development Plan Review included in Head's Report
14. Link Governors
15. Staff Appointments
16. Approval of Educational Visits
    (a) Approvals by Chairman since last meeting
    (b) Approvals required
17. Reports of Committees
    (a) Curriculum Liaison Committee
       The Committee has met once since the last Governors' Meeting 28 February 2017. An oral report will be given of the February meeting.
    (b) Pupil Welfare and Discipline Committee*
       The Committee has met once since the last Governors' Meeting on 27 January 2017. Minutes are enclosed.
    (c) Health & Safety Committee*
       The Committee has met once since the last Governors' Meeting on 27 January 2017. Minutes are enclosed.
    (d) Budget Committee*
       The Committee has met four times since the last Governors' Meeting, on 7 October, 11 November, 1 December and 16 December 2016. Minutes of the October, November and December meetings are enclosed.

18. Income and Expenditure Accounts to 31 December 2016*
    MOVE: That the Income and Expenditure Accounts to 31 December 2016 be approved.
19. Condition Survey Summary*
20. Capital Projects Update*
21. Appointment of Auditors
    MOVE: That Baker Tilly be appointed Auditors for the period ending 31 August 2017.
    MOVE: That a tender process be undertaken for the 2017/2018 academic/financial year.
22. Admissions Policy*
23. Charging and Remission Policy*
24. Best Value Statement*
    MOVE: That the Policies and Best Value Statement be approved.
25. Political Developments/Report from Foundation Grammar Schools' Committee
26. Dates of Next Meetings (Suggested dates: Tuesday 20 June 2017; Tuesday 10 October 2017 at 6.00pm at the School)

* = Note enclosed

NOTICE INCORPORATING THE AGENDA

Company Number: 1234567
NOTICE is hereby given that a Meeting of the Governors will be held on Tuesday 4th October 2016 at 6.00pm

1. Declarations of interest
2. Election of Chair and Vice Chair
3. Apologies for absence
4. Matters to be raised under AOB
5. Approval of the minutes of the Governors' Meeting held on 5th July 2016 (attached)
6. Matters arising
7. Governor vacancies
8. Governor Self Evaluation
9. Chair's Report
10. Headmistress' Report (attached)
11. SEF/School Development Plan
12. Admissions
13. Reports from:
    (i) Finance Committee

    (ii) Personnel Committee
    (iii) Premises Committee
    (iv) Curriculum Committee
14. Governors' visits
15. Governor training
16. Policies
    (i)   Appraisal policy
    (ii) Pay policy
17. Correspondence
18. Items for agenda of next meeting of the Governing Body
19. Any other business

By order of the board

K Paxton-Doggett

Katie Paxton-Doggett
Company Secretary

DATE ISSUED: 26 September 2016

It is useful to set time limits for individual items to avoid wasting time. It will be for the chair to ascertain whether a guillotine should be imposed at the end of that time period and trustees asked to vote, or whether further time is necessary to fully consider the issue.

A meeting cannot decide to rescind (i.e. repeal or withdraw) a decision of a previous board meeting or to vary it, unless it is specifically included as an item of business on the agenda for that meeting.

Opinion is split about including a general 'Any Other Business' heading. Clearly it is poor practice to give an open invitation for anyone to raise any issue. However, there will be times when items arise after the agenda has been circulated which will need to be noted formally by the board. Requiring trustees to notify the chair of AOB items prior to the meeting is generally an acceptable middle course.

ANY OTHER BUSINESS

Presdales School Academy Trust includes Any Other Business on its agendas. As well as items that have arisen subsequent to the circulation of the agenda, trustees note successes enjoyed by the school and pupils such as sporting achievements, successes in inter-house competitions and other outstanding achievements by the girls. At the end of the meeting it is good evidence of the progress of the school and the impact of strong leadership and management.

Reports and other documentation

All papers to be discussed at the meeting should be attached when the notice and agenda are circulated. Clearly, the meeting should be used to discuss issues rather than the trustees being presented with documentation that they will need time to read and digest.

Where there are a significant number of documents it is useful to cross-reference the paper with the agenda items to which they relate or to number the papers.

The person responsible for a particular report will generally 'speak to the report' (i.e. they will comment on the contents and outline the issues). They should not summarise the report. A well-run meeting will not spend time outlining the contents of a previously circulated document which trustees will be assumed to have read. Discussion of the item should be limited to questions relating to the content of the report or discussion of issues arising or decisions to be made.

Unfortunately there may be occasions where it is not possible to provide a written report ahead of the meeting. In this instance, a short synopsis should be given. However, decision making requires trustees to be fully informed and conversant with the matter at hand and great care should be taken when making decisions without the opportunity to fully consider any implications. Reports given without a written report pre-circulated should be an exception and never become the rule.

Annual schedule of business

It is good practice to draft an annual schedule of business for board consideration in the same way that maintained schools would set up a year planner for their full governing body. The schedule timetables issues for consideration and decision over the course of the academic year. This ensures:

- all items are considered on a timely basis to meet applicable deadlines
- the work of the board is spread across the course of the year.

Naturally, unforeseen circumstances occur which may impact on the schedule and additional items arise for consideration, but modifications can be made across the year to meet the requirements of the company and the board.

Managing the meeting

Briefing the chair

The chair is key to ensuring the productivity and smooth running of any board meeting as it is their job to ensure that each item of business on the agenda is addressed and that discussions and decisions are conducted in an orderly way. Where there is a decision to be made, the chair will formally propose a resolution to the meeting, take a vote and then declare the result (i.e. that the resolution is carried or defeated).

The chair may not have experience of conducting a meeting under the specific requirements of academy trust administration. The procedure is more formal than that required under the maintained system, so it is good practice for the clerk to brief the chair prior to the meeting. A good relationship between the clerk and the chair is essential for the smooth running of a meeting and it is essential to discuss what level of support is required as many chairs will not want a formal briefing. Some may find a series of notes helpful or may wish to talk through the main items of business prior to the meeting. Nevertheless, the clerk will be required to provide support and advice as required throughout the meeting.

A briefing document or 'script' provides all the information that the chair will need, although few chairs will rely on the document word for word. In particular, the briefing should contain information on the elements of the meeting that are required under statute and set out the wording of any proposed resolutions.

EXAMPLE   8 June 2016 – A Meeting of the Governors of
King Edward VI Handsworth School

PRESENT: Mrs S Roberts, Chairman

Mr G Andronov	Mr A Patel
Mr J Cammish	Dr T Purewal
Rev P Challis	Miss K Reid
Mr P Cotterill	Mr G P Thomas
Ms A Lloyd	Mrs E Wager
Mr R A Mansell	Mr P Williams
Mrs U Minchin	Mrs J Wilson

Mr J Collins, Secretary, Mrs P Cole, Clerk and Mrs S Soni will attend.

1. **FAREWELL TO REV P CHALLIS**

2. **APOLOGIES**
   Apologies have been received from Mr A Crampton, Professor T Norris.

3. **MINUTES**
   Copies of the minutes of the meeting held on 25 February 2016 have been circulated to members of the Governing Body.
   MOVE: that the Chairman be authorised to sign the minutes.

4. **MATTERS ARISING FROM THE MINUTES**

5. **HEAD'S REPORT**
   The Head has circulated a written report.

6. **BUSINESS INTERESTS**
   In accordance with Sections 177 and 182 of the Companies Act 2006, governors are required to declare their interest in directorships, share-holdings and other appointments of influence within organisations that

may have dealings with the school, or declare there are no such interests. Governors are reminded of their obligations to note ongoing conflicts of interest under Articles 98 & 99 of the Articles of Association. The register of business interests is a public document available for inspection. Governors are asked to check the details in it are accurate and, where appropriate, to complete a new form and give it to the Clerk. Please sign the 'date reviewed' on the second sheet as well as initialling the first page to indicate no changes.

7. **FIVE-YEAR FINANCIAL PLAN**

   The Director of Finance will comment and this item will be taken together with item 8 Threats and Challenges Paper.

8. **THREATS AND CHALLENGES DISCUSSION PAPER**

   A note has been circulated to members of the Governing Body.

MOVE: that, in principle, the recommendation to increase the Published Admissions Number for Year 7 from 128 to 150 for September 2017 be accepted subject to the following:

(i) the Budget Committee gives further consideration to strategies to address the impact of funding cuts; such consideration to be coordinated with an assessment of the impact of cuts by the Curriculum Committee and to include consideration of the increase to the Published Admissions Number for Year 7 from 128 to 150 for September 2017

(ii) the Committees report back to the Governing Body in the autumn term with recommendations either at the next scheduled meeting (2 October) or at a Special Meeting arranged specifically to consider such recommendations

(iii) such consultation and approvals as may be required by the Foundation Board.

Quorum

The quorum is the minimum number of persons required to validly conduct business at a meeting. Only trustees will count towards the quorum and any other persons present at a meeting such as observers or advisors, even if they are there legitimately, cannot be included.

The quorum for a board meeting is set out in the Articles as the greater of:

- three trustees; or
- one-third (rounded up to a whole number) of the total number of trustees holding office at the date of the meeting.

The quorum must be present, either in person or via telephone/video conferencing, so that a meeting can take place.

It is important that the quorum remains present throughout a meeting. Great care must be taken to note if any trustee leaves the meeting, even if only for a few moments, or where any trustee has a conflict of interest (meaning that they cannot participate in the consideration of an issue) as they will not be counted in the quorum.

If the number drops below the quorum then the meeting cannot continue and it will be 'terminated forthwith' or immediately brought to a close. If all business on the agenda has not been covered, the clerk must call another meeting as soon 'as is reasonably practicable' but this must be within seven days of the original date of the meeting.

Any decision taken when the quorum is not present will not be valid and can be challenged.

If at any time the total number of trustees appointed is less than the quorum, then the remaining trustees may act 'only for the purpose of filling vacancies or of calling a general meeting' (i.e. a members' meeting where further trustees can be appointed). Such a situation is only likely to occur in the event of a mass resignation by trustees leaving fewer than three in office!

The role of the chair

The chair is the cornerstone in the corporate governance structure and pivotal to the success of the board. Whilst their ability to chair meetings effectively is important, their role is much wider and demands a talented individual.

There is, of course, no simple formula for what makes a good chair and it will differ from school to school, but the main attributes may be:

- the ability to build effective teams;
- a good working relationship with the chief executive/head teacher;
- willingness to have the 'difficult' conversations;
- PR champion;
- credible public speaker;
- understanding of the educational environment and current changes;
- excellent knowledge of the academy and key staff;
- ability to delegate;
- effective chairing of meetings; and
- the ability to recognise the skills that the team has and to use them effectively.

CASE STUDY

Bob Wintringham is chair of the Faringdon Academy of Schools, a multi-academy trust which has recently expanded from three to eight schools. It is a ground-breaking arrangement which includes infant, junior and primary schools alongside the secondary school. Most importantly it is one of the first to have Church of England schools in a multi-academy trust with community schools. Bob has been extremely successful in his roles; he has chaired five Interim Executive Boards and has been Chair of Faringdon Community College for over 20 years.

'I build teams,' he explained. 'I build teams that are prepared to put in the work to achieve results.'

With a team largely composed of unpaid volunteers, this is no mean feat. But Bob does create remarkably cohesive teams who work well together.

Bob also feels the Chair's relationship with the head teacher is key to effectiveness in the role. But this is not some cosy, symbiotic relationship which does little to challenge the head teacher or the organisation. In fact, quite the reverse.

'The Chair must be able to have those difficult conversations. Sometimes there is no option but for the head teacher to leave and the Chair must be able to recognise this and tell them.'

In fact, what Bob says really sums up the 'support and challenge' or 'critical friend' role that is at the heart of good governance.

What is more, Bob is a charismatic speaker and fantastic PR champion for the MAT. Although he is relatively softly spoken, he conveys an authority so that others stop to listen when he speaks. He has a credibility that comes from a deeply held conviction that the actions of the board, led by the chair, can really make a difference to the children.

Experienced chairs of governors can apply to become National Leaders of Governance (NLGs) through a programme developed by the National College for Teaching and Learning. They must demonstrate a proven track record of contributing to school improvement through the effective leadership of a governing body.

NLGs use their skills and experience to increase the leadership capacity of other chairs to help raise standards so that improvements can be sustained.

Voting

Decisions made by the board, known as 'resolutions', are passed by a majority of the votes cast by the trustees present at a meeting.

Every trustee has a right to be heard on a subject, so adequate time should be given for consideration of a proposal before it is put to the vote. Every board will operate in its own way, but the chair should ensure that all get an opportunity to speak if they so wish.

Each trustee has one vote, although if the number of votes cast for and against a resolution are equal, the chair will have a casting vote in addition to his/her normal vote. However, this will not apply if the chair is not eligible to be counted in the quorum for the purposes of the particular decision.

Only the trustees have a vote and any others present, albeit invited in an advisory role such as the school business manager, do not have a vote.

It is for the trustees to decide on the best way to facilitate voting, but generally it will be on a show of hands with the chair declaring that the resolution is carried. In accordance with the collective responsibility that the board has for decisions, the number of votes for, against and abstentions should not be included in the minutes.

Once a resolution is passed, it is binding on all trustees irrespective of whether they personally voted in favour of it.

There are occasions when it is preferable to conduct a secret ballot. This could be where a resolution is contentious or where trustees may not wish to publicly declare their vote (e.g. in a situation where a staff trustee may wish to vote contrary to the wishes of the head teacher!).

Conducting a secret ballot need not cause administrative difficulties. Each trustee is given a piece of paper on which to identify their choice. This could be a blank piece of paper on which the trustee can indicate acceptance or rejection. In a situation such as a contested election for chair, the names of the nominees can be printed on the paper with the trustee indicating which one gets their vote. The clerk will then collect and count the votes.

Conflicts of interest

It is essential that a fair and just process is applied at all times in trustees' meetings and all should be diligent to note any conflict of interest that arises. If any trustee has other interests which could possibly influence or corrupt their motivation or decision making – or could be seen to do so – then these should be declared (see Chapter 14).

Such a conflict could occur from a 'direct' personal interest or an 'indirect' interest arising through a relative such as where the spouse of a trustee runs a business that is offering services to the trust or any one of its academies.

The trustee must declare any interest and will be excluded from the discussion and decision-making process. They will not be eligible to vote on any resolution in which they have an interest.

Clerk to the board

The DfE recognises that the clerk to the board has an important part to play in the organisation of a governing body's work.

Clerks are appointed by the board of trustees but they report to the chair of the board. Where the role of the clerk is undertaken by the school secretary, bursar or other member of staff, the individual concerned should be clear that clerking the governing body is outside their normal reporting arrangements. Appointing a clerk who is employed in another capacity in the trust can lead to difficulties as a result of any conflict that may arise.

The value of a professional, independent clerk is increasingly recognised. As well as being able to offer appropriate legal and regulatory guidance when applicable, they bring an unbiased view.

The National Governors' Association's (NGA) Clerking Matters campaign has four main aims:

- to increase the understanding of the importance of the work of clerks and what can be expected of a well-trained clerk
- to help governing boards find good clerks where there is difficulty in doing this
- to help clerks know where continuing professional development can be found
- to encourage appropriate remuneration of clerks.

The NGA has published a model job description which sets out the expectations of the role.

It will be for the board to decide if the clerk should be appointed to a particular committee.

The clerk cannot be a trustee or the principal/head teacher. They cannot vote at board meetings (although a trustee who acts as clerk for a meeting if the clerk fails to attend may take part in discussions and vote).

Depending on the conditions of service on which the clerk is engaged, the board may have the power to remove them from office.

The importance of the role should not be underestimated. The minutes prepared by the clerk are among the first documentation viewed by Ofsted inspectors and other external bodies in assessing the effectiveness of a school.

Telephone/video conferencing

The Articles include a provision that trustees can participate in board meetings 'by telephone or video conference'. This very practical provision allows those trustees who may be unable to be physically present to attend meetings. Teleconferencing is now used as a matter of course for many organisations and the majority of trustees working in professional or business roles outside of education have considerable experience of it.

The trustee must give at least 48 hours' notice and suitable equipment must be accessible; if reasonable efforts do not enable access to the 'appropriate equipment' to facilitate participation by telephone or video conference, then the meeting may still proceed provided it is quorate despite the absence of the trustee.

HELPFUL HINTS

Here are some guidelines for trustees to bear in mind:

1. Be careful of your surroundings. Consider confidentiality and sensitivity of information and do not conduct your conversation in a place where you will be overheard. NEVER take part in a meeting if you are travelling on a train – apart from inadvertently sharing information, it is extremely annoying to other passengers!

2. Pay attention! It will very quickly become clear to everyone if a person is not listening to the proceedings, particularly if they are asked for their vote. Focus on the matters being discussed and do not try to multi-task by reading e-mails or watching TV.

3. Conferencing enables trustees to 'participate in meetings'. This does not mean that they simply dial in for the items on the agenda that they are interested in!

4. Identify yourself if you speak. This is more relevant for the people in the meeting room. Whilst everyone present can see who they are, the person on the other end of a telephone line can't.

5. Be respectful. This should, of course, apply to all meetings of trustees but it is more pronounced where some attendance is via conferencing. Try not to interrupt or overtalk – it is confusing and ultimately wastes time.

Adjournments

The trustees can decide to adjourn a meeting before all items on the agenda have been dealt with. If so, they must set the date and time that a further meeting will take place for considering the outstanding items. The clerk will be directed to formally convene such a meeting.

ICSA Code for Good Boardroom Practice

The Institute of Chartered Secretaries and Administrators (ICSA) has formulated a code for trustees and company secretaries setting out matters that it believes 'should be addressed and, wherever applicable, accepted formally by boards of trustees in recognition of a commitment to adhere to an overall concept of best practice'.

Although it is accepted that there will be differences in style of boardroom management between organisations – even between trusts – ICSA has identified basic principles of good boardroom practice which are 'universally applicable'.

Appropriate boardroom procedures should be implemented as well as being made subject to periodic review.

1. The board should establish written procedures for the conduct of its business which should include the matters covered in this code. A copy of these written procedures should be given to each director. Compliance should be monitored, preferably by an audit committee of the board, and breaches of the procedures should be reported to the board.

2. The board should ensure that each director is given on appointment sufficient information to enable him/her to perform his/her duties.

In particular, guidance for non-executive directors should cover the procedures:

- for obtaining information concerning the company
- for requisitioning a meeting of the board.

3. In the conduct of board business, two fundamental concepts should be observed:

- each director should receive the same information at the same time
- each director should be given sufficient time in which to consider any such information.

4. The board should identify matters which require the prior approval of the board and lay down procedures to be followed when, exceptionally, a decision is required before its next meeting on any matter not required by law to be considered at board level.

5. As a basic principle, all material contracts, and especially those not in the ordinary course of business, should be referred to the board for decision prior to the commitment of the company.

6. The board should approve definitions of the terms 'material' and 'not in the ordinary course of business' and these definitions should be brought to the attention of all relevant persons.

7. Where there is any uncertainty regarding the materiality or nature of a contract, it should normally be assumed that the contract should be brought before the board.

8. Decisions regarding the content of the agenda for individual meetings of the board and concerning the presentation of agenda items should be taken by the chair in consultation with the company secretary.

9. The company secretary should be responsible to the chair for the proper administration of the meetings of the company, the board and any committees thereof. To carry out this responsibility the company secretary should be entitled to be present at (or represented at) and prepare (or arrange for the preparation of) minutes of the proceedings of all such meetings.

10. The minutes of meetings should record the decisions taken and provide sufficient background to those decisions. All papers presented at the meeting should be clearly identified in the minutes and retained for reference. Procedures for the approval and circulation of minutes should be established.

11. Where the Articles of Association allow the board to delegate any of its powers to a committee, the board should give its prior approval to:

- the membership and quorum of any such committee;
- its term of reference; and
- the extent of any powers delegated to it.

12. The minutes of all meetings of committees of the board (or a written summary thereof) should be circulated to the board prior to its next meeting and the opportunity should be given at that meeting for any member of the board to ask questions thereon.

13. Notwithstanding the absence of a formal agenda item, the chair should permit any director or the company secretary to raise at any board meeting any matter concerning the company's compliance with this Code of Practice, with the company's Memorandum and Articles of Association and with any other legal or regulatory requirement.

Written resolutions

The most recent version of the Articles permits trustees to make decisions using the written resolution procedure. This may be applied to full board or committee decisions.

The usual rules regarding conflicts of interest apply so that any trustees with an interest are not eligible to vote in favour of a written resolution (see Chapter 14). If the number of trustees excluded from voting due to a conflict of interest means that the quorum requirements are not satisfied, then it is not possible to pass a written resolution.

A copy of the proposed resolution must be sent to every trustee entitled to receive notice of a board or committee meeting, as appropriate. The resolution will only be passed if there is a unanimous vote in favour, with each trustee signing the resolution. This may be difficult to achieve not least on a practical level to secure the relevant paperwork!

Consent to or acceptance of the resolution may be by way of several 'instruments in like form' (i.e. identical copies of the same document) each agreed by one or more trustees. This means that a copy of the resolution could be returned signed by each trustee individually yet the resolution would be valid.

The resolution is passed only when all trustees have signed and returned the written resolution.

Copies of each of the signed written resolutions must be kept in the minute book.

Although written resolutions are useful on occasion, they cannot replace regular board meetings.

Local Governing Bodies

Local Governing Bodies (LGBs) may be established within a MAT with various governance functions delegated to it by the board. However, the LGB does not have a legal personality and is akin to a committee of the MAT. Individuals appointed as governors of the LGB are not trustees by virtue of the position (though they could also be appointed as a trustee).

However, the functions or decision-making powers of the LGB are delegated by the MAT board which remains accountable. The board can decide what to delegate and the remit of any LGB decision making; the model Articles state:

'Any such delegation shall be made in writing and subject to any conditions the Directors may impose, and may be revoked or altered.'

A scheme of delegation defining the lines of responsibility and accountability should be agreed by the board. The NGA has developed a series of Model Schemes of Delegation which can be adopted.

The LGB must report to the board:

'in respect of any action taken or decision made with respect to the exercise of that power or function at the meeting of the Trustees immediately following the taking of the action or the making of the decision'.

Although decisions made by the LGB (or any other committee) need to be reported to the next board meeting, the board does not need to ratify the decision but merely note that it has taken place.

It is good practice to run LGB meetings and prepare minutes in the same way as board meetings. Minutes of meetings will be produced to the next board meeting and will then become publicly accessible in the same way as the board minutes to which they become attached.

Board effectiveness

It is essential that regular reviews take place to ensure that the board remains effective. This can be done as part of an annual review. The NGA has produced a useful skills audit which can be used as part of this process. Results should be analysed to form the basis of a report which can be used to foster growth and development within the board. (See also Chapter 15.)

ICSA has developed a Maturity Matrix which can be used in a self-assessment governance review. The Matrix can assist in highlighting 'factors that would indicate an academy having fledgling governance arrangements to those leading good practice and being sought out as "best in class".'

COMMENT

Louise Thomson FCIS, ICSA's Head of Policy (Not for profit), explains:

'Good governance in academies and MATs can present some challenges. There is no single blueprint for what good governance looks like in academy trusts. As one organisation can have different strengths and challenges to those of another, governance arrangements should be fit for purpose in each organisation at its particular stage in development. What good looks like in one school might not be appropriate for another. The governance maturity matrix helps academy boards to review their governance development and provides criteria for helping academy trusts to improve their governance in a proportionate manner which is appropriate for enabling the school, and its pupils, to thrive.'

11 Minutes of trustees' meetings

A formal record of proceedings at board meetings must be taken (CA 2006, s. 248). These requirements are also contained within the model articles which state that minutes 'shall be drawn up and entered into a book kept for the purpose'.

Once approved by the trustees, the minutes are signed 'at the same or next subsequent meeting by the person acting as chairman thereof'.

Once approved and signed by the chair at the next trustees' meeting, minutes are evidence of the proceedings at the meeting. Minutes also act as evidence that trustees are complying with their duties in running the company and have a central role in the leadership and management of the trust in terms of Ofsted. In some limited situations, trustees can be personally liable (see Chapter 9) so great attention should be given when drafting minutes to reflect the consideration given by trustees.

Minutes are also a very useful practical tool for everyone involved in the board meeting to recognise decisions made, delegation of authority and any subsequent actions for which they may be responsible.

Given the importance of accurate minutes, drafting, as well as subsequent checking and approval, should be undertaken with care. Inaccuracies should always be corrected prior to approval.

Practical considerations

There are no specific rules regarding the way in which minutes must be written. However, there is generally a 'house style' in drafting minutes and a clerk should endeavour to mirror this approach when appropriate. Minutes can follow a fairly traditional style with trustees referred to by their title and surname (e.g. Mrs Bolton) or a more modern approach where initials (e.g. RAB), previously set out against names in the heading (e.g. Mrs Bolton (RAB)), are used. Despite any efforts to modernise minutes, they remain a legally required document and should not be overly informal. Whatever approach is adopted it should be consistent across all board minutes.

In essence, the minutes provide an explanation of the issue, the reasoning behind any decision made and any resultant actions.

- Minutes should be written in the past tense.
- Minutes must always be written in the third person (i.e. 'he', 'she', 'it' and 'they').
- Number paragraphs. It is useful to use a reference system that can be carried forward into other minutes (e.g. a simple increasing numeric system or a system indicating the calendar year such as 01/17 for the first item in the first meeting of 2017).
- Use plain English and avoid acronyms where possible (if they are unavoidable, make sure they are defined).
- Use short sentences and paragraphs to make the minutes reader-friendly.
- Layout should encourage accessibility and easy reading of the content. Action points and resolutions should be easy to identify.
- Make reference to supporting documentation but do not replicate information.
- Any legal or procedural advice given by the clerk should be recorded.

It is useful to identify the individuals participating in a board meeting – a signing-in or attendance sheet can be used to evidence who was present. Getting trustees to sign an attendance sheet which also notes any identified conflicts of interest is another method of jogging their memories to confirm that any declarations are up to date.

Name cards are helpful, particularly with larger boards where trustees may have difficulty in remembering newer members. In addition, the clerk can ask for everyone to introduce themselves and can prepare a simple diagram of the meeting and attendees. This is a good reference tool when noting when individuals leave the room or when actions are delegated (see opposite page).

Minutes of board meetings are also a tool used by Inspectors in Ofsted inspections. It is, therefore, essential that the challenge provided by the trustees (and equally the governors at any LGB where oversight has been delegated) is clearly reflected. One common way of doing this is to include the question posed and the response provided and literally highlight the question in red/bold font.

What evidence was there that pupils made progress following interventions?

The board has a collective responsibility for decision making. Once a decision is passed it is binding on all, whether or not they voted for it. Furthermore, minutes should provide a subject-based record so that it is the nature of the discussion that is important rather than who said what. Individual trustees will not generally be identified in the minutes except where they:

- have been tasked with a particular action;
- have requested that their objection to a decision is noted; or
- are being thanked for their efforts.

The relationship between the chair and clerk is very important for the efficient and effective running of a meeting and they should sit together so that practical support can be given during the course of the meeting. The company secretary/clerk provides appropriate legal and procedural guidance when necessary and is, in fact, one of the most important individuals present as they are responsible for preparing the legal record of what has happened.

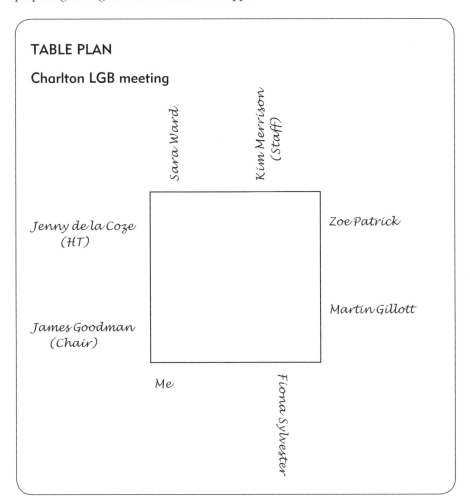

TABLE PLAN

Charlton LGB meeting

Sara Ward

Kim Merrison (Staff)

Jenny de la Coze (HT)

Zoe Patrick

Martin Gillott

James Goodman (Chair)

Me

Fiona Sylvester

Board minutes and members' meetings

It is extremely important to ensure that board minutes remain just that! There may be a temptation where the members are present for a necessary decision to be taken in the course of the board meeting. This is not legally permitted. If a decision is required before the board meeting can continue, then the meeting must be adjourned and subsequently reconvened. Obviously this is only likely to be an issue either where there is a flat governance structure and all trustees are also members, or when the members are a sub-section of the board.

> It was agreed that the meeting be adjourned to enable a members' meeting on short notice and immediately thereafter reconvened.

Drafting the minutes

Heading

Minutes should be headed with the practical details about the meeting:

- Name of the academy/trust.
- Company registered number. (It may be easier and look more professional to use headed paper, which would include the company number.)
- Date, time and location.
- Names of those present. If any trustee is not physically present (i.e. attending by other means such as telephone conferencing) this should be noted.
- Names of those 'In attendance'. Other persons present in a role as observer or advisor to the meeting should also be noted.
- Apologies. Names of those not present who have informed the meeting beforehand that they would not be able to attend and the apologies have been accepted.
- Absent. Where apologies are not given or they have not been accepted.
- Name of the chair.
- Confirmation that the meeting was quorate. If a meeting is not quorate, no valid decision making can take place.

Modern minute style tends to list the various names in columns, although some trusts prefer to list in a paragraph. Whichever way, it is best to avoid any hierarchical order to the list apart from the chair, who should be identified first. The board acts as a body and individuals are present as trustees rather than as representatives of a particular body or group.

It is possible to refer to participants by either their:

- full name – Katie Paxton-Doggett;
- title and surname – Mrs Paxton-Doggett; or
- initials – KPD. The initials to be used should be identified after the individual's full name in the heading.

Whichever approach is selected should be used throughout the minutes.

If the meeting started at a different time to that notified, it is good practice to note the actual time that it started.

See Appendix 3 for useful minute-taking checklists for before, during and after a meeting.

MINUTES OF MEETING

Company Number: 07977368

**MINUTES of a Meeting of the Trustees
held on Thursday 20 October 2016
at Faringdon Community College at 7.00pm**

Present:
Bob Wintringham – Community (**BW**)
  CHAIR
Alex Bond – Parent FCC (**ABo**)
Heather Hambridge – Head FIS (**HH**)
Liz Holmes – Chair FCC (**LH**)
Peter McGurk – Parent FIS (**PM**)
Mark Mobey – Chair FJS (**MM**)
Lisa Proctor – Community (**LP**)
Paul Turner – Head FJS (**PT**)
Alun Williams – Community (**AW**)

Apologies:
Alex Bannister – FJS parent (**ABa**)
Roger Cox – Chair FIS (**RC**)
Rachel Kenyon – Staff (**RK**)
David Wilson – Head FCC (**DW**)

Absent:
Dan Read – FIS parent (**DR**)

In attendance:
John Banbrook – Business Manager
  (**JB**)
Kathryn Hall (**KH**)
Katie Paxton-Doggett – Clerk (**KPD**)
Ian Wright – Chair Watchfield (**IW**)

The meeting was quorate and commenced at 7.15pm

Quorum

The meeting cannot take place unless a quorum is present. The Articles state that the quorum is the greater of:

- three trustees; or
- one third (rounded up to a whole number) of the total number of trustees holding office at the date of the meeting.

Trustees attending by telephone or video conferencing count towards the quorum. However, any other persons present at a meeting, such as observers or advisors, do not count.

The quorum must be maintained throughout any meeting. Therefore, if any trustee leaves the meeting, even if only for a few moments, it should be noted. If a trustee has a conflict of interest and cannot participate in the consideration of an issue, they will not be counted in the quorum.

When any trustee joins or leaves the meeting this should be noted and the quorum confirmed.

> 4.15pm RA left the meeting
> The clerk confirmed that the meeting was quorate.

Introduction/chair's welcome

Although the agenda may have an introductory item or welcome by the chair, often this will not appear on the minutes. One exception is where faith academies use the opportunity to open the meeting in prayer. In such cases, the introduction is included in the minutes as an indication that the board have the faith aspects of the academy uppermost in their minds. It is also useful evidence where an inspection takes place in accordance with s. 48 of the Education Act 2005.

> *Welcome and opening prayers*
> KW welcomed everyone and AW opened the meeting with prayer.

Apologies

Apologies should be considered in respect of each trustee individually. It is for the meeting to decide whether apologies should be accepted and give consent. Failure to give apologies, or for apologies not to be accepted, will be relevant when a trustee has been 'absent without the permission of the trustees' from all meetings within a six-month period. In this case, the trustees can resolve that their office be vacated.

> *Apologies*
> Apologies were received and accepted from ABa, RC, RK and DW. PM would be late.

Declaration of interests

It is good practice for trustees to complete a declaration of interests form annually and for the Register of Interests to be updated accordingly (see Chapter 7). The Register of Interests should be laid before each board meeting for reference and updating.

In addition, at the beginning of each meeting, trustees should be asked whether they have any particular interest in any item on the agenda. Interests need not be pecuniary (i.e. financial) but could be any wider business interest that could affect their decision and lead to a conflict of interest.

Where an interest is declared in a particular item, the individual should be asked to leave the room during the discussion and will not be able to participate in any vote. They will not count towards the quorum during the part of the meeting where the item is to be discussed.

> *Declarations of interest*
> The Register recording governors' interests was laid on the table. No new interests were declared.

Appointment of chair and vice chair

The model articles require that the board elect a chair and a vice-chair of the board annually. All trustees, with the exception of staff, are eligible to stand.

It is good practice to ask the nominees to leave the room to enable a full and frank discussion and to take a vote, even when individuals are standing uncontested. It is also good practice to conduct a secret ballot.

> *Election of chair and vice-chair*
> Nominations had been received for JG for chair and for SW for vice-chair. JG and SW left the room.
>
> The clerk conducted a secret ballot and confirmed that JG was duly elected as chair and SW as vice-chair for the academic year 2016–17.

Minutes of the last meeting

The minutes of the last meeting are formally approved and signed by the chair on behalf of the board. Until this point, minutes are technically 'draft' even though they might have been approved by the chair. Where minutes are in loose-leaf, which is currently the norm, the chair should sign and date each page. This is to prevent any subsequent (potentially fraudulent) changes to a page or pages of the minutes.

Approval indicates that the minutes are accurate as to fact. Any errors should be amended by hand on the copy of the minutes that is subsequently signed by the chair with the amendment initialled. The amendment is also noted in the minutes of the meeting:

> *Approval of the minutes of the Governors' Meeting held 5 July 2015*
> The minutes were amended to show that apologies had been received from Dr J Downs.
>
> The minutes were then accepted as an accurate record, approved by the governors and signed by the chair.

Trustees should have read the minutes prior to the meeting. The content and any updates are not discussed at this point in the meeting, nor should individuals be reporting back in relation to specific actions. The chair should sign the minutes on each page to signify that they are an accurate version of events that has been approved by the meeting.

Approved minutes are evidence that:

■ the meeting was duly held and convened;
■ proceedings of the meeting are deemed to have taken place; and
■ appointments at the meeting are deemed valid.

The minutes cannot be changed after approval unless they are challenged on the basis of proof of inaccuracy of a fact or proof of bad faith which can be proved.

The minutes provide an audit trail of what has happened and that it was done appropriately. The minutes are amongst the first documents to be available to Ofsted inspectors or other external bodies looking at an academy/trust. It is absolutely essential that minutes reflect the meeting but also demonstrate that the trustees are doing their job of strategic oversight, considering progress and providing appropriate challenge to the head teacher and senior leadership team.

Minutes of the board meeting held on 17 October 2016
The minutes were agreed as an accurate record of the meeting and signed by BW.

Matters arising from the minutes

Brief updates can be given of any items discussed and minuted from the last meeting. Each action point should be reviewed to establish whether it has been completed and, if it has not, when it will be done. Any issues that have arisen in connection with an outstanding matter can be raised. The minutes provide an audit trail on action taken in relation to items discussed at a board meeting; as the board should have a strategic focus, these actions should be fundamental to the future direction of the trust. However, in general, board minutes will have fewer action points and greater focus on delegation of duties to progress matters.

It is sometimes possible to identify items that will be covered under 'Matters arising' (e.g. where there is an action point to find out specific information to be reported back to the board). In this case it is useful, particularly for the chair, to include that item as a sub-heading. Any matters which are likely to require significant feedback or necessitate a discussion should be given a dedicated place on the agenda and action points related to that item should be reviewed and discussed at that time.

Reports

Trustees can delegate authority to an individual or committee (see Chapter 14). The board minutes should clearly record any delegation and the terms on which it was made. It should be evident who is able to make decisions and what is required to be brought back to the main board. When any delegated authority is exercised 'in respect of any action taken or decision made with respect to the exercise of that power or function', the party should report back to the board at their next meeting.

Reports should, therefore, be provided by any individuals, whether a trustee such as the chief executive or a member of the executive such as the academy business manager, or committees with delegated authority.

A significant amount of the work done by trustees is conducted through committees. Minutes of committee meetings should be circulated with the agenda prior to the board meeting.

The trustees can require the head teacher or chief executive to report to meetings providing such information that they require. Again, a written report should be provided prior to the meeting for circulation with the agenda.

Any reports required should be circulated with the agenda. The assumption at the meeting is that reports have been read and the person presenting it should be asked only whether they have anything to add or highlight. The agenda item will allow questions to be put to the party responsible for the report and discussion confined to areas that require further debate or formal decision making.

The minutes should confirm that a report was circulated:

Finance committee
The minutes of the meeting held on 25 September 2016 had been circulated.

Sometimes it is not possible to circulate a report or paper, but it is important that it is seen by the trustees and considered at the meeting. In such a case the document is handed out at the meeting and this should be specifically noted in the minutes:

Copies of the full Trust Development Plan were tabled.

All reports and documentation put before the meeting are filed with the minutes and must be made available for public inspection.

Items of business and resolutions

The minutes should record a summary of the items of business. No attempt should be made to recreate a verbatim record of conversations or debate, but they should set out the issue or situation being considered, any decision and the basis on which it was made as well as any action points. Minutes should make sense to anyone who was not present at the meeting!

'Resolutions' are decisions made by a meeting and must be recorded in full using the exact words used. The minutes will then indicate whether the resolution was passed.

> **1089. School term dates**
>
> The Head sought a change to the provisionally agreed end of term date for summer term 2017. It was proposed that Friday 14 July 2017 should be the last day of term, rather than the following Monday.
>
> RESOLVED: that the School year 2017 ends on Friday 14 July 2017

Trustees have a collective responsibility and, therefore, the actual number of votes cast in favour, against and abstaining should not be recorded. In some cases, a board will have a 'proposer' and 'seconder' in connection with formal resolutions.

> *Appointment of Responsible Officer*
> Directors RESOLVED that JM be appointed as Responsible Officer, proposed by RC and seconded by DR.

Correspondence

Communications received such as from the DfE, LA or Diocese could be reported to the board either in a specific agenda item or as part of any report from the chair.

Any other business

The chair should ensure that the item remains focused on matters of strategic importance. Generally, items for 'any other business' should be submitted to the chair in advance of the meeting to avoid discussion without sufficient preparation. Items should be urgent matters that have arisen after the agenda has been drawn up. It may be necessary for the chair to adjourn any such matter to the next meeting or delegate it for further consideration to a committee or working party.

Presdales School often has an 'and finally' feel to AOB which informs governors of the outstanding achievements of pupils which are their focus:

16/13	**Any other business**
	The PE department had enjoyed a number of fantastic achievements including the regional finals for table tennis, cross country and football. A gold medal had been won at a national diving event by a pupil and another pupil had been selected for the England under-16 squad for rounders.
	Two pupils had qualified in the European maths championship.
	There would be a celebratory assembly held on 15 April at 9am at which presentations would be made. All pupils from years 7–13 attend which gives a sense of cohesion.

Next meeting

It is good practice for the board to set dates for full board and committee meetings for the year. In any event, trustees should not leave a board meeting without having a date for the next meeting identified.

Action points

It is important for any actions to be clearly defined and the individual or group responsible to be identified. A clear format is extremely useful so that actions and the person or group responsible are easily identified even on skimming. The clearest layout is a dedicated action column.

55/13	*Governor self-evaluation*	
	All were encouraged to complete the form for consideration at the next board meeting.	**ALL**
	Although it was not a skills audit, it could help in appointments to link governorship or committees. The committee list would be circulated and reviewed at the next meeting.	**KPD**

Alternatively, the action can be identified at the end of the section to which it applies.

4.2 *Delegation of governor's responsibilities*
Governors went through the plan of governor's responsibilities and the annual plan showing what to review and when this is necessary. Lisa will update and put onto the Learning Platform. Action: Lisa Smith.

Where there are a lot of action points arising, it can be useful for a schedule to be prepared and appended to the minutes.

Minute reference	Action point	Person responsible
6.1	Pupil Premium statement to be sent to all governors	**AR**
8	Computer Science Development Project – Phase 2 /Lecture Theatre implementation	**AR/HH**
9.1	Access to Blue Sky	**AH/relevant governors**
9.2	Training session for governors on Blue Sky	**AH/Clerk**
10	Updating and dissemination of school policies	**Clerk**
11(a)	Reports on the examination outcomes and the university destinations of leavers to be circulated to all governors	**SN/Clerk/TH**
11(b)	Offer of free influenza vaccinations to the staff	**AH/SB**
11(d)	Amendment to Property Committee minutes	**Clerk**
13	Chair to write to Mary Chaplin	**PCHM**

Close of meeting

The closing time of the meeting can be included as part of the heading. However, it is generally easier to note at the very bottom of the minutes. The starting and closing time for the meeting will indicate the length of meetings. If board meetings regularly go on for more than three hours, consideration should be given to whether more meetings should be scheduled. Productivity will dip in long meetings, particularly when there is no break. If meetings are too long, consideration should also be given by the board as to whether their focus is truly strategic or whether they are getting too closely embroiled in the day-to-day.

Very short meetings can seem to be a bonus, particularly to the clerk! However, although the board can delegate its powers and authority, it retains overall responsibility for running the trust. If meetings are regularly short, then it must be queried whether the board is effectively overseeing the delegated responsibility and whether it has a proactive strategy that it is progressing.

Confidential items

Items requiring confidential discussion should be listed on the agenda in general terms so that the details are not provided. Commonly, confidential items are put at the end of the agenda to enable any person who cannot be present for the discussion to leave.

The minutes will contain a simple reference to the confidential item:

> 07/14   A confidential staffing matter was discussed.

Separate confidential minutes are prepared and headed up in exactly the same way as the main minutes. The confidential item is outlined and referenced with the same number taken from the main minutes:

> 07/14   A disciplinary hearing had been held and allegations deemed to have merit. As a result a member of staff had been dismissed. They had now lodged an appeal which would be heard before Christmas.

Great care should be taken when discussing confidential items, particularly when they relate to ongoing complaints, disciplinary or capability hearings. Panels are, initially, drawn from trustees appointed to the board. It is important that they are not given too much information, which could be construed as removing their impartiality and disqualifying them from taking part on a panel.

It is always important to remember that discussion of individuals in a meeting situation will constitute 'publication' for the purposes of defamation and any false derogatory comments will be 'slander'. These will be 'libel' if they are repeated in the minutes.

It is usual practice to print confidential minutes on pink paper so that they are easily identifiable. Once approved, they should be stored separately from the main board minutes in a lockable filing cabinet which is accessible only to authorised persons.

Preparation of minutes

A first draft of the minutes should be produced as soon as possible after the meeting, ideally the following day. These should be forwarded to the chair to check for accuracy and approval. The chair should not add extra information that was not available at the time of the meeting or amend the minutes to give a more favourable slant. The chair should, however, check the contents of the minutes, amending errors or making changes to clarify the proceedings.

When the approved minutes are returned from the chair they should be circulated to all board members and anyone else who receives a copy.

Storing minutes

Minutes must be kept for at least ten years from the date of the meeting. Failure to comply with the requirements for producing and storing minutes will mean that every officer of the company who is in default (which could potentially be every trustee and the secretary/clerk) commits an offence. Anyone found guilty could be liable to payment of a fine.

The model Articles of Association provides that the trustees must make various documents available to 'persons wishing to inspect them'. They should be made available at every academy and the registered office 'as soon as is reasonably practicable'. The documents concerned are:

a. the agenda for every meeting of the trustees;
b. the draft minutes of every such meeting, when approved by the person acting as chairman of that meeting;
c. the signed minutes of every such meeting; and
d. any report, document or other paper considered at any such meeting. This will obviously include the minutes of any LGB meetings in a MAT.

The same documentation is also required to be sent to the Secretary of State 'as soon as is reasonably practicable'. However, in practice, few trusts forward all such documentation and the EFA will specify if the trust is to forward the documentation in accordance with these measures. Instead, the trust should ensure secure storage of documentation at the registered office (or such other location identified as the SAIL – see Chapter 7) at each academy and make available to the Secretary of State and their officers as required.

The signed minutes must be kept securely together with the notice and agenda for the meeting and supporting documentation provided for consideration at the meeting. Documentation is generally filed in a dedicated minute book which is usually in the form of a loose-leaf binder to which additional pages can be added easily.

12 Financial management

Accounting reference date

The financial year for an academy will run from 1 September to 31 August so that, unlike maintained schools, the academic year and the financial year will be brought into line. The date of the financial year-end is known as the accounting reference date (ARD). This is also the date that determines when accounts are due to be delivered to Companies House.

COMMENT

Martin Wyatt, Director with Witley Stimpson Limited, explains:

'The date to which accounts are prepared is referred to as the accounting reference date. This is a formal registered date and recorded at Companies House. Academy trusts must have the date of 31 August as their accounting reference date.

Academy trusts must ensure that their accounting reference date is registered as 31 August at Companies House to correspond with the date required under their Funding Agreement. When the academy trust is first formed the accounting reference date will automatically be set by Companies House to the last day of the month in which the academy trust is incorporated. For example, if the academy was incorporated on 10 May 2016, its first accounting reference date would be 31 May 2017, and unless amended, 31 May for every year thereafter.

After incorporation the academy must ensure it changes its accounting reference date at Companies House to 31 August.'

Immediately after setting up a trust by whichever means, it is necessary to change the ARD at Companies House. As this is a requirement of the funding agreement, no resolution of the trustees is required to facilitate this. The change must be formally notified to Companies House (see Chapter 7).

Accounting officer

The funding agreement requires every trust to appoint an accounting officer and notify the Secretary of State of that appointment.

The *Academies Financial Handbook* states that the accounting officer should be a 'fit and suitable person' for the role. The accounting officer should be the senior executive of the trust, so that in a single academy trust, it will be the principal/head teacher, and in a MAT the chief executive or executive principal/head teacher. The *Academies Financial Handbook* makes clear that this role may not rotate.

The accounting officer has a personal responsibility for:

- regularity (i.e. that all items of expenditure and receipts are dealt with in accordance with the appropriate legislation, funding agreement and the *Academies Financial Handbook*);
- propriety (i.e. that expenditure and receipts are dealt with in accordance with Parliament's intentions and the principles of parliamentary control); and
- value for money (i.e. that the best educational outcomes are achieved through the economic, efficient and effective use of resources).

The accounting officer must complete and sign a statement on regularity, propriety and compliance each year which is submitted to the EFA with the audited accounts. The accounting officer must also demonstrate via the governance statement which forms part of the financial statements how the trust has secured value for money.

The accounting officer also has responsibility for ensuring that proper financial records are kept and 'for the management of opportunities and risks' and is 'accountable for the trust's financial affairs'.

The accounting officer must 'take personal responsibility (which **must not** be delegated) for assuring the board that there is compliance with the *Handbook* and the funding agreement'. They must also notify the board in writing if at any time 'any action or policy under consideration by them is incompatible with the terms of the articles, funding agreement' or the *Handbook*.

It is an onerous role which is generally undertaken by an individual with little or no formal training in accounting or financial processes.

Chief financial officer

Of course, whilst the accounting officer has overall responsibility and is accountable for the trust's financial affairs, in practice the role will be fulfilled by a finance director or academy business manager. The *Academies Financial Handbook* specifically states that a trust **must** have a chief financial officer who is appointed by the board of trustees and who is 'the trust's finance director, business manager or equivalent' who will lead on financial matters.

The CFO should ensure that 'sound and appropriate financial governance and risk management arrangements are in place, preparing and monitoring of budgets, and ensuring the delivery of annual accounts'. Not only should the CFO fulfil a 'technical' role in being responsible for making sure that proper processes are in place but they must play a 'leadership role' ensuring that sound financial governance systems are in place and understood across the trust.

The CFO can delegate their duties. However, all trust finance staff must be 'appropriately qualified and/or experienced'.

COMMENT

Rachael Warwick, Executive Head teacher of Didcot Academy of Schools:

'One thing I have learnt over the last couple of years is that it is crucial to have an effective and appropriately qualified Finance Director to run a successful MAT!'

Exempt charity status

Academy trusts are charitable companies limited by guarantee. However, they are exempt charities, which means that they do not need to register with the Charity Commission. The Secretary of State for Education is the principal regulator for schools and the DfE is responsible for overseeing the compliance by trusts with charity law.

As well as not being required to submit their accounts to the Charity Commission, there are other advantages of exempt charity status:

- exemption from corporation tax; and
- business rate relief – 80% compulsory and 20% at the discretion of the local authority.

Subsidiary trading companies

As a charity, an academy trust is not permitted to trade and make a profit. It is, however, possible to set up a subsidiary trading company which can sell products or services and Gift Aid profits back to the trust.

EXPERIENCE

Cabot Learning Federation:

'CLF owns houses which were part of the leasehold that we were granted from the foundation. The houses are rented out and the income goes through a trading company, John Cabot Ventures. This company receives any commercial income such as fees for consultancy work or any charged-for courses that we put on.

Having a separate trading company helps CLF to manage corporation tax issues and the whole profit is gifted to CLF at the end of the year.'

Gift aid

The funding agreement provides that 'the academy will establish an appropriate mechanism for the receipt and management of donations and shall use reasonable endeavours to procure donations through that mechanism for the purpose of the objects specified in the Articles'. The presumption is that donations will be encouraged and maximised to further the interests of the trust.

It is possible to 'gift aid' donations to increase the sum by way of tax relief. The trust does not need to register with HMRC for the purposes of gift aid but will need to apply formally to HMRC for recognition as a charity. Tax on the 'gross' equivalent of any donation (i.e. their value before basic rate tax was deducted) can be reclaimed.

As of 6 April 2013, the Gift Aid Small Donations Scheme (GASDS) has meant that gift aid can also be claimed on 'bucket collections' up to a total of £5,000 in a tax year provided that donations are cash of £20 or less (i.e. in bank notes or coins). The trust must have:

- existed for at least the last two complete tax years (6 April–5 April);
- made a successful gift aid claim in at least two out of the last four tax years, without a gap of two or more tax years between those gift aid claims or since the last claim made; and
- not incurred a penalty on a gift aid or GASDS claim made in the current or previous tax year.

There are proposals to simplify the GASDS by removing the first two of these requirements and exploring whether donations made by contactless credit cards and debit cards could be brought within the scope of the scheme. Irrespective of whether these go ahead, the scheme will not be extended to include donations made by cheque, text message or direct debit.

A GASDS claim cannot be more than 10 times the Gift Aid claim. However, this does mean that £1,000 worth of donations through GASDS can be claimed even if only £100 of Gift Aid donations has been received in the same tax year.

Records must be kept of:

- the total cash donations collected
- the date of the collection
- the date it was paid into a bank account.

Tax relief

As a charity, a trust does not need to pay tax on income which is used for charitable purposes, i.e. that complies with the objects clause of the Articles. It is possible to arrange for interest to be paid without tax deducted by presenting the letter of recognition from HMRC to the bank or building society.

Alternatively, a trust can claim tax back on income received on which tax has already been paid. For the current tax year, this is done by making a claim to the bank or building society; for previous tax years it is necessary to claim direct from HMRC.

Investment policies

Trusts should set out their strategy for investment and enshrine this in a formal investment policy. However, whilst interest rates are low, many see little real need for this to be done, as it costs more in terms of man hours to shuffle funds between accounts than would ever be achieved in interest. In any event, the *Academies Financial Handbook* makes clear that 'exposure to investment products **must** be tightly controlled so that security of funds take precedence over revenue maximisation'.

COMMENT

John Swift, the Business Manager at The Knights Templar School, explained:

> 'There is no formal investment policy in place and business rates of interest for school cash deposits are very low presently. We continue to consider the merits of placing deposits for greater financial reward.'

John Banbrook MA FCMI FNASBM is Business and Finance Director at the Faringdon Academy of Schools, and elected Council Representative for the South East for ASCL. He agrees:

> 'With interest rates so low it has not made sense to spend a lot of administrative time making use of the provisions suggested by the bank. We also do not wish to risk losing our free banking!'

As interest rates rise, there will be a greater need to take advantage of investment opportunities. However, in the meantime, there is a need to establish a policy which reflects risk, return and the liquidity challenges of the organisation. Following the example of the failed Icelandic banks, academies should avoid holding amounts greater than £75,000 in any one account. (This is the amount covered by the Financial Services Compensation Scheme (FSCS).)

COMMENT

Mike Lawes, Finance Director at Bartholomew School, Eynsham:

'Whilst interest rates have been at a historical low level for a considerable period of time, we are generating in excess of £7,000 from our investment, which is four times what our bank account earns annually. As such, it should not be ignored.

The following is taken from our investment policy.

AIMS

The School aims to manage its cash balances to provide for the day-to-day working capital requirements of its operations, whilst protecting the real long-term value of any surplus cash balances against inflation. In addition, the School aims to invest surplus cash funds to optimise returns, but ensuring the investment instruments are such that there is no risk to the loss of these cash funds.

The School does not consider the investment of surplus funds as a primary activity, rather it is the result of good stewardship as and when circumstances allow.

OBJECTIVES

- To ensure adequate cash balances are maintained in the current account to cover day-to-day working capital requirements.
- To ensure there is no risk of loss in the capital value of any cash funds invested.
- To protect the capital value of any invested funds against inflation.
- To optimise returns on invested funds.

IMPLEMENTATION

The School will construct such budgets and cash-flow forecasts as are required by legislation to ensure the viability and sustainability of the activities of the School and to ensure there are adequate liquid funds to meet all payroll-related commitments and outstanding supply creditors that are due for payment.

From time to time, operational and strategic decisions will result in substantial cash balances at the bank over a sustained period.

Where the cash flow identifies a base level of cash funds that will be surplus to requirements these may be invested only in the following:

- Interest-bearing deposit accounts with any of the following banks only:
  - Lloyds TSB
  - Barclays
  - RBS
  - HSBC
- Treasury deposits, with maturity dates which do not result in the cash funds being unavailable for longer than eight weeks.

Prior to investing funds, the head teacher must satisfy himself that the cash flow predictions provided by the finance director and finance officer are accurate and that the amount/time period of the investment will not compromise the viability and sustainability of the activities of the School.

In making decisions regarding where and how any surplus funds should be invested, due regard will be given to the "Risk that the return on investments is not being maximised" and "Risk that trustees are not acting in accordance with their Investment Policy" (e.g. investing in high-risk investments which are not in the best interests of the School).'

Reserves Policy

The DfE previously set limits on the amount of General Annual Grant (GAG) funding that could be carried forward from year to year. The limits have now been removed for many trusts. However, the *Academies Financial Handbook* states:

'Trusts should use their allocated GAG funding for the full benefit of their current pupils. If a trust has a substantial surplus they should have a clear plan for how it will be used to benefit their pupils, for example a long-term capital project.'

However, since the collapse of charity Kids Company, there has been much discussion on the appropriate levels of reserves that should be held. Many now claim that charities, including academy trusts, should keep one month's worth of expenditure in reserves.

COMMENT

FAoS is a MAT in Oxfordshire consisting of one secondary school (the Community College), five primary, one junior and one infant school. John Banbrook MA FCMI FNASBM explained:

'It's often said that a MAT should keep a month's worth of expenditure in reserve. But if we couldn't pay salaries because we hadn't received our funding there would be some form of national emergency and a risk that should sit in someone else's risk register! There is a lot of uncertainty and no real best practice regarding the size of reserves.

One of the committee members is an accountant working in the third sector. We looked at setting a contingency for each school which reflected risk to property, a reserve for staffing and a small amount to cover uninsurable risks such as a server failing. It is unlikely that all schools will have all risks occur at the same time, so the Resources Committee applied the assumed risk level to calculate a total figure. The final figure is close to a month's salary costs but is more justifiable.'

Value Added Tax

VAT is a tax charged on the supply of goods and services and will apply to most business transactions. There are currently three rates of VAT depending on the goods or services provided, as well as limited exemptions.

Companies including academy trusts can register for VAT purposes; this means that they can generally reclaim any VAT that they have paid. Companies that are not VAT-registered may reclaim VAT paid on goods and services through the submission of Form 126, although they cannot charge VAT and to do so could be construed as fraud.

A threshold based on turnover is set, above which it is compulsory to register for VAT. However, trusts may find it advantageous to voluntarily register for VAT and specific advice should be sought from a relevant professional.

COMMENT

Martin Wyatt, Director with Whitley Stimpson Limited:

'The mere mention of the three letters, VAT, sends shudders down many a well-qualified and experienced accountant. For the School Business Manager VAT is a totally alien tax. It is a tax that prior to conversion to an academy trust had been administered for them by the local authority.

With the application of certain VAT rules by academy trusts remaining unclear and a loud silence in lieu of any guidance from HMRC on academies, VAT in the academy sector could be seen as a financial accident waiting to happen.

Background
Provision of education by a state school is not regarded for VAT purposes as a business activity. Normally VAT incurred on costs would not be recoverable. However, s. 33 VAT Act provides for certain bodies [i.e. local authorities] to reclaim VAT on costs.

Academy schools are an entity recognised as a Section 33 body. Their inclusion, however, was under a new section, section 33B, specifically for academy trusts.

Academies can therefore claim back VAT on costs incurred in providing state-funded education. This is done either via submitting a VAT return where the academy trust is VAT registered or via submitting a VAT126 claim where the academy trust is not VAT registered.

Registration
Always take professional advice when reviewing the impact of VAT on the academy trust and whether or not to register for VAT with HMRC.

VAT registration involves an initial formal application to HMRC.

VAT is then reclaimed via the completion and submission of VAT returns to HMRC.

If the academy trust does not formally register for VAT, it can still reclaim any VAT incurred by the completion and submission of form VAT126.

If an academy trust's 'taxable turnover' exceeds the VAT registration threshold then it is obliged to register for VAT. At the time of writing, the threshold is £83,000.

The golden rule is always to seek professional advice to carry out a review of the activities of the academy to ascertain if the registration principles and limit apply. With advantages and disadvantages to both registration and VAT126, ensure the route opted for is right for your academy trust.

A VAT-registered academy will be able to submit either monthly or quarterly VAT returns. Form 126 claims may be made monthly, quarterly or any combination of whole calendar months.

The priority for the academy trust must be to recover as soon as possible VAT incurred on its costs. My advice to all my academy clients is to do a monthly return or VAT126 reclaim.

I am currently seeing academy trusts' VAT126 repayments being handled swiftly and without challenge by HMRC. But VAT and academies are new bedfellows and it will not be long before HMRC will begin to review, challenge and then visit academy trusts to inspect the records being maintained to support the reclaims.

Some of the more frequent encountered activities that may generate income and need close review for the application of VAT are:

- catering
- letting of buildings and rooms
- sports facilities
- use of transport
- provision of staff to other schools.'

Apprentices

All schools and academies are effectively service industries with typically around 80% of their budget expended on staffing costs. As MATs get bigger, so the total payroll bill will rise. From April 2017, any employer with an annual pay-bill in excess of £3 million will be required to pay an apprenticeship levy which will be charged at a rate of 0.5%, based on total employee earnings subject to Class 1 secondary NICs. The levy will be payable through Pay As You Earn (PAYE) and will be payable alongside income tax and National Insurance.

Each employer will receive one annual allowance of £15,000 to offset against their levy payment. There will be a connected persons rule, similar to the Employment Allowance connected persons rule, so employers who operate multiple payrolls will only be able to claim one allowance.

The levy is intended to 'help to deliver new apprenticeships and it will support quality training by putting employers at the centre of the system'.

In addition, all public sector organisations with more than 250 employees will also be subject to an apprenticeship target. This means that any such trust will have to hire a number of apprentices each year equivalent to 2.3% of the sum of their full-time equivalent workforce.

COMMENT

FAoS is a MAT in Oxfordshire consisting of one secondary school (the Community College), five primary, one junior and one infant school. John Banbrook explained:

'The MAT was hugely supportive of education and training for young people. However, the policy on apprentices could be as much as £100,000 costs by 2020. Paying the apprenticeship levy plus the need to take on ten apprentices would mean that the existing staff would need to be reduced.

It may be possible to take on apprentices in IT, catering and some administrative posts. We tried to hire an IT apprentice last year and failed despite advertising three times – it also worked out as more expensive than a qualified technician due to the minimum hour requirements. Hiring an apprentice will also cost more than a TA and this will impact on other staffing levels.

It has now been recognised that apprentices cannot do 52 weeks in a school so the policy has now changed to 60 weeks for a level 2 apprentice and 70 weeks for a level 3 apprentice – these do not align with the school year!

We will now look at appointing people who are already in position within FAoS. In the early years, we may use the opportunity for existing staff to gain qualifications. Unlike the traditional apprenticeship, this temporary apprenticeship arrangement will allow the individual to return to their job at the end of the period. Apprenticeships are not a perfect fit for academies, but FAoS is embracing the opportunity and looking for other opportunities.'

Budgeting

The board of trustees is responsible for approving a balanced budget each year. The approval must be formally minuted in the board minutes.

The trust must submit its **budget forecast return** to the EFA using the online form by 31 July each year.

Trusts are not permitted to go into a deficit position and there are strict guidelines about loans including overdrafts. The *Academies Financial Handbook* states that the board of trustees:

'. . . must notify EFA if the board of trustees formally proposes to set a deficit revenue budget for the current financial year which it is unable to address, after unspent funds from previous years are taken into account.'

Capital funding

The Condition Improvement Fund

Single academy trusts, smaller MATs and sixth-form colleges can apply to the EFA for additional funding from the Condition Improvement Fund (CIF) to improve the condition of their school buildings and expand their facilities.

The stated core priority of the scheme is to support condition projects: keeping 'buildings safe and in good working order is a key priority' and issues will include 'poor building condition, building compliance, energy efficiency and health and safety'.

CIF also supports a small proportion of expansion projects for academies rated good or outstanding to:

■ increase the number of admissions in the main year of entry
■ address overcrowding, including cases of recently approved age-range expansion and sixth-form expansions.

Trusts must apply within specific time-scales. Great care should be taken that applications conform with the detailed requirements relevant to the programme priorities and assessment criteria. However, the window of opportunity for applications is small and trusts should make sure that they are well prepared.

Trusts may submit applications for up to two projects via the CIF online portal or one application for an expansion project. Primary and special schools can apply for funding from £20,000 to £4 million for each project, and secondary schools, all-through schools and sixth-form colleges can apply for between £50,000 and £4 million for each project. Any capital works required below these limits should be funded from the revenue and DFC funding.

The process is highly competitive, with demand exceeding available fund allocation: less than a quarter of applicants were successful in previous rounds. The guidance states:

CIF 2015 to 2016 was 4 times oversubscribed. It is expected that there will be similarly high levels of demand this year. Only applications which demonstrate a high project need and align closely with the priorities of CIF are likely to be successful.

COMMENT

John Swift, the Business Manager at The Knights Templar School, explained:

'We were successful in a bid for significant capital funding from the EFA in 2015.

We engaged the services of an architectural practice that provided good consultancy advice and support through the bidding process. The bid was based on condition need given the very poor state of some of our buildings that needed urgent replacement.'

Trusts are expected to show their commitment to the building works proposed by contributing part of the total funds required. However, trusts may now take out a loan for all or part of the project costs in their CIF proposal. Such loans are offered at Public Works Loan Board rates of interest, the same rate that local authorities can access to invest in their schools. Loans repayments are made through abatement of revenue funding paid to the academy or college and reinvested into future capital budgets.

Formula funding

MATs with at least five academies and more than 3,000 pupils will generally receive a *formulaic allocation* of capital funding. The formulaic allocation is determined by aggregating a notional allocation for each of the academies in the trust. The sum can then be deployed strategically across all academies within the trust to meet priority need.

Formula funding is not likely to be available where the DfE has 'concerns about a MAT's ability to manage capital funding allocations effectively'.

The DfE believes that there are significant benefits for MATs, including:

- allowing trusts to plan and budget more effectively, with funding more easily consolidated into accounts and reporting systems;
- affirmation of independence and self-reliance, with priorities identified and decisions made by trusts rather than EFA;
- flexibility in how the funding is deployed (within the overall priorities and terms and conditions of grant); and
- resource savings and procurement efficiencies can be obtained, and less time and money wasted on preparing and submitting unsuccessful CIF applications.

COMMENT

Simon Spiers, Chief Executive of the Vale Academy Trust:

'As the trust has grown so has the way we access capital funding from the EFA. For the first couple of years we applied through the bidding process and, whilst very successful, we never knew if we were going to be successful until the bidding round closed and the results announced months later. This was hugely frustrating, expensive and made it impossible to plan capital work across academies.

However, this year, after expanding to six academies and more than 3000 students, we received formulaic funding for capital.

Whilst this limits the amount we may get, we do know that it is definitely coming and the best news is that we have already received indicative funding for year 2 as well. This finally allows us to plan capital work across the academies over a longer period. As such we now have a transparent approach to capital funding overseen by the central team. We can explain to head teachers and governors what work is due to be carried out on their academy and when it will happen. Most importantly, condition surveys are all commissioned by the central team so this ensures work is only carried out based on need. This is definitely the future!'

Salix funding

Salix Finance is a not-for-profit company funded by the Department of Energy and Climate Change and the Welsh and Scottish Governments which has been set up to remove the upfront capital cost of investing in energy-efficient technologies. Salix provides interest-free loans for projects that fall within its compliance criteria: namely, that returns on investment and carbon savings must be achievable within a stipulated time period.

Salix funding is now the EFA's preferred method to support heating system replacements at academies. Although Salix is loan-based, academies must bid in the same way as CIF.

Loan repayments can be made for a minimum of four years up to a maximum of eight years, depending on the specific project. Payments are made by direct debit every March and September over the agreed period.

It is hoped that Salix funding will prove to be successful and a 'sustainable initiative' through which all projects will be funded in future.

MATs receiving a condition funding allocation cannot make separate applications for energy and heating projects funded through Salix as allocations are drawn from the same funding source used to support Salix loans.

PFI academies

PFI trusts/academies will generally be obliged to contract with the PFI provider for condition work and maintenance issues. This means that the MAT/SAT must negotiate with the PFI provider to seek agreement for them to either take on the project or approve a third party coming on site to complete the works.

▥ Procurement

The board is under an obligation to ensure value for money (i.e. that funds are used economically, efficiently and effectively). In any event, good procurement is a means by which financial savings can be made and funds diverted to best benefit the pupils. A number of procurement consortiums now offer access to national contracts and frameworks for commonly purchased categories of goods and services.

However, trusts will now be regarded as a 'contracting authority' for EU public procurement purposes. Therefore, great care should be taken in respect of procurement, particularly for higher-value contracts. There are detailed rules that apply where the value of a contract is above a certain threshold. The thresholds are revised every two years. As at January 2016, the relevant thresholds are €209,000 (around £164,176) for supply and service contracts and €5,225,000 (around £4,104,394) for works contracts.

There are onerous obligations to be followed if these thresholds are exceeded and specialist advice should be obtained where necessary. MATs should take particular heed of the relevant limits.

There are some 'Part B' services which will generally not fall within the procurement rules despite the value of the spending. Relevant services include catering, health and legal services.

▥ Financial monitoring

Academy trusts are under an obligation to ensure that financial operations reflect regularity, propriety and value for money. The accounting officer carries a personal responsibility to ensure that this is achieved.

In order to do this, trustees must make sure that financial affairs are properly conducted and accounts are correct on an ongoing basis as well as setting up internal controls to ensure that the trust's money is spent wisely and fraud is avoided. The board and committees should meet regularly enough to discharge their responsibilities and there should be a finance committee to which the board delegates financial scrutiny and oversight.

The *Academies Financial Handbook* requires that finance staff are 'appropriately qualified and/or experienced'. The contrast between a maintained school

and a trust is stark with respect to finances and accounting and this is a requirement that trustees overlook at their peril!

COMMENT

Catherine Barnes, Business Development Manager of The Propeller
Academy Trust:

'As an academy, it is necessary to know a lot more about the finances.
Getting involved with the accounting side is a great deal more onerous and
involves things that a local authority school doesn't even know exist!

From the moment of conversion, the local authority safety net has
gone. We need to work at the highest level and be able to stand up to scrutiny. There is nobody out there to save us. The biggest area of challenge is,
without a doubt, the finance and administration side.'

Monitoring and management

The trust is under an obligation to monitor the current and forecast financial
position. Bank and control accounts should be reconciled regularly and financial
reports should be presented to the board at least termly. It is very important to
remember that, unlike maintained schools, trusts cannot go into a deficit position and all efforts must be made to ensure this does not happen.

Budget monitoring is essential so that spending can be tracked and controlled.
Not only does this ensure that spending is within overall totals, but it also serves
to identify any circumstances that may require corrective action. The *Academies
Financial Handbook* makes clear that 'variances between budget and actual
income and expenditure must be understood and addressed'.

In addition, forecasting cash flow is key to safeguarding the trust's financial
position by making sure that it does not run out of cash. Trusts cannot resort to
loan funding, even on a short-term basis such as with an overdraft, so running
out of cash could have serious implications.

The *Academies Financial Handbook* states:

'The trust should manage its cash position, avoid going overdrawn, and
reconcile bank and control accounts regularly.'

It also makes clear that:

'Where there are concerns about financial management in a trust we are
explaining that the trust may be required to report information about its
cash position to EFA.'

COMMENT

Catherine Barnes, Business Development Manager of The Propeller Academy Trust:

'Budget monitoring is much as it was as a maintained school, though reporting is into the board rather than into the local authority.

Cash flow forecasting will be a bigger challenge, especially in a special school. Personnel take up a much higher proportion of the budget so that there is less flexible income every month. At the most basic level, we need to make sure that there is money in the bank each month for payroll otherwise we won't be able to pay staff!

Getting the whole school community to understand that even though the budget says that there is money available for something doesn't mean that you can buy it when you want to – the cash flow dictates when in the year you can buy. We are in a stable position now, but it could get more challenging if the budget gets used up and I have to say to someone who wants something that they can't buy it just yet.

The academy must, therefore, carry out regular monitoring checks, usually on a monthly basis.'

COMMENT

Sarah Chambers FCA, School Business Manager and self-employed consultant/advisor on school and academy finance:

'The aim of budget monitoring is to look at the actuals (i.e. income and expenditure in the month and more particularly year to date) and compare them to the budget to see how the academy's finances are progressing. Variances need to be investigated and more importantly acted upon. Income from funding generally doesn't change significantly – if it does the assumptions in the budget should be carefully reviewed because this is generally what drives the academy's core activity expenditure. Other income can be more difficult to forecast so assumptions may need to be updated. With regard to expenditure, if the payroll is being reconciled each month any variances to budget should be understood. Payroll costs are relatively fixed, so if there is an overspend, there needs to be a plan to accommodate this and the governors need to understand how this has happened. If there is an underspend, why? Is the underspend offset by overspends elsewhere (e.g. supply teachers)?

The other areas of expenditure typically account for 20–30% of the budget. If there is an underspend are we happy that we haven't incurred the expense but it still hasn't been invoiced (in which case consider accruing the expense) or is it just that we budgeted an amount that we haven't yet incurred but will still spend (phasing in the budget is different) or have our plans changed and we no longer plan to spend it on this line item (in which case do we want to allocate it to other priorities)? If there is an overspend again, consider whether it is phasing (whether we've spent it all up front but budgeted to spend it over the year) or if there is a real over-spend, in which case corrective action will be required. Can a stop be put on further spending? Can other sources of finance be found?

Ideally the academy needs to update the budget/at least have a more up-to-date forecast on a regular basis as the budget is only a plan and plans change. The academy should consider processes around this (i.e. how much governor/director involvement is required in developing and approving an updated budget/forecasts to ensure that governors are up to speed with the latest view and associated plans?).

Cash flow is something that finance staff and governors need to pay attention to and I'd suggest this should be reported on at least monthly. As a maintained school, cash flow is rarely an issue. Academies don't have the local authority to rely on, so need to monitor their cash flow to ensure that they have sufficient funds available at the right point to pay their staff, suppliers, HMRC etc. Insufficient cash flow is a primary cause of business failure. The cash-flow forecast should take into account any major projects (e.g. IT programmes, building works etc.) as well as day-to-day expenditure. The forecast will identify whether there are sufficient funds and may drive decisions about the timing of discretionary spend. The academy may even be in the fortunate position of having spare funds. Cash-flow forecasting will enable the academy to make better use of its funds (e.g. by placing what is not immediately required in term deposits) subject to its investment policy.'

Sarah has devised a checklist for use at month end to make sure that everything has been covered. (See Appendix 4 for the month-end checklist.)

Internal scrutiny

Trusts are required to have in place 'sound internal control, risk management and assurance processes'.

All trusts must establish a committee 'to provide assurance over the suita-bility of, and compliance with, its financial systems and operational controls'. However, only trusts with an annual income over £50 million are required to have a dedicated audit committee – all other trusts have flexibility to decide whether to have a dedicated audit committee or whether another committee has the functions. The *Academies Financial Handbook* states:

'the audit committee's oversight of its trust **must** extend to the controls and risks at its constituent academies, where the trust has them. Oversight **must** also ensure that information submitted to DfE and EFA that affects funding is accurate and compliant.'

The audit committee or other committee carrying out that function must review the risks to internal financial control and agree a programme to address any risks identified.

Trust employees should not be members of an audit committee but they can attend to 'provide information and participate in discussions'. Employees can be members of a finance committee but may not be members when the committee is considering audit matters.

COMMENT

Matthew Hall, Finance Manager at the Diocese of Bristol:

'The Diocesan MAT, Diocese of Bristol Academy Company, originally named a responsible officer to conduct internal audits after it was set up. The EFA then said it was possible to do it another way.

Now the internal audit is run by the Diocesan finance team which is independent of the academy's finance. They have the relevant experience but also have an understanding of the way things work in the Diocese. It ties in the Diocesan advisory role whilst providing a critical eye reporting direct to the board.'

The programme of risk review and internal controls can be carried out in whatever way the board sees fit and the *Handbook* sets out several possible options:

- use of an internal audit service (either in-house, bought-in or provided by a sponsor);
- a supplementary programme of work undertaken by the trust's external auditor;
- the appointment of a non-employed trustee with an appropriate level of qualifications and/or experience who does not charge or get paid by the trust for their work; and
- use of peer review.

COMMENT

Catherine Barnes, Business Development Manager of The Propeller Academy Trust:

'PAT has an audit committee which is composed of directors, although their remit and accountability is very different. PAT also currently contracts with the local authority which acts as a responsible officer and undertakes audits four times a year. However, in the future I am looking to set up a reciprocal arrangement with another academy. It is a good opportunity to build relationships with other schools which is important as we move forward. It can assist with sharing good practice as well as offering a learning experience for those involved.

The board must decide on the most appropriate method of fulfilling the requirements and must be confident that the financial responsibilities are being discharged in an appropriate way. There is, however, no standard specification as far as the extent of review and sampling necessary, or the approach to be taken.'

COMMENT

Mike Lawes is Finance Director at Bartholomew School, Eynsham. He supports 14 schools as responsible officer.

'I have developed an audit programme which is broadly based on FMSiS and its replacement, SFVS, that maintained schools had to complete annually and the minimum requirements set out in the original *Academies Financial Handbook*. I go to the academy and prepare a report which identifies any areas of concern and gives recommendations. I give a rating for each of the areas we look at and generally give three months for academies to resolve them. If a serious issue is identified, a shorter deadline will be set, such as recently when I attended an academy where the safe was sitting on the floor!

There is no definition of what is required and it will be down to the board and audit committee to direct the work of the responsible officer. I have noticed a move away from a focus on control systems and transactions to a more risk-based approach.'

▨ Financial management and governance self-assessment

New trusts are generally required to complete a Financial Management and Governance Self-Assessment (FMGS) which must be submitted via an online form to the EFA within four months of the trust's opening date. Trusts may agree to provide an alternative form of assurance that the financial management and governance arrangements are acceptable. Academies which are joining an existing MAT which has previously prepared audited accounts must confirm via the online form that they intend to adopt the same financial management and governance arrangements.

The self-assessment checklist is part of the EFA's assurance programme that the trust's financial management and governance arrangements meet the requirements. The completed self-assessment must be approved by the trustees or an appropriate delegated committee prior to submission.

The EFA reserves the right to visit an academy 'to review the evidence used to inform your self-assessment'.

13 Accounts

As charitable companies, academy trusts are required to comply with the Companies Act 2006. As charities, they must comply with the requirements of the Charities Act 2011.

In addition, trusts are classified by the Office for National Statistics as 'central government public sector bodies' which means that they are subject to public standards of accountability, involving a higher level of transparency.

The funding agreement requires compliance with the *Academies Financial Handbook* which sets out financial requirements. This states that the EFA expects academies to 'take full control of their financial affairs and apply the letter and the spirit of this handbook'.

At the present time, trusts fall under a variety of legislation and accounts directions.

COMMENT

Martin Wyatt, Director with Whitley Stimpson Limited, states:

'The legislation and regulations governing the financial statements reporting process are an amalgam of direction and guidance and are essentially embodied within the Companies Act 2006, the Charities' Statement of Recommended Practice (SORP) and the annual Accounts Direction guidance issued by the EFA. With the number of academies continuing to increase each year, it cannot be long before specific accounting standards and practice are issued for the academy sector.

Care should be taken that guidance is sought to ensure that accounting practice adopted is up to date with the latest requirements and guidance.'

The *Academies Financial Handbook* is supplemented by the Academies Accounts Direction, which is issued annually and sets out the technical details to fulfil the requirements to:

- prepare an annual report and financial statements to 31 August;
- have these 'accounts' audited by an independent registered auditor;
- submit the audited accounts to the EFA by 31 December;
- file the accounts with Companies House as required under the Companies Act 2006; and
- arrange an independent audit of regularity at the academy trust and include an independent reporting accountant's report on regularity as part of the trust's accounts.

The latest version of the Academies Accounts Direction must be referenced when preparing the annual report and accounts as this will change from year to year.

As charitable companies, accounts must be prepared under the Charities' Statement of Recommended Practice (SORP) issued by the Charity Commission. This provides a 'comprehensive framework of recommended practice for charity accounting and reporting'.

Annual report and accounts

It is a condition of the funding agreement that trust accounts must be produced for the 12-month accounting period ending on 31 August.

The annual report and accounts must be submitted to the EFA by 31 December and filed with Companies House by 31 May and should include the following elements:

Reports:
- a trustees' report;
- a governance statement;
- a statement on regularity, propriety and compliance;
- a statement of trustees' responsibilities;
- an independent auditor's report on the financial statements; and
- an independent reporting accountant's assurance report on regularity.

Financial statements:
- a statement of financial activities;
- a balance sheet;
- a cash-flow statement; and
- notes which expand on the statements.

The financial reporting environment is constantly changing, but the *Academies Financial Handbook* and the Accounts Direction are both essential to understanding the requirements for academies. (The Accounts Direction provides model reports and financial statements which can be used by academies when preparing their own.) Although there is no requirement to have a qualified accountant, the reality is that the accounting standards do need someone with suitable experience to apply them. You will therefore need to review the skills within your team and supplement either through training, recruitment or the use of external advisors.

Reports

Trustees' report

The trustees are responsible for the preparation of a trustees' report which supports the financial statements. The report fulfils the requirements for a directors' report as set out in ss. 415–419 CA 2006 as well as a trustees' report under charity law as set out in the Charities' SORP. The main objective is to supplement the financial information with such further information as necessary for a full appreciation of the company's activities.

The report describes what the trust is trying to do and how it is going about it, demonstrates whether and how the trust has achieved its objectives during the year and explains its plans for the future.

The trustees' report should cover the following matters:

- Reference and administrative details:
  - The names of any members in office on the date the financial statements are approved and any others who served during the year.
  - Basic information relating to the trustees in office on the date the financial statements are approved and any others who served during the year including their appointment or resignation/expiration of term of office.
  - The Company Secretary.
  - Senior Management Team.
  - Trust name, principal and registered office, and company registration number.
  - Independent auditor, bankers and solicitors.

- Opening section:
  - A non-compulsory 'scene setter' can be included. There is no specific wording required but the Accounts Direction suggests something like:

    'The trust operates an academy for pupils aged 11 to 16 serving a catchment area in north Coketown. It has a pupil capacity of x and had a roll of y in the school census on [date]'
    Or
    'The trust operates x primary/secondary/special academies in Coketown/ the south east/across England. Its academies have a combined pupil capacity of x and had a roll of y in the school census on [date]'

- Structure, governance and management:
  - Constitution – this must include the details of any other names by which the trust makes itself known.
  - Members' liability in the event of the company being wound up.

- Trustees' indemnities in respect of qualifying third-party indemnity provisions as required by s. 236 CA 2006.
- Method of recruitment and appointment/election of trustees including the name of any person or body entitled to nominate or appoint trustees and the approach taken to recruiting new trustees.
- Policies and procedures adopted for the induction and training of trustees.
- Organisational structure showing how decisions are made.
- Arrangements for setting pay and remuneration of key management personnel including benchmarks, parameters or criteria used and including the trust's senior leadership team as well as senior leadership teams in individual academies in a multi-academy trust (MAT).
- Related parties and other connected charities and organisations including membership of a federation or other wider network. Details are also required of relationships with related parties and other charities/organisations with which it cooperates in pursuit of charitable activities. The role and contribution of the sponsor should be explained.

■ Objectives and activities:
This should assist the reader to understand the purpose of the trust.
- Objects and aims.
- Objectives, strategies and activities.
- Public benefit including a statement confirming that the trustees have complied with their duty to have due regard to the guidance on public benefit published by the Charity Commission.

Strategic review

Trusts are required to produce a strategic report which must contain a fair review of the trust's business and a description of the principal risks and uncertainties it faces. It will specifically include:

■ Achievements and performance:
- Analysis against key financial performance indicators and analysis against other key performance indicators including information relating to environmental and employee matters.
- A statement on the trust's ability to continue to operate as a going concern including disclosure of any financial uncertainties facing the trust.

■ Financial review:
This must include a review of the financial performance and position of the trust during the period and any factors likely to affect these going forward.
- Reserves policy identifying value of free reserves held (income funds that are freely available for general purposes) and information on the policy and other reserves such as restricted general funds. Where material funds have been designated, these should be quantified and the purpose of the

designation explained and, where it has been set aside for future expenditure, the likely timing. If any fund is materially in deficit, details of the circumstances giving rise to the deficit and details of the steps being taken to eliminate the deficit must be given. Steps being taken to bring the level of reserves into line with the level identified by trustees as appropriate should be explained.
- The powers of the trust with regards to investments must be included. Description and objectives of the investment policy and the extent to which social, environmental or ethical considerations are taken into account.
- Disclosure of principal risks and uncertainties facing the trust linked to the risk management process. This should include financial risks such as credit, cash flow and liquidity risks. Reference should be made to its defined benefit pension schemes, particularly where there is a deficit.

■ Plans for future periods:
- Aims and key objectives set for future periods together with details of activities planned to achieve them.

■ Funds held as custodian trustee on behalf of others:
- Details of assets and arrangements for safe custody and segregation where the academy trust or its trustees are acting as custodian trustees. Details should be given of the name and object of the charity on whose behalf they are being held and how this activity falls within their own objectives.

■ Auditor:
There should be a clear statement that the trustees' report including the strategic report was approved by the board of trustees.

COMMENT

Phil Reynolds, Academies Audit Manager at Reeves & Co LLP, advised:

'The introduction of the Strategic Report does not represent a change to the content of the Trustees Report but a revision in the way in which it is presented. Therefore the introduction of the Report should not be too onerous on academy schools.

Until the EFA release the latest Accounts Direction it will not be clear what format they will require the Strategic Report to take. This stresses the importance of ensuring the latest Accounts Direction is reviewed each year prior to the statutory financial statements being produced to ensure all relevant changes have been included.

The EFA may even choose not to adopt the Charity SORP. The Charity Commission have been consulting about the potential effect the change in UK Generally Accepted Accounting Practice will have, with a new SORP likely to be released for 2015. The EFA will be looking at the currently used Charities SORP and the Further & High Education (F&HE) SORP during this process.

Academies should talk to their auditors in the lead-up to the audit process so that they are aware of the key changes to their sector.'

Governance statement

Trusts are recipients of public funding and so must prepare a governance statement which is a requirement by HM Treasury for all public bodies. It must be signed by the chair and accounting officer on behalf of the board. The statement provides assurance that the trust is appropriately managed and is controlling the resources for which it is responsible. The governance statement should include information on the governance framework and confirm that trustees have carried out their responsibility for ensuring that effective systems, including financial monitoring and control systems, have been put in place.

The Academies Accounts Direction contains a model Governance Statement. However, the Catholic Education Service recommends that Catholic trusts use the model 'Governance Statement for Boards of Directors of Catholic Academies'. This model, based on the Academies Accounts Direction model, reflects the fact that the functions of the corporate board in a Catholic academy trust must be carried out in such a way as to comply with the overarching function of the board to ensure that the academy is, at all times, conducted in accordance with its Catholic character.

- *Scope of responsibility*
  - This generic section is applicable to all academies. The wording from the model accounts can be incorporated without alteration unless the principal is not the accounting officer.
  - The trustees acknowledge their overall responsibility for ensuring that effective and appropriate management systems, including both financial monitoring and control systems, are in place.

- *Governance*
  The governance structure is outlined and details of the trustees, changes in composition of the board and number of meetings attended are provided. The committee structure together with membership, the purpose of the committee and details of particular issues dealt with during the year should also be given. A review of governance should be conducted by all new trusts in their first year and established trusts on an annual basis. The outcome should:
  - describe the evaluation or review undertaken on the impact and effectiveness of the board of trustees

- describe the findings, any actions taken and the impact they had
- indicate when the trust intends to carry out its next self-evaluation or external review of governance.

Extract of the section of Reading School's Governance section:

The Finance Committee is a sub-committee of the main governing body. Its purpose is to assist the decision making of the governing body, by enabling more detailed consideration to be given to the best means of fulfilling the governing body's responsibility to ensure sound management of the academy's finances and resources, including proper planning, monitoring and probity and to make appropriate comments and recommendations on such matters to the governing body on a regular basis. Mr D Jubb, who is a qualified accountant, chairs the committee.

■ *Review of value for money*

Standard wording is set out to confirm that the trust has delivered 'good value in the use of public resources'. In addition, the accounting officer must describe how they have improved their use of resources to deliver better value for money in their trust during the year.

COMMENT

Martin Wyatt, Director, and Andy Jones, Director, with Whitley Stimpson Limited:

'Academy accounting officers are personally responsible and publicly accountable for achieving the best possible value for money in their academy trust. The trustees will also come under scrutiny on the basis they should be challenging spending decisions to ensure that funding is used effectively.

Accounting officers must make an annual statement, which is included as part of the trustees' report in the annual financial statements, which demonstrates to parents and the public that the academy trust's use of public assets and funds has provided good value for money during the period and to identify opportunities for potential improvement.

The requirements of this value for money review essentially consist of two elements – a standard declaration by the accounting officer acknowledging their responsibility for value for money and then a number of examples illustrating how the academy trust has delivered value for money during the year.

Trusts are free to decide how to set out the examples, which do not need to be lengthy. Instead they should be concise and focused on the information that is most relevant and appropriate to the academy trust, emphasising those issues that had the greatest impact on the academy's use of resources. The EFA have set out that they consider up to three brief examples to be sufficient, but that these should cover the following:

- the areas where the academy's activities have contributed to achieving value for money
- the areas of future focus.

Trusts may describe how educational outcomes have been improved with the same resource (for example through targeted intervention or through collaboration), how the curriculum has been delivered in a different way to reduce costs, how financial oversight and governance has been strengthened (for example through robust challenge of spending and other decisions), how purchasing has been improved (for example looking at benchmarking tools, where appropriate, or by delivering economies of scale), how income generation has been maximised, or other activities specific to the trust.'

- *The purpose of the system of internal control*
Suggested wording is included in the model accounts which should be tailored to the needs of the individual academy. The statement explains that the system of internal control is designed to manage risk to a reasonable level rather than to eliminate it. The trustees must also confirm that the system of internal control has been in place for the year and up to the date of approval of the accounts.

Extract of Reading School's Governance Statement:

THE PURPOSE OF THE SYSTEM OF INTERNAL CONTROL

The system of internal control is designed to manage risk to a reasonable level rather than to eliminate all risk of failure to achieve policies, aims and objectives; it can therefore only provide reasonable and not absolute assurance of effectiveness. The system of internal control is based on an on-going process designed to identify and prioritise the risks to the achievement of Reading School's policies, aims and objectives, to evaluate the likelihood of those risks being realised and the impact should they be realised, and to manage them efficiently, effectively and economically. The system of internal control has been in place in Reading School for the year ended 31 August 2016 and up to the date of approval of the Governors' annual report and financial statements.

- *Capacity to handle risk*
  Again, suggested wording is provided which should be tailored to the individual trust. The trustees confirm that operating, financial and compliance controls that have been implemented to mitigate key risks have been in place for the period, on an ongoing basis and are regularly reviewed.

Extract of Reading School's Governance Statement:

CAPACITY TO HANDLE RISK

The Governing Body has reviewed the key risks to which Reading School is exposed together with the operating, financial and compliance controls that have been implemented to mitigate those risks. The Governing Body is of the view that there is a formal ongoing process for identifying, evaluating and managing the Academy School's significant risks that has been in place for the period ended 31 August 2016 and up to the date of approval of the Governors' Annual Report and financial statements. This process is regularly reviewed by the board of Governors.

- *Risk and control framework*
  This sets out the framework for the risk management process including the segregation of duties and system of delegation and accountability whether by way of internal or external auditor. Confirmation should be given as to whether the internal auditor/reviewer has delivered their schedule of work as planned, provide details of any material control issues arising as a result of the internal auditor's/reviewer's work and, if relevant, describe what remedial action is being taken to rectify issues.

Extract of Faringdon Academy of School's Governance Statement:

THE RISK AND CONTROL FRAMEWORK

The academy trust's system of internal financial control is based on a framework of regular management information and administrative procedures including the segregation of duties and a system of delegation and accountability. In particular, it includes:

- comprehensive budgeting and monitoring systems with an annual budget and periodic financial reports which are reviewed and agreed by the board of trustees;
- regular reviews by the academy resources committee of reports which indicate financial performance against the forecasts and of major purchase plans, capital works and expenditure programmes;
- setting targets to measure financial and other performance;
- clearly defined purchasing (asset purchase or capital investment) guidelines;
- delegation of authority and segregation of duties; and
- identification and management of risks.

The board of trustees has considered the need for a specific internal audit function and has decided to maintain the requirement for an audit committee. The composition and function of the audit committee is highlighted on page 22 of this report. The academy provides funding for a Peer Reviewer for 6 full days each year. The work of the Peer Reviewer is determined by the priorities of the audit committee to ensure full independence.

- *Review of effectiveness*
  The accounting officer is responsible for ensuring that the system of internal control is effective and this section confirms that this is reviewed and gives details of the mechanisms informing the process. Details are also given of any action required to address weaknesses identified and to ensure continuous improvement of the system.

Extract of Reading School's Governance Statement:

REVIEW OF EFFECTIVENESS

As Accounting Officer, A.M. Robson has responsibility for reviewing the effectiveness of the system of internal control. During the year in question the review has been informed by:

- The work of the external auditor and the school's responsible officer;
- The financial management and governance self-assessment process;
- The work of the executive managers within Reading School who have responsibility for the development and maintenance of the internal control framework.

The accounting officer has been advised of the implications of the result of their review of the system of internal control by the finance committee and a plan to ensure continuous improvement of the system is in place.

Statement on regularity, propriety and compliance

Although there is a straightforward model format included within the Accounts Direction which provides the contents, this statement is extremely important. It includes confirmation that public money has been spent for the purposes intended by Parliament (regularity) in line with the relevant authorities and legislation. The accounting officer must specifically make a formal declaration that they have met their personal responsibilities to Parliament for the resources under their control during the year.

Connected to this is the concept of 'propriety'; the accounting officer must confirm that appropriate standards of conduct, behaviour and corporate governance have been maintained when applying the funds under their control. There are no guidelines over what propriety could cover, but it could include matters such as fairness, integrity, the avoidance of private profit from public business, even-handedness in the appointment of staff, open competition in the letting of contracts and avoidance of waste and extravagance.

Oversight of internal control processes should be performed throughout the year to ensure that the trust is working within the boundaries of regularity and propriety. This could include:

- review of management reporting documents;
- review of trustees'/governors' minutes;
- confirming compliance with the trust's scheme of delegation;
- ensuring outcomes and recommendations from the FMGS report have been implemented; and
- adherence to tendering policies.

The audit committee and internal auditor (or equivalent) also provide independent checking of financial controls, systems, transactions and risks, which can be used to inform the accounting officer.

The accounting officer also has a responsibility to advise the board and the EFA of any instances of irregularity or impropriety, or non-compliance with the terms of the trust's funding agreement. The accounting officer must, therefore, confirm that there have been no instances of material irregularity, impropriety or funding non-compliance, but if there are they must confirm that such instances have been reported to the board and the EFA.

Statement of trustees' responsibilities

After the trustees' report, governance statement and the statement on regularity, propriety and compliance, a statement of trustees' responsibilities must be included. This acknowledges the requirements imposed by company law. Trustees are required to prepare the trustees' report and financial statements, maintain adequate accounting records, safeguard the assets and must not approve the financial statements unless they are satisfied that they give a true and fair view of the state of affairs of the trust. It should also set out the financial reporting framework that has been applied, which will comprise UK Generally Accepted Accounting Practice, and the Accounts Direction issued by the EFA.

Independent auditor's report on the financial statements

The auditors are independent accountants who are registered to carry out the auditing function. They certify that the accounts are drawn up in accordance with the requirements of the Companies Act and appropriate accounting standards including the Academies' Accounts Direction issued by the EFA. The form of the audit report is governed by the International Standards on Auditing (UK and Ireland), standard ISA 700.

The auditor must confirm that in their opinion the financial statements:

- give a true and fair view of the state of the trust's affairs as at 31 August and of its incoming resources and application of resources, including its income and expenditure, for the year then ended
- have been properly prepared in accordance with United Kingdom Generally Accepted Accounting Practice
- have been prepared in accordance with the requirements of the Companies Act 2006
- have been prepared in accordance with the Charities SORP and Academies Accounts Direction.

Independent auditor's report on regularity

An additional report by the trust's reporting accountant (external auditor) must express the conclusion on regularity. The auditor explains the basis on which the audit was conducted and confirms that nothing has come to their attention which suggests that in all material respects the expenditure disbursed and income received during the period have not been applied to purposes intended by Parliament and the financial transactions do not conform to the authorities which govern them.

COMMENT

Martin Wyatt, Director at Whitley Stimpson Limited:

'Under the requirements of the academy trust's Funding Agreement, the annual financial statements must be audited. The requirement for an audit of the annual financial statements is also set out in the *Academies Financial Handbook* and the Companies Act 2006.

The purpose of the audit is to provide an opinion to the members of the academy trust as to whether the annual financial statements present a "true and fair" view of the financial position and results of the academy trust for the year/period.

There is also a requirement, under the *Academies Financial Handbook* and related guidance issued by the EFA, to report on the Regularity and Propriety of public funds. This is that public funding provided by the Government to the academy has been used for the purposes intended.

What does this all mean?
It is about providing assurance to the EFA (and DfE), the Government and the public on the governance and accountability of the academy trust and on the appropriate use and application of public funds.

It is a process which is aimed at identifying whether there are any material oversights, accounting errors and over-optimistic predictions included within the annual financial statements. Sometimes, it can unearth serious issues such as fraud.

The process involves gathering the evidence required to work out whether an organisation's claims about income and expenditure and its financial position are true and fair.

Auditors do not test and look at everything. It is about focusing on the "key" risks in each academy trust and gathering sufficient evidence through various tests, observations and enquiries that can support a conclusion that the financial statements are "true and fair".

Auditors do not specifically test for fraud when undertaking an audit, but they do ensure there is review of areas where fraud could occur and ensure their tests and enquiries are directed at these areas. Auditors also have a responsibility to report to the trustees/directors of the academy trust whether any instances of fraud have come to their attention during the course of the audit.

An important concept to remember is "going concern". The financial statements are prepared on the assumption that the academy trust will be in a position to carry on its activities for a period of 12 months from the date the financial statements are approved by the trustees.

If the auditor finds good reasons to doubt the academy trust's ability to carry on as a going concern, then this must be reflected in the Auditor's Report.'

Financial statements

Producing the statutory accounts is a complex matter and should be done by a qualified accountant or suitably experienced person. The process will vary depending on the accounting software used by the trust and what method is being used for converting the accounting records into the statutory accounting format.

Overspending is absolutely forbidden for academies, so meticulous budget monitoring is essential.

Statement of financial activities for the year (including income and expenditure account and statement of total recognised gains and losses)

The accounts are made up of a number of financial (or 'primary') statements:

- The Statement of Financial Activities (SOFA) is a record of income and expenditure, although it does not follow the format of a conventional income and expenditure account. Disclosure of comparative information for all amounts presented in the SOFA, including the split between unrestricted and restricted income funds, must be presented.
- The balance sheet provides a snapshot of assets, liabilities and capital as at 31 August. There is a model format included in the Accounts Direction.
- A cash-flow statement will record movements of cash into and out of the trust.
- Notes to the financial statements should provide further information including details of the trust's accounting policies. The notes provide a detailed analysis and are a major part of the accounts. Only 'material and relevant' accounting policies need to be disclosed; 'an item is material when its omission or misstatement could influence the economic decisions that users make on the basis of those accounts'.

A note is required for trusts subject to a limit on the amount of GAG carry forward allowed by their funding agreement confirming whether the limits have been exceeded. Trusts should make all efforts to keep within the amount equal to 12% of the GAG awarded for the year (except by agreement) or risk any unspent GAG in excess of this threshold being surrendered. Trusts not subject to GAG carry forward limits should declare that the limits do not apply.

There has been some consternation about the requirement for staff governors' remuneration to be disclosed. The notes must provide details of the number of employees whose employee benefits exceeded £60,000 during the period and present it in £10,000 bandings. Employee benefits include salary and other taxable benefits in cash or in kind and termination payments.

Details must be given of any related party transactions. Any such transactions should be given 'fully and openly' to give readers of the accounts 'a proper understanding of them, and any issues that might have influenced them'. Setting out details provides assurance that potential conflicts of interest are identified and managed. Disclosure must include:

- Names of related parties
- Description of relationship between the parties
- Description of the transactions
- Amounts involved
- Amounts due to or from the related parties at the balance sheet date, and any provision for doubtful debts or amounts written off
- Details of any guarantees given/received
- Terms and conditions, including whether they are secured, and the nature of the consideration to be provided in settlement
- Other elements of the transactions which are necessary for the understanding of the accounts.

Multi-academy trusts

MATs must prepare a single set of accounts combining the results of all the academies within the trust.

Additional disclosures must be included to:

- Identify the share of funds attributable to each academy at the end of the current and comparative period
- Provide a narrative describing the action being taken by any academy in respect of which the total of these funds is a deficit
- Identify the amounts spent during the period by each academy on:
  o Teaching and educational support staff
  o Other support staff
  o Educational supplies
  o Other costs.

The trust must disclose details of central services provided by the trust to academies during the year and an illustrative format is included in the Accounts Direction. A note must describe:

- The types of central services provided
- The trust's policy for charging for those central services
- The actual charges placed on each academy for the services during the year.

Subsidiary companies and group accounts

A trust must prepare consolidated 'group' accounts where it has a subsidiary which it controls:

- The trust's accounts must include a consolidated SOFA for the group
- The trust's accounts must include a consolidated balance sheet for the group in addition to a balance sheet for the parent
- The notes to the accounts should give the position of the group as well as the parent

–   The trustees' report must include relevant information about their subsidiary undertakings
–   The trust's accounts must include in the group accounting policies a statement that the accounts are consolidated
–   The notes to the accounts must give specific information in relation to each material subsidiary.

Approval

Once the annual reports and accounts are prepared they are formally approved by the board. The trustees' report, the statement of trustees' responsibilities and the financial statements must be approved by the board of trustees and all documents are signed on behalf of the trustees, generally by the chair, with the date of approval and name of signatory stated.

The annual reports and accounts are also presented to the members. Historically this was done at the AGM; however, private companies no longer have to hold an AGM unless their articles of association contain the requirement (some versions of the model articles include the requirement) (see Chapter 8). In these circumstances, the accounts must be sent to all members by the time they are due to be filed with Companies House.

It is feasible for the articles of association to be amended so that documentation including accounts can be provided to members by means of publication on a website. This is a provision more generally used by large companies with great numbers of members and is unlikely to be required by most academies. In any event, members will retain the right to request paper copies.

Filing

Academies must submit accounts to Companies House within nine months of the date to which the accounts are made up (i.e. by 31 May). Filing may be done through the Companies House e-filing service or through submission of a paper filing.

The deadlines for filing are initially set by the incorporation date of the company, which may not correlate with the date of conversion or the date when the trust commenced operations. For the first period, accounts may be prepared for a period of more than 12 months. These must be delivered to Companies House either:

■   within 21 months of the date of incorporation; or
■   three months from the accounting reference date, whichever is longer.

For filing, the copies of the accounts must state the following:

- the copy of the balance sheet must be signed by a trustee;
- the copy of the balance sheet must show the printed name of the trustee who signed it on behalf of the board even if the signature is legible;
- the copy of the trustees' report must include the printed name of the trustee or company secretary who signed the report on behalf of the board; and
- the copy of the auditor's report must state the auditor's name. Where the auditor is a firm the auditor's report must state the name of the auditor and the name of the person who signed it as senior statutory auditor on behalf of the firm.

COMMENT

Martin Wyatt, Director with Whitley Stimpson Limited, sets out a timetable for submission and publication of the academy trust's annual financial statements:

'I would describe the current reporting deadline of 31 December as at the very least nonsensical and at the most as farcical.

With most schools concentrating on end-of-year plays and concerts in reality an academy trust has little more than three months to have its financial statements completed, audited and approved by the board of trustees.

The example financial statements included within the annual Accounts Direction issued by the EFA, Coketown Academy Trust, consist of 46 pages. It is not unusual to have financial statements with many more pages than this, such are the disclosures currently necessary for the financial statements.

Action required by 31 December – reporting to the EFA
The following documents must be submitted to the EFA by 31 December:

- A copy of the audited financial statements, comprising:
  - a trustees' report – signed by the chair of trustees, or another trustee;
  - a governance statement – signed by both the chair and the accounting officer;
  - a statement on regularity propriety and compliance – signed by the accounting officer;
  - a statement of trustees' responsibilities – signed by the chair of trustees;
  - an independent auditor's report on the financial statements – signed by the auditor;
  - an independent accountant's auditor's report on regularity – also signed by the auditor as the reporting accountant; and
  - a set of financial statements and supporting notes – including a balance sheet signed by the chair of trustees, or another trustee.

- A copy of the auditor's management letter. This will provide details of the auditor's findings from their audit, including any significant concerns and adjustments if arising. The academy trust's response to the issues raised in the letter must also be submitted.

The audited financial statements and auditors' management letter must be submitted to the EFA as electronic documents only, in pdf form, using the EFA's Document Exchange portal.

The board of trustees should prepare, and agree with their auditor, an accounts preparation and audit timetable that enables the 31 December deadline to be achieved.

The timetable should incorporate the date of the trustees' meeting at which the accounts will be approved and signed, as well as meetings prior to this with the trustees or relevant sub-committees such as a Finance Committee or Audit Committee at which the auditors' report and key issues are discussed and presented to the trustees.

The above is easily written in two very short paragraphs; in reality this can soon become a distant and moving target.

Accounts action required by 31 January – publication of financial statements on academy's website
Academies are required to publish their audited financial statements in full on their website. To maximise transparency and openness this should be done as soon as possible after the financial statements are approved and signed by the trustees, but by no later than 31 January each year.

Accounts action required by 31 May – reporting to Companies House
In addition to submitting audited financial statements to the EFA, academies must also file them with Companies House each year. Under section 442(2a) of the Companies Act 2006 the financial statements must be filed with Companies House within nine months of the end of the accounting period. For academy trusts this will be no later than 31 May.

However, where an academy trust is preparing financial statements for its first period after incorporation and is preparing them for a period of greater than 12 months, then under s. 442(3) of the Companies Act 2006 the financial statements must be filed within 21 months of incorporation, or within three months of the end of the accounting period, whichever is later.

Companies House will levy automatic penalties on a rising scale if financial statements are filed late.'

Accounts action no longer required – reporting to the Charity Commission
As exempt charities, academies are not required to submit their accounts to the Charity Commission.

Academies should notify HMRC that the entity is a charity, or it will be asked to complete a tax return. This will require iXBRL tagged accounts at extra cost.

New academies

The Companies Act allows newly converted academies to have their first accounting period other than the usual 12-month period. As long as the period is more than six months, it can be up to 18 months from the date of incorporation of the company and ending with its accounting reference date (i.e. 31 August).

COMMENT

Martin Wyatt, Director with Whitley Stimpson Limited, provides an example:

- An academy trust incorporated on or before 28 February 2016 would have to prepare the first financial statements from the date of incorporation up to 31 August 2016 because deferral to 31 August 2017 would take it beyond the permitted 18-month maximum period.
- An academy trust incorporated on or after 1 March 2016 may, if it wishes, defer preparation of the first financial statements to 31 August 2017. These financial statements would cover the period from the date of incorporation to 31 August 2017.

Note that it is the incorporation date (i.e. the date of company registration at Companies House), not the academy trust's operational opening date (or conversion date) which is relevant to these provisions.

Auditors

The funding agreement requires that accounts be audited annually by independent auditors. The auditor must be independent of the trust and hold a current audit-practising certificate issued by a recognised supervisory body. The audit will be carried out in accordance with International Standards on Auditing and will examine evidence relevant to the amounts and disclosures in the financial statements.

Members appoint the auditor who will produce a report stating whether the trust has prepared financial statements in accordance with company law and relevant accounting standards and the financial reporting framework. The auditor will also state whether the accounts give a true and fair view of the affairs at the end of the financial year.

An auditor can be removed from office at any time during their term of office. The members or trustees give 28 days' notice of the intention to put to a members' general meeting a resolution to remove the auditor. A copy of the notice of the general meeting must be sent to the auditor who has the right to provide a written response which must be circulated to members. The auditor also has the right to attend and speak at the meeting when the resolution will be considered. Members will pass an 'ordinary resolution' to remove the auditor on a simple majority (i.e. at least 50% plus one of the votes cast). It is not possible to remove an auditor using the written resolution method.

Within 14 days of the resolution being passed, Form AA03 'Notice of resolution removing auditors from office' must be filed at Companies House (see Chapter 8).

Care should be taken when removing an auditor during their term of office as they may be entitled to damages for breach of contract or another form of compensation. A better approach would be to consider not reappointing the auditor for a further term.

When an auditor ceases to hold office, for whatever reason, he must deposit a statement at the registered office setting out any circumstances connected with his ceasing to hold office that he considers should be brought to the attention of the members and the EFA. The company must send a copy of this statement to all members or apply to the court to avoid having to do so within 21 days of the statement being deposited with the company. If the auditor does not receive notification of an application to the court within 21 days, they must send a copy of the statement to Companies House within a further seven days.

Where the auditor resigns or is removed, the auditor and company are obliged to notify the 'appropriate audit authority' (i.e. the EFA) under ss. 522–525 CA 2006.

Whole of Government Accounts

Academy trusts are classified as central government public sector bodies and must comply with central government accounting practices. This means that they are required to produce returns in respect of Whole of Government Accounts (WGA) each year.

COMMENT

Martin Wyatt, Director with Whitley Stimpson Limited:

'We are given no time for smug satisfaction that year-end financial statements and documents have been submitted by the deadline of 31 December. The old adage "It's not over 'til the fat lady sings" is very true. In this instance it's not over until the Academies Accounts Return (AAR) is submitted to the EFA.

Having completed, reviewed and indeed provided an assurance report the AAR, I can confirm it is a voluminous spreadsheet to complete and you are inclined to break into celebratory singing on successful submission of the return.

In order for the EFA to complete its own accounts it must first obtain data from all academy trusts on their financial performance and position for each year. Academy trusts that have completed accounts for the period ended 31 August must complete and submit the AAR by, currently, the following 31 January.

For those new academy trusts who have not completed accounts for the preceding 31 August period end, they must complete an AAR for the period from opening to 31 March each year and submit to the EFA by 31 May. For an existing MAT that has opened new academies since the 31 August period end and before 31 March, they will need to complete and submit an AAR for those new academies for the period to 31 March.

The EFA issue a very detailed spreadsheet to academy trusts to capture and collate the accounts data needed for their consolidated accounts, which in turn feed into the DfE's consolidated accounts and the Whole of Government Accounts (WGA).

Academy trusts will need to commission from their external auditors an assurance report on the 31 August AAR each year.'

Dormant accounts

If a trust company has made no 'significant transactions' during its financial year then it is dormant. Financial transactions will not be regarded as significant if they relate to fees or penalties paid to Companies House. If any other transactions have taken place, the trust will be considered trading and full accounts must be prepared.

If a trust has been dormant for the full period between incorporation and 31 August, it can prepare dormant accounts. These consist of a balance sheet and a signed statement by a trustee that the trust was dormant during the period.

It is not necessary to include a statement of income and expenditure or a trustees' report and these do not usually need to be audited.

Dormant accounts must be submitted in line with the deadlines for full accounts.

A pro-forma is included in the Academies Accounts Direction.

14 Corporate governance

There is no recognised definition of the term 'corporate governance', but it is generally used to refer to the way in which a company is directed and controlled with a framework that monitors actions and decisions. The interests of the various stakeholders need to be balanced through a system of rules and procedures.

Major scandals such as Enron, Parmalat and BCCI have already arisen in the corporate world, and have led to an increased focus on corporate governance. The Cadbury Committee published a report entitled *Financial Aspects of Corporate Governance* in 1992, which made recommendations on the arrangement of company boards and accounting systems to mitigate risks and failures. The resultant UK Corporate Governance Code expanded this to state that the purpose of corporate governance is 'to facilitate effective, entrepreneurial and prudent management that can deliver the long-term success of the company'. The principles contained in the Code are primarily aimed at listed companies, although non-listed public and private companies are also encouraged to comply with the requirements. The principles relating to the operation of the board should be considered by free schools and academy trusts, not least because they are the recipients of public funding.

- Every company should be headed by an effective board which is collectively responsible for the long-term success of the company.
- The board and its committees should have the appropriate balance of skills, experience, independence and knowledge of the company to enable them to discharge their respective duties and responsibilities effectively.
- The board should present a fair, balanced and understandable assessment of the company's position and prospects.

Failure to observe these principles leaves a board of directors/trustees open to criticism that it has not acted appropriately and has failed to fulfil the requirements of the funding agreement.

Academy trusts are autonomous organisations free of local authority control. This also brings greater emphasis on effective, accountable and more independent governance.

Corporate governance mechanisms

All trusts must establish and adopt mechanisms to promote good corporate governance and increase accountability.

Trustees in academies are generally not entitled to be remunerated and this is reflected in the model funding agreement. Apart from the chief executive officer (CEO)/principal and any member of staff, no trustee may be employed by, or receive any remuneration from, the trust. The remuneration paid should be 'reasonable in all the circumstances' and the individual trustee concerned should be absent from any discussion of his/her employment, remuneration, or performance in the employment. Furthermore, the total number of trustees employed by the trust must be no more than one-third of the total number of trustees – this figure is calculated including the principal, executive principal or chief executive.

There is a widespread recognition of the importance of the role of the chair and there have been calls to allow academies to offer remuneration particularly for a trust or academy that is in a category and will require considerable time and experience to support it. However, the model articles of association currently prevent payment of trustees for their services as a trustee. It may be possible to seek the approval of the Charity Commission for payment of a trustee for their services as a trustee in exceptional circumstances.

However, high levels of remuneration for board members, particularly in public companies, have been the subject of much media criticism. It is essential that where any pay or other rewards are made to trustees, whether executive/staff or non-executive, these are granted through transparent mechanisms. The UK Corporate Governance Code states:

> There should be a formal and transparent procedure for developing policy on executive remuneration and for fixing remuneration packages of individual directors. No director should be involved in deciding his or her own remuneration.

The Code also recommends establishment of a remuneration committee comprising three independent non-executive directors (NEDs) which sets the level of remuneration for executive directors. With the greater freedoms available to trusts in setting staff pay and rewards, this is likely to become of greater importance as time goes on.

Trustees' remuneration must be disclosed in the annual accounts within £5,000 bandings. Confirmation is also given that they only receive remuneration in respect of their staff roles and not for their services as trustees. Disclosure must be given of:

- The amount of employer pension contributions paid in respect of trustees
- The total amount of expenses reimbursed to trustees or paid directly to third parties
- Any other related party transactions with trustees including payments for services under commercial contracts.

The National Governors' Association recognises eight key elements of effective governance:

- the right people around the table;
- understanding roles and responsibilities;
- good chairing;
- professional clerking;
- good relationships based on trust;
- knowing the school – the data, the staff, the parents, the children, the community;
- commitment to asking challenging questions; and
- the confidence to have courageous conversations in the interests of the children and young people.

The board is required to plan strategically and to produce a board development plan which is both informed by and feeds into the trust/academy development plan, training and development plan and budget.

Independent trustees

The role of the non-executive director (NED) (i.e. a director who is not an employee of the company) has gained increasing prominence over recent years. The Higgs Report, published in 2003, called NEDs the 'custodians of the governance process'; they bring a level of independence which is essential for robust governance. Their impartial viewpoint will assist in developing policy and constructing effective development plans and, as they are not involved in the management of the trust, they can objectively monitor the activities of the executive.

It is important to note that trustees who do not work for the trust may not necessarily be independent. A classic situation is where a trustee is married to a trust employee and may well have a personal interest in some of the decisions made. Whilst there is no need to exclude such individuals, it is extremely important that their relationship or circumstances are clearly noted and the situation managed appropriately and reflected in the notes of the financial statements.

Of course, although a non-executive trustee may not work for the trust, they may work elsewhere or have other significant commitments. Their role is fundamental to the running of the trust, helping to set the strategic direction and providing oversight of the day-to-day, yet they are volunteers and receive no financial benefit. Concerns are regularly expressed over the amount of time that trustees have to devote to become truly involved in the business of the trust. There may be a tendency for trustees to rely on the executive to draw attention to areas that need consideration and this is a weakness in the system of oversight. They must be proactive in seeking information and understanding the workings of the organisation.

The appointment of NEDs is extremely important and care should be taken over the process of selection (see Chapter 9). However, the Articles of Association may provide that certain appointments to the board are made through an election process.

Ofsted

Ofsted makes clear the requirements undertaken by governors which relate to trustees in academies. The performance of the board contributes to the overall evaluation by Ofsted. The *School Inspection Handbook* (August 2015) states:

> 'The contribution of governors to the school's performance is evaluated as part of the judgement on the effectiveness of leadership and management.'

Trustees other than staff trustees are not expected to be routinely involved in the day-to-day activity of the academy and would only visit lessons where there were clear protocols and the purpose was understood by academy staff and trustees alike.

However, the judgement on 'the effectiveness of leadership and management' does not look at the role of trustees in isolation but takes an overview of leadership through school/academy leaders, managers and trustees. The Common Inspection Framework (effective from September 2015) outlines the role that leaders, managers and trustees are expected to fulfil. They need to:

- demonstrate an ambitious vision, have high expectations for what all children and learners can achieve and ensure high standards of provision and care for children and learners;
- improve staff practice and teaching, learning and assessment through rigorous performance management and appropriate professional development;
- evaluate the quality of the provision and outcomes through robust self-assessment, taking account of users' views, and use the findings to develop capacity for sustainable improvement;
- provide learning programmes or a curriculum that have suitable breadth, depth and relevance so that they meet any relevant statutory requirements, as well as the needs and interests of children, learners and employers, nationally and in the local community;
- successfully plan and manage learning programmes, the curriculum and careers advice so that all children and learners get a good start and are well prepared for the next stage in their education, training or employment;

- actively promote equality and diversity, tackle bullying and discrimination and narrow any gaps in achievement between different groups of children and learners;
- actively promote British values; and
- make sure that safeguarding arrangements to protect children, young people and learners meet all statutory and other government requirements, promote their welfare and prevent radicalisation and extremism.

Code of Governance

'Good Governance – A Code for the Voluntary and Community Sector' sets out clear key principles that organisations should abide by:

An effective board will provide good governance and leadership by:
1. Understanding their role.
2. Ensuring delivery of organisational purpose.
3. Working effectively both as individuals and as a team.
4. Exercising effective control.
5. Behaving with integrity.
6. Being open and accountable.

The aim of the Code is to help organisations improve their governance by applying the six principles. However, as its website points out: 'It is about flexibility and proportionality, not uniform standards', taking account of 'an understanding of people and their roles as well as policies and systems'.

COMMENT

Lindsay Driscoll, former Independent Chair of the Governance Code Steering Group, explained:

'The Code of Governance was drafted for all voluntary and community organisations including registered and exempt charities and non-charitable bodies. The high-level principles are applicable to all these organisations. The examples given for the application of the Principles are not intended to be prescriptive and not all the examples given will be relevant for all organisations. We have tried to indicate where a point is only applicable to registered charities or to companies. The Code would need to be read in conjunction with any special rules for academies but the Principles and much of the examples should be relevant.'

Self-regulation

Although the principles of corporate governance must apply to trusts, they are run by volunteers acting as trustees who may lack the skills or experience to understand their obligations. They are not aware of the requirements, never mind ignoring them. Most corporate bodies have professional individuals involved with the administration of their corporate governance. If errors can occur in this situation, what hope is there for academy trusts?

Just like the corporate governance scandals that occupied the media in previous years, the instances of failures in trusts are few and far between. This is, of course, no reason to ignore the problems.

A robust process to ensure ongoing financial and regulatory oversight is required to ensure that all trusts and their trustees are appropriate guardians of funding and use it for the benefit of their pupils. One way of ensuring that the obligations are being met at school level is to engage the services of a company secretarial advisor who can highlight the areas of risk and ensure that a robust system is put in place.

Effective governance is something that the trust must put in place itself; it will not be imposed by any external body or via government intervention. In fact, DfE strategy appears to have noted its inability to get involved in the governance of each trust and favours the role of overseeing regulator.

COMMENT

Graham Burns, Partner with Stone King:

Removal of the Secretary of State's Powers of Intervention

Prior to the publication of the DfE's updated Model Articles in January 2013, the Secretary of State was able to exercise his powers to appoint members and also to appoint governors onto the board of the academy trust. Since this power has been removed the Secretary of State is no longer able to 'flood' the board of directors.

As a compromise the Secretary of State now has the power to terminate the funding agreement if an academy is designated as requiring significant improvement.

This change in approach seems to indicate a realisation by the DfE that as the number of academies continues to grow the power to flood the board of an academy trust is an increasingly impractical tool for a centralised regulator without the local resources to implement it. In addition, it does not seem appropriate for a seemingly independent charitable company to be subject to such intervention in its governance. In practical terms, it is envisaged the DfE would no doubt prefer to have greater powers to terminate the funding agreement.

Conflict of interest

It is essential that a fair and just process is applied at all times in the governance process. One obvious way in which this may be skewed is where a person involved in that process has a conflict of interest (e.g. where the individual has other interests which could possibly influence or corrupt their motivation or decision making).

There is often a focus on financial or 'pecuniary' interests which are easier to quantify objectively. However, conflict can arise in connection with any interests such as recommending a specific group of people or personal promotion.

Section 175 of the Companies Act 2006 states:

> A director of a company must avoid a situation in which he has, or can have, a direct or indirect interest that conflicts, or possibly may conflict, with the interests of the company.

A conflict of interest may arise both from a 'direct' personal interest and an 'indirect' interest (e.g. arising through a relative or another business that the trustee is involved with). Trustees have a duty to avoid conflicts of interest and must declare any interest in any transaction or arrangement or any proposed transaction or arrangement prior to it taking effect. The *Academies Financial Handbook* states that trusts must ensure that:

> 'trustees understand and comply with their statutory duties as company directors to avoid conflicts of interest, not to accept benefits from third parties, and to declare interest in proposed transactions or arrangements.'

There are strict rules regarding the benefits which may be received by trustees under charity law. In general, trustees cannot be employed by, or receive any remuneration from, the trust in their role as a trustee. Trustees may receive a benefit from the trust in the capacity of a beneficiary of the trust (i.e. with no preferential treatment arising due to their role as trustee). They can sell goods, services or any interest in land to the trust, or receive interest on money lent to the trust, only if the amounts concerned are 'reasonable in all the circumstances' and 'it is in the interests of the academy trust to employ or to contract with that governor rather than with someone who is not a governor'. Any benefit received must be disclosed in the annual report and accounts.

It is essential that any potential conflict of interest is identified and managed. To ensure transparency, this should extend to situations where the trustee's interests may appear to influence the trustee's decision making or be seen to have the potential to do so. The conflict will be seen to arise if circumstances reasonably indicate a risk that decisions may be unduly influenced, whether or not an individual actually is, or would be, so influenced.

It is good practice to have a policy on conflicts of interest which, in the interests of transparency, is available publicly and is applied consistently across the whole trust. Appropriate procedures to be followed when a trustee is subject to a conflict of interest could include:

- the removal of the trustee concerned from the decision-making process;
- managing the conflict of interest once a decision has been made; and
- recording details of the discussions and decisions made.

It should be noted that where a trustee is absent from part of a meeting due to a conflict of interest, they will not count towards the quorum.

All members, trustees, local governors (where applicable) and senior employees must complete the register of interests. Relevant business and pecuniary interests must also be published on the trust website (see Chapter 17). The register should be presented at each board meeting for confirmation that the details contained are accurate.

Upon first appointment, members, trustees, local governors (where applicable) and senior employees should be asked to complete and sign a declaration indicating any interests that could potentially conflict with those of the trust. The declaration should be repeated and the register subsequently updated annually. If circumstances change for any individual, they should update their declaration in respect of any actual or potential conflicts as soon as they arise.

A version of a Declaration of Interests form following the ICSA version can be used. It reflects the principles highlighted in 'The Code of Governance for the Voluntary and Community Sector', but remains accessible and user-friendly.

School Academy Trust
Company Number: 1234567
Declaration of Interests

I .... as Member/Governor of * * * * * * * * *
School Academy Trust have set out below my interests:

Category	Please give details of the interest and whether it applies to yourself or, where appropriate, a member of your immediate family, connected persons or some other close personal connection.
Current employment and any previous employment in which you continue to have a financial interest.	
Appointments (voluntary or otherwise), e.g. trusteeships, directorships, local authority membership, tribunals etc.	
Membership of any professional bodies, special interest groups or mutual support organisations.	
Investments in unlisted companies, partnerships and other forms of business, major shareholdings and beneficial interests.	
Gifts or hospitality offered to you by external bodies and whether these were declined or accepted in the last 12 months.	
Any contractual relationship with the Academy.	
Any other conflicts that are not covered by the above.	

I certify that I have declared all beneficial interests which I, or any person closely connected to me, have with businesses or other organisations, which may have dealings with this school. To the best of my knowledge, the above information is complete and correct. I undertake to update as necessary the information provided, and to review the accuracy of the information on an annual basis.

Signed: ....

Date: ....

Below is an alternative version, produced by the Cabot Federation:

CABOT LEARNING FEDERATION

ANNUAL DECLARATION OF PECUNIARY AND OTHER INTEREST 2016/17

As part of the Cabot Learning Federation's financial regulations the Federation Board is required to maintain an annual register that lists each member of the board, the principal and senior members of staff and records their individual pecuniary and other potential conflicts of interest.

Staff Interest:	*Board and Council Member's Interest:*
It is important that every staff member completes this record, even if there is nothing to declare, that individuals are aware that they should notify the academy immediately of any changes which would affect their declaration and that individuals should make an annual declaration that the information is accurate.	Board and council members are required to register any interest that they or their partners or immediate family may have which could have association with the trading activity of the Federation. This may mean a company or individual that is a supplier to the Federation or a company that purchases services from the Federation or its subsidiary, John Cabot Ventures Ltd. The obligation to disclose also relates to any non-business organisation that may hire premises from the Federation.

Please complete the sections below. **[NIL returns are required]**

1. Board / Council / Staff Member Name: ————————————
[Please Print]
2. Do you have a business/pecuniary interest? **Yes/No** [delete as appropriate]. If Yes, provide details below (please attach additional sheets if there is insufficient space below):
3. Names of Company / Organisation's details:
   [1] ————————————————————————————
   [2] ————————————————————————————
4. Indicate the type of work carried out in each case:
   [1] ————————————————————————————
   [2] ————————————————————————————
5. Relationship of the Company or Organisation to the person completing this form:
   [1] ————————————————————————————
   [2] ————————————————————————————

Signature ————————————————————

Date ————————————

Delegation of authority

The board is responsible for the operation of the trust as a company. It has authority as a body rather than individually so that any decision making is a collective process of the board; once a resolution has been passed it is binding on all trustees, not just those that voted in favour of it.

However, the Articles permit the board to delegate the responsibility for tasks and grant the necessary authority to carry them out to:

- board committees including local governing bodies;
- individual trustees such as the chief executive officer/principal; and
- members of the executive (e.g. the business manager).

Responsibility and accountability will, nevertheless, remain with the board.

The trustees can decide on the limit of such delegation and the conditions that should be imposed. No committee or individual should have unfettered powers. The extent and remit of their authority should be made clear. Levels of expenditure are commonly established so that each level in the hierarchy knows what size of contract or purchase agreement they can legally enter. The *Academies Financial Handbook* states:

> 'Whilst the board cannot delegate overall responsibility for the academy trust's funds, it **must** approve a written scheme of delegation of financial powers that maintains robust internal control arrangements.'

It is, nevertheless, good governance that major decisions are made by the board as a whole and the matters 'Reserved for the Board' (i.e. which can only be decided upon at board level) should be established and made explicit.

When any delegated authority has been exercised, the person or committee must report to the board 'in respect of any action taken or decision made with respect to the exercise of that power or function'. They must, therefore, formally report to the next board meeting.

A Delegation Planner used at Rush Common School, a single primary academy in Oxfordshire, can be found in Appendix 5.

Committees

The board can set up as many committees as is felt to be appropriate.

A MAT will generally have committees known as local governing bodies (LGBs) linked to each individual school. The LGB is often delegated responsibility for oversight of teaching and learning.

COMMENT

Emma Knights, Chief Executive of the National Governors' Association:

'There may be others involved in governance of academies who are not directors or members. This is particularly the case in multi-academy trusts (MATs), where the trustees govern all the academies in the MAT, but then each school has a local layer of governance. Increasing numbers of academies now belong to MATs. These are often local governing bodies, and sometimes advisory councils. The roles of a local governing body differ between different academy trusts. It may involve full financial delegation to each school, possibly with a percentage slice for centralised services, or may be a structure that is much more centralised, with local governing bodies looking only at attainment and progression of pupils. The roles should be set out clearly in a delegation document.'

The *Academies Financial Handbook* states that, as a minimum, there should be a finance committee 'to provide assurance over the suitability of, and compliance with, its financial systems and operational controls'.

Trusts with an annual turnover of over £50 million must also have a dedicated audit committee to provide 'internal scrutiny which delivers objective and independent assurance'. All other trusts have the flexibility to establish either a dedicated audit committee, or to include the functions of an audit committee within another committee.

Constitution and terms of reference for committees should be drafted and reviewed annually. Non-trustees can be appointed to committees and be given voting rights as long as the majority of the committee are trustees. The Articles do not set out a quorum for meeting so an appropriate quorum can be decided by the board and incorporated in the Terms of Reference. The majority present and voting at any valid committee meeting must be trustees.

In a MAT, the trustees may appoint separate committees known as LGBs for each separate academy or in respect of a group of academies. The requirements in respect of trustees making up the majority of a committee do not apply in the case of LGBs. The functions and proceedings of LGBs are subject to regulations made by the trustees from time to time.

However, apart from a finance committee, there is no requirement for the board to appoint any committees. There may be other ways of working which are more appropriate for a trust.

COMMENT

John Banbrook MA FCMI FNASBM is Business and Finance Director at the Faringdon Academy of Schools, and elected Council Representative for the South East for ASCL. FAoS is a MAT which expanded from three to eight schools at the end of 2013:

'Previously there was too much consideration at board level of details which could be dealt with elsewhere. We now have a much more strategic approach and have introduced a business cycle which sets the business to be dealt with on the agenda at a particular point in the year.

The committees do not have individual representatives from each school although they do represent schools. This has helped to move to the strategic view.

We may, in time, give consideration to evolving to a model with fewer committees. We would have named leads for each area who would meet regularly with the executive responsible. Ad hoc meetings to deal with committee-type business would be called when required. The board will continue to set the strategy and check it is being done.'

Chief executive officer/principal

The Articles recognise that day-to-day management of the trust will be delegated to an individual. In a single trust this will be the principal (head teacher) and in a MAT the chief executive officer. This individual plays a central role in the trust but may be known by any one of a number of names: CEO, principal, head teacher, executive head teacher, director of learning, etc.

However, there is currently some conflict with regards to where that individual sits within the organisation. The CEO/principal is automatically a member of the board within the model articles if they agree 'so to act'. However, the Charity Commission are uncomfortable with this blurring of the board and senior executive. It seems likely that in future the CEO/principal will appear before the board as chief advisor and accountable to the board, but not a part of it.

COMMENT

John Banbrook MA FCMI FNASBM is Business and Finance Director of the Faringdon Academy of Schools, and elected Council Representative for the South East for ASCL. FAoS is a MAT in Oxfordshire consisting of one secondary school (the Community College), five primary schools, one junior and one infant school. He explained:

'Originally, we were steered by the DfE to appoint our executive head teacher as a director as they were seeking for someone to be accountable. At that time that was met with opposition from the Charity Commission, which did not feel that the executive head teacher should be a director but would prefer them as an advisor to the board.

The NGA now recommend a model where the chief executive/executive head teacher is not appointed to the board.

FAoS is in the process of reviewing governance and leadership structure over the course of the coming year.'

Vision and strategy

Fundamental to any successful organisation is a coherent vision that encapsulates core values and purpose whilst envisioning a future that the organisation hopes to become or achieve. That vision should set the core principles which underpin everything the organisation does and informs the creation of operational strategies and practices.

Strategy is the direction and scope of an organisation over the long term. That strategy puts into action the vision in a way that is both proactive and also responsive to change.

Trusts should consider and set their own vision and strategy. That vision should be a constant that informs and underlies everything that the trust does in the long term. A strategic plan should flow from that.

CASE STUDY

Rush Common School in Oxfordshire:

Vision and Strategy

'Our vision is to be an outstanding school where all learners have wide-ranging opportunities to develop their talents and abilities.

In response to the ever-changing demands of the 21st century, the school provides a safe, continually improving and inspirational educational environment, making innovative and appropriate use of technologies, so that pupils, staff and the community develop as confident, independent learners with high aspirations. Effective teaching and learning ensures that all learners' capacity to be resourceful and adaptable individuals is developed, so that change and challenge is embraced and the qualities of resilience and self-confidence are fostered.

At the core of the vision is a concept of Rush Common School as the dynamic heart of a flourishing learning community, where high quality on-going professional training and development plus mutually beneficial relationships with wide-ranging agencies and organisations enhance the opportunities and experiences for all learners. Our partnerships encompass the local community and connect with wider learning communities nationally and internationally.

Underpinning the vision is the following set of core values. All pupils and staff are required to:

- Be self-respecting individuals who take personal responsibility for their own learning.
- Work hard and achieve their very best.
- Show respect for, and tolerance of, others and the world in which we live.
- Be sensitive to the needs of others with the capacity to empathise with the experiences of people from diverse communities and backgrounds.
- Display determination, self-discipline and perseverance and to be confident to take risks.
- Be able to respond positively to the challenges they will encounter in the changing learning, work and social environments they will encounter in the 21st century.

Rush Common Academy Trust is a multi-academy trust. The board of directors are discussing the school's long-term strategy within the current educational landscape to develop the multi-academy status of RCAT.'

In a multi-academy trust, the vision and strategy will be set by the board. Strategy is multi-layered and the over-arching strategic direction will feed down into the strategic plans of individual academies and departments. The board of a trust should be concerned only with the highest level of such strategic planning, but it will ensure that the strategy directs the executive and operational thinking throughout.

CASE STUDY

Vision and strategy is a bigger issue for MATs formed from a coming together of various schools with different histories and structures. A good example is the Faringdon Academy of Schools (FAoS) in Oxfordshire, a MAT consisting of a secondary school (Faringdon Community College), five primary schools, an infant and a junior school. Some of these schools had previously been Community schools whilst others were Church of England VC schools.

Bob Wintringham, Chair of the Board, explains:

'To understand our vision, we have to start long before schools were encouraged to become academies.

The governing body of the Community College (FCC) has been evolving over at least 20 years with a low turnover of governors and staff for the majority of that time. This has meant that the level of expertise has remained high and the strategic direction has evolved steadily, taking account of the perpetual change in education whilst always being aware of what is best for FCC. Governors see teaching as a vocation and schools only keep the best teachers if they can retain the motivation and challenge. This means that the whole school team (governing body and staff) need to be at the cutting edge of educational development, with every change part of the long-term push to continually raise standards and create a wider school partnership; a community school, a college, a specialist school, Charter mark etc., etc. – each has had a part to play in our development.

A clear vision and strategy has meant that we have been able to assess the rainstorm of initiatives from successive governments; each carefully weighed against our own clear objectives to increase the quality of the education of our students.

But an academy must be built on trust particularly where schools agree to work together, and the Faringdon Partnership has a long history of mutual trust and support that provided the natural base for closer collaboration.

So, the journey to academy status took more than two years to complete. We shared and augmented the FCC vision for the future with our potential partners, and built on it to provide the overall FAoS vision. We were adamant that the pace of improvement would not relax; that smaller primary schools would not feel railroaded by the big secondary; that we needed to build on the successful parts of the local authority education provision and most importantly, that academy status must bring added value.

The single vision gives us stability and sustainability, future-proofing and credibility – more than a glib statement but a philosophy for the member schools to follow.

All schools build their own plans around the strategic objectives which are derived from the central vision.

The practical application of this vision has led to a proactive academy School Improvement team, a programme of collaboration between schools towards an all-through curriculum and an altruistic sharing of resources to the greater good of the whole academy.'

The Strategic Objectives & Key Indicators document used by Faringdon Academy of Schools is contained in Appendix 6.

Trust name

Choosing the name of a trust may not always be straightforward, especially where there is a MAT arrangement with a number of different parties involved. The name encapsulates the vision of that organisation for the future.

COMMENT

One Twitter user, Brian Walton, Head Teacher at Headley Park Primary School, summed it up:

@PrimaryHead1 'Thinking of names for our new multi trust academy . . . Inspire Learning Corporation . . . It's like choosing a band name!'

Ensuring cohesion

In a MAT, the individual academies are united in a single unit from a legal perspective. Many MATs believe that it is important for them to unite on a practical level as well. A strong and cohesive trust can share best practice and develop a single vision.

COMMENT

Sujata McNab, Chief Operating Officer of the Cabot Learning Federation:

'The academy chairs meet as a group with the CEO and the chair of the board. They have a free agenda.

It is a really good way for them to air issues and talk through the details. They can share good practice, for example that a particular teacher has achieved a specific qualification which could be of benefit to other academies. They also have an opportunity to discuss things or to escalate anything they wish the board to consider formally. It is a key way that the board links itself to the academies.'

Clerks and company secretaries

Clerk to the board

The DfE recognises that the clerk to the board has an important part to play in the organisation of a governing body's work, irrespective of the governance structure of the school, and it states:

'It is helpful if the clerk is able to offer information and advice to the governing body, particularly on matters involving the law and procedures to be followed at meetings.'

Clerks are appointed by the board of trustees but they report to the chair of the board. Where the role of the clerk is undertaken by the school secretary, bursar or other member of staff, the individual concerned should be clear that clerking the governing body is outside their normal reporting arrangements. Appointing a clerk who is employed in another capacity in the trust can lead to difficulties as a result of any conflict that may arise.

The value of a professional, independent clerk is increasingly recognised. As well as being able to offer appropriate legal and regulatory guidance when applicable, they bring an unbiased view.

The National Governors' Association (NGA) runs the Clerking Matters campaign with four main aims:

1. to increase the understanding of the importance of the work of clerks and what can be expected of a well-trained clerk
2. to help governing boards find good clerks where there is difficulty in doing this
3. to help clerks know where continuing professional development can be found
4. to encourage appropriate remuneration of clerks.

NGA has published a model job description which sets out the expectations of the role.

The board must decide whether the same clerk should be appointed to the committees/LGBs. Whilst clerking support must be provided, for a MAT it may simply be unfeasible for one person to provide services to all.

The clerk cannot be a trustee or the principal/head teacher. They cannot vote at board meetings (although a trustee who acts as clerk for a meeting if the clerk fails to attend may take part in discussions and vote).

Depending on the conditions of service on which the clerk is engaged, the board may have the power to remove them from office.

The importance of the role should not be underestimated. The minutes prepared by the clerk are among the first documentation viewed by Ofsted inspectors and other external bodies in assessing the effectiveness of a school.

Secretary/clerk

The model articles provide that the trustees should appoint a clerk or secretary to the board 'at such remuneration and upon such conditions as they may think fit'. The person appointed cannot be a trustee, principal or chief executive, although the board may appoint a trustee to act as clerk for any meeting where the clerk fails to attend. The 'clerk' in this sense is akin to the clerk to the full governing body in a maintained school.

> **COMMENT**
>
> John Banbrook MA FCMI FNASBM, Business and Finance Director at the
> Faringdon Academy of Schools and elected Council Representative
> for the South East for ASCL:
>
> 'Communication in the MAT is really valuable. We have now appointed an
> academy secretary whose role is significant in terms of effective commu-
> nication between the LGBs, the board and ops. She takes some company
> secretarial responsibility and is the "go to" person for the academy. She is
> also the line manager for clerks at each of the LGBs.'

The clerk has a central role in organising and directing the work of the board just
as in a maintained school. The importance of the position has not gone unno-
ticed. In their *Report on the Role of School Governing Bodies* published in July
2013, the House of Commons Education Committee commented:

> 'As professional bodies, school governors need professional support. The
> role of clerk to a school governing body should be classed as a professional
> post.'

The clerk should be able to provide support on a much wider basis than simply
attending to take the minutes of meetings. They should be well versed in the
law and procedures relevant to meetings and the particular requirements of the
funding agreement and Articles of Association that apply to their own trust. The
requirements are often very different to those of the maintained sector, and the
clerk should be well trained and conversant in the legalities.

Historically, the role of clerk to the governing body was undertaken by the
school secretary. This is no longer appropriate. Not only is the role important in
its own right, requiring particular knowledge and training, but it also presents
a difficult dilemma for the individual who reports not only to the head teacher
as part of their day job, but to the board, and specifically to the chair, when they
operate as clerk to the board. An independent and appropriately qualified clerk is
recommended.

There is a legal obligation on the trust to compile and retain minutes of board
meetings; a record of board decisions should also be kept, whether passed in a
board meeting or via a written resolution. The requirements are too onerous not
to be given the attention they deserve.

There is obviously a distinct overlap in the roles of clerk and company secretary, and consideration should be given to the most appropriate arrangements to
meet the needs of a trust and their academies. It may be the case that a company
secretary or governance specialist be appointed at trust level and then clerks

appointed to the individual academies. In such a case, those clerks will be guided by the specific requirements of their own trust and need not have training or experience at trust level, though obviously this is a bonus.

The company secretary

Since the Companies Act 2006, there has been no legal requirement to appoint a designated company secretary in a private company provided that there is no specific requirement to do so within the Articles of Association.

The Department for Education has provided model Memorandum and Articles of Association which trusts are not expected to change (see Chapter 6). There is no specific requirement to appoint a company secretary included in the model articles. It is, of course, still open to a trust to choose to appoint a company secretary.

Normally, a company secretary will act as the chief administrative officer of the trust. Their specific responsibilities will differ depending on the requirements of the trust but they are likely to advise on legal and regulatory matters, finance and accounting, governance and the development of strategic planning. In fact, they could be responsible for any of the matters covered by this book – and more.

A company secretary is a high-ranking professional whose role is often combined with that of the director of finance. The company secretary enables the directors to retain a strategic focus managing the business of the trust. The company secretary will carry legal responsibilities; however, ultimate responsibility for administration of the trust lies with the trustees.

Unfortunately, smaller trusts may not have the financial resources to appoint a specialist company secretary directly. Various organisations such as solicitors offer a company secretarial service which will fulfil the requirements relating to Companies House and company law. However, many more trusts are opting to appoint a member of staff to take responsibility for the company secretarial function rather than using external providers. Often this will be the bursar/director of finance or business manager.

Whatever the approach, trusts must fulfil their obligations. The company secretarial function is fundamental and whoever undertakes the role should not underestimate the level of responsibility involved. It is incumbent on the trustees to make sure that any person appointed knows what they are doing. As well as possible liability implications for the trustees and company secretary, failure to meet these requirements could see trusts threatened with fines from Companies House, followed by a visit from the EFA or Ofsted.

The role of the company secretary is not dictated by legislation or regulation, so the remit of any person appointed will be established by the terms of their contract of employment. There is no 'typical' company secretary, but the role should be recognised as a key operational one.

A trust is not legally bound to appoint a company secretary, and where no company secretary has been formally appointed, the liability will fall on the trustees as a whole.

COMMENT

Simon Osborne FCIS, Chief Executive of ICSA:

'Academisation changes the way in which a school is governed. Responsibility for leading the academy trust lies with the trust board, which has a remit that encompasses not just the role of governor but that of trustee and company director as well. This is not always clear to those on the board or to those that work with them, especially local governing bodies or advisory councils. Recent media stories highlighting poor governance in some academies reinforce the importance of good governance and how pivotal a company secretary is in supporting the board of trustees.

The role of company secretary to an academy trust board is one for which chartered secretaries are well qualified and suited. They are grounded in business and company law, governance, strategy, financial management and decision making. They also have expertise in the sound principles of secretaryship and administration. They have the know-how to advise the chair of trustees and the trustee board as a whole across a wide spectrum of issues and knowledge of the appropriate governance framework for the organisation. In short, to borrow a slogan for a quite different industry, they know how to help keep an organisation like an academy "legal, honest, decent and truthful".'

The governance professional

It is clear that with the further development of MATs growing in size and becoming more diverse, there is an increasing need for robust governance, advice and support. Trustees can continue to engage legal advisors, but this is a costly and often time-consuming process. It is now almost essential to have dedicated governance support within the organisation and many MATs already employ their own company secretary or head of governance.

However, there is little need to appoint an individual with company secretary-type responsibilities at LGB level. Many MATs have already developed a two-tier system where LGBs have a clerk or minute-taker who reports to the company secretary.

COMMENT

Mark Johnson, Solicitor & Chartered Secretary, Elderflower Legal, Independent Audit Committee Member, The Dean Trust MAT:

'One of the difficulties in embedding sound governance practice is a current lack of clarity about who is responsible in academy trusts for setting up the framework for sound governance and embedding good practice. In my experience, CEOs and executive principals are not usually the best people to lead on this – they are tasked with driving the organisation forward and taking measured risks. Similarly, finance directors and school business managers may be too immersed in the day-to-day operations and short of time to take an overview of governance. The best person to implement the system is a trained governance professional, such as an ICSA-qualified chartered secretary. They have the necessary experience and rigorous qualifications beyond financial and legal aspects to help you succeed.'

Professional recognition

ICSA, the Institute for Chartered Secretaries and Administrators, is the professional body for those working in governance. Through a combination of examinations and relevant professional experience, it is possible to become a chartered secretary, which ICSA believes represents the 'gold standard of the company secretarial field'. Associate status requires six years of experience, and Fellowship requires eight.

However, not all clerks desire or require the level of qualification or the wide scope of the subjects covered by ICSA. Consequently, the Accredited Clerk is one accreditation programme which has been run for over 14 years. Externally moderated by ISCG or Qualifi, the programme is used by local authorities and offered to their own clerks and independent clerks in their area. Clerks need to obtain relevant training separately to ensure that they are able to produce the evidence portfolio required.

COMMENT

Matt Lake, Senior Clerk to Governors, Islington Governor Services and co-founder of the National Association of School Governance Officers:

'The massive increase in the number of academy schools and more latterly multi-academy trusts in recent years has delivered a commensurate growth in the attention given to the governance of these institutions, especially as they hold responsibility for the distribution of significant amounts of public money.

'However, whilst we have seen a number of high-profile cases of poor governance in the academy sector, usually related to conflicts of interest and the ineffective systems in place to prevent these, we have as yet seen little concerted focus on ensuring that all school and academy boards of governors have access to high-quality governance support, guidance and advice from those who are best placed to provide this in real time, the clerks to the board.

The first attempt to provide this on a national scale through the NCTL Clerks Development Programme should be applauded. However, the experience of its delivery across England has been patchy with some programmes led by appropriate experts but with some licensees having programmes facilitated by those that have never worked as a clerk to a school governing board.

The clerk as the guardian of the governance processes as they are being operated acts like the oil that ensures an engine works smoothly. Poor-quality oil, or oil that needs replacing (or perhaps in this instance some focused professional development), can lead to the engine failing, bringing the vehicle to a sudden, shuddering halt.

Much has been made by DfE Ministers in the face of the increasingly complex responsibilities being taken on by school and academy governors of the importance of recruiting and appointing governors with the skills required to ensure that their board is effective. However, the linked requirement to invest in the provision of quality governance support from professionally trained and experienced clerks remains the missing link of school and academy governance.

Some first steps towards this are being taken by the NGA and ICSA who come to this from their own perspective and with their own priorities. The ICSA submission to the Education Select Committee on multi-academy trusts stated, "Given the complex structures being put in place between MAT boards, local governing bodies (LGBs) or advisory councils and stakeholders it is essential that appropriate and professional governance expertise is available to the MAT board. It is vital that MATs have appropriate company secretarial and clerking support in place."

It is welcome that organisations with an engagement in the world of school and academy governance are increasingly recognising the importance of the role of the clerk but the next stage in the professional development of this role must be led by those with direct experience of working as clerks. To ensure the appropriate professional development of clerks and a full appreciation of the complete range of skills, knowledge and activity that comprise the core of the work involved, the time is right for the creation of a collaborative network of clerks working in partnership to raise the profile of the role, to develop professional standards and provide support to the individuals engaged in this important work across the country.'

Performance management and CPD

No matter how they are engaged or the nature of their role, all clerks/company secretaries should be subject to the normal performance management system in place in the trust. As well as a written job description setting out their role, each year the clerk/company secretary should be involved in a process that reviews the year just gone to learn from mistakes and build on successes. A more developed system will include the setting of formal objectives which are then reviewed at year end.

Although the trust board may not be aware, the role of the clerk has been subject to significant change over the last few years and this is likely to continue, at least in the short term. The responsibilities falling on the trust board are considerable and the clerk/company secretary needs to be conversant with the latest requirements and able to give the best advice to the board. This means that the need for good continuing professional development (CPD) is more important than ever.

Trusts engaging clerks/company secretaries through a local authority or other third-party provider should ask about qualifications and ongoing support including quality assurance processes and CPD.

15 Risk management

Every organisation faces risk in their everyday operation. However, management of risk by identifying and monitoring it is a key part of effective governance and is essential for the successful running of an academy trust.

The International Organization for Standardization (ISO) defines risk management as 'coordinated activities to direct and control an organisation with regard to risk'. The ISO has established International Standards which sets out principles and guidelines for managing risk in a 'systematic, transparent and credible manner'.

Every trust should develop and adopt a framework for effective risk management which is incorporated into the overall management and strategy as well as reflected in policies and procedures and underlying culture and values. The framework itself should also be subject to continuous review and improvement.

An effective risk management process involves:

- establishing a risk policy;
- identifying risk;
- analysis of specific risks;
- evaluation and, if appropriate, modification of risk; and
- ongoing monitoring.

The framework should be created to fit the specific risks faced by the particular trust reflecting the activities, structure and environment in which it operates. Possible risk categories could include:

- governance;
- operational risk, including health and safety;
- finance risk;
- environmental and external risk; and
- law and regulation compliance risk.

Risk management should consider the effect of uncertainty both in terms of positive and negative impact. Risk could arise as a result of an event that will occur to impact negatively on the trust as well as from the potential that something good will happen.

Risks are then prioritised according to the likelihood of occurrence and the potential loss or impact. Risks with the greatest potential loss and greatest probability of occurring should be managed first.

The resulting 'risk management plan' should identify mitigation strategies. One common mnemonic for a risk strategy is SARA:

- **S**hare risk. Outsource the activity or transfer the risk through insurance.
- **A**void risk. Change the activity or plan so that the problem will not arise.
- **R**educe risk. Take steps to control or mitigate the risk.
- **A**ccept risk. Take the chance that some or all of the potential risk will arise.

Academy trusts are effectively 'service' businesses, so some consideration should be given to 'knowledge risk' where there is deficient knowledge either in trust staff or the board, or 'relationship risk' where there is ineffective collaboration from departmental level across academies in a MAT. These risks will reduce staff efficiency and/or effectiveness, potentially impacting on pupil performance and results and, consequently, increasing reputational risk.

COMMENT

Mark Taylor, Director of Lucas Fettes & Partners, highlights issues involved in managing the risk of staff absence:

'Supply cover is probably the least predictable area of expenditure for most academies and can often be the main contributory factor in budget overspends. But the cost of staff absence is more than just financial – the absence of a valued team member can have a significant impact on the school community and the continuity of teaching.

Comparing insurance quotes on a like-for-like basis can be difficult because there is a huge variety of policy wordings available, each offering varying levels of cover and limitations. An independent broker should be able to arrange the appropriate cover to meet your individual needs. We have been able to save some academies up to £100,000 on their budgets by rearranging their existing staff absence insurance.'

Despite the importance of risk management, it is important that the cost in time and resources of risk management is proportionate and balanced against other pressing needs of the trust.

One key aspect of risk management is effective financial oversight. The *Academies Financial Handbook* contains detailed requirements that must be observed by trusts. As the recipient of public money, the obligations on a trust are understandably onerous. Financial monitoring and appropriate internal controls are considered in detail in Chapter 12.

Figure 15.1: Faringdon Academy of Schools Risk Management Model

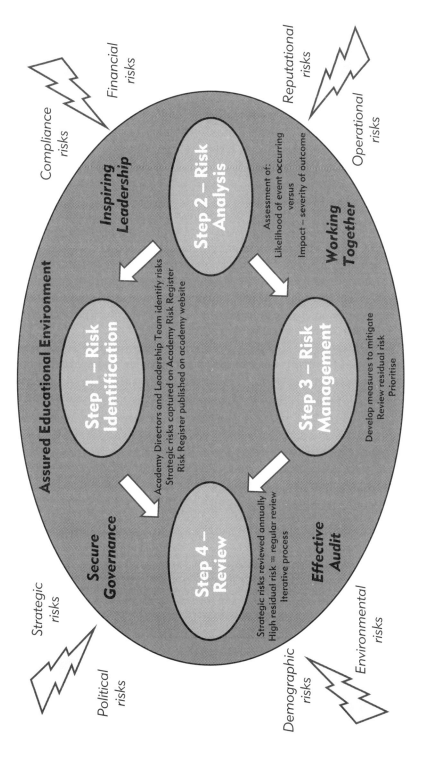

The *Academies Financial Handbook* specifically states that:

> 'The trust must cooperate with risk management auditors and risk managers and implement reasonable risk management audit recommendations that are made to them.'

The risk management process should be continually or periodically re-assessed and enhanced and improved whenever possible. The process should become integral to the corporate governance processes, informing board decision making.

Examples of a risk assessment and risk register are included in Appendices 7 and 8.

■ Health and safety

Academy trusts are employers of staff and must ensure, as far as possible, the 'health, safety and welfare at work' of all employees as well as protecting other people such as pupils or visitors who might be affected by their activities. Further, as a trust will generally also have responsibility for maintenance and repair of its premises, it must ensure that they are 'safe and without risks to health' (Health and Safety at Work Act 1974).

The provisions of the Act are qualified by the words 'so far as is reasonably practicable' so a trust is not required to eliminate the risks entirely if that would be technically impossible or the cost of doing so would be disproportionate to the risk. Trusts are, however, required to carry out appropriate risk assessments and take sensible measures to manage any risks identified. Risk management for health and safety is an ongoing process that needs to be kept under constant review. In simple terms, there is a three-step process:

1. Know the risks.
2. Control the risks that need it.
3. Make sure that risks stay controlled.

However, there is a lot of regulation in this area and specialist advice is recommended.

More specific requirements on the trust as employer are set out in the Management of Health and Safety of Work Regulations 1999 (SI 1999/3242) These include:

- making arrangements for implementing the health and safety measures identified as necessary by the risk assessment;
- appointing competent people to help implement the arrangements;
- setting up emergency procedures;
- providing clear information and training to employees; and
- working together with other employers sharing the same workplace.

COMMENT

Solicitor Stuart Armstrong of SV Armstrong has developed a Health & Safety Leadership Checklist as an introduction for those managing trusts:

'In the event of a serious incident occurring on or off premises, it is likely that there may be an investigation by the police and/or the health & safety executive. Individual governors, trustees, board members as well as officers and employees may all be required to demonstrate that they did everything so far as was reasonably practicable to prevent the incident from happening.

Do board members know what they should be doing to avoid incidents occurring?

The HSE and the Institute of Directors in their Guidance to Directors (INDG 417) suggest three essential principles of effective leadership in health and safety. These apply to governors, trustees, officers, directors and their equivalent senior managers. These are as follows:

1. Strong and active leadership with:
   - visible, active commitment from the board;
   - established downward communication systems; and
   - good health and safety management integrated with business decisions.
2. Worker involvement that includes:
   - engaging the workforce in the promotion of safe and healthy conditions;
   - effective upward communication; and
   - high-quality training.
3. Assessment and review processes that:
   - identify and manage risks;
   - allow access to competent health and safety advice and require that advice to be followed; and
   - include monitoring, reporting and reviewing of health and safety performance.

How should boards put these principles into practice?
- Agree a health and safety policy statement that the board then ratifies and the senior executive signs – for and on behalf of the board. This should be reviewed after 12 months, and then on a regular basis after that.
- Agree on the practical arrangements for managing safety and checking on the understanding of those arrangements. Consider the following:
  o Who gives the board its competent advice? This should be someone with the relevant safety competence (knowledge, skills training, experience etc. Training should be a Diploma Level qualification in

safety and membership of a professional body (CMIOSH, MIIRSM or above); experience in education and relevant knowledge of the industry; experience in working with the same systems, etc.). Internal advice is preferable to external advice of the same level, since internal advisors will have greater access to documents, people and facilities in the trust.

o The board should also consider carrying out a Training Needs Assessment to identify who else may need additional health and safety training to carry out their roles (first response, manual handling, risk assessment, etc). Training needs may be identified in a matrix of skills required for each level of post.

o To what extent is everyone aware of their responsibilities for safety, and do they understand their roles, etc.?

■ Agree on the policies/procedures operating in the organisation.

■ Agree on who will and how to review policies/procedures, implement changes in policy/procedure, monitor the effectiveness of change, and consider whether the changes are working in practice. Continue to review on a regular basis.

■ Recognise that a formal management system may take 12–18 months to implement.

Consider whether you could answer the following questions:

1. Who is responsible for health and safety in the organisation?
2. How does the board demonstrate its commitment to health and safety?
3. What information does the board receive to enable it to monitor health and safety performance?
4. How does the board communicate and implement its policies on safety?
5. What information does the board review?
6. Who decides what risks to assess?
7. At what level is competent advice given within the organisation?
8. Who monitors contractors working on the premises?
9. Are the principal risks from premises or activities?
10. How does the board ensure adequate supervision of its employees?
11. How do employees inform the board if there are problems? Are there examples of these problems, and how were the issues resolved?
12. Who is responsible for managing asbestos, and how is it managed? In several school refurbishment projects, the schools were criticised for not managing asbestos properly.

If board members are unsure what they should be doing, or whether their organisation is doing the right thing, then they should consider their own health and safety training needs. There are varying levels of health and safety training and qualifications available.'

Particular areas that should be considered for health and safety hazards are:

- Provision of a safe place of work including workstations (Health and Safety (Display Screen Equipment) Regulations 1992 (SI 1992/ 2792)).
- Slips and trips.
- General fire safety.
- Machinery safety (Provision and Use of Work Equipment Regulations 1998 (SI 1998/543)).
- Plant and equipment maintenance.
- Gas- and oil-fired equipment (Gas Safety (Installation and Use) Regulations 1998 (SI 1994/3140)).
- Workplace Transport (Workplace (Health, Safety and Welfare) Regulations 1992 (SI 1992/3004) and the Provision and Use of Work Equipment Regulations 1998 (SI 1998/2306)).
- Electrical equipment (Electricity at Work Regulations 1989 (SI 1989/635)).
- Harmful substances including asbestos (Control of Asbestos Regulations 2012 (SI 2012/632)) and COSHH (Control of Substances Hazardous to Health Regulations 2002 (SI 2002/2677)).
- Outdoor play equipment.
- Managing health including sickness absence and return to work and work-related stress.
- Adventure activities using licensed providers (Adventure Activities Licensing Regulations 2004 (SI 2004/1309)).

COMMENT

Catherine Barnes, Business Development Manager of The Propeller Academy Trust, a MAT of two special academies, Kingfisher School and Fitzwaryn School, which has the additional expertise of a sponsor organisation, Abingdon and Witney College:

'The head of health and safety at the college is a qualified individual. I can ask him to come to do a health and safety audit for me which he does in a friendly way, offering help and support.

He has a health and safety qualification and is able to provide expertise when we need it. For example, he can provide support in connection with COSHH – we have a Jacuzzi at Fitzwaryn and a swimming pool at Kingfisher which require chemicals.'

The HSE website has a great deal of useful guidance relating to health and safety and includes a health and safety checklist which can be used to identify issues in classrooms.

All staff should be given appropriate health and safety training, although this may only require providing basic instructions. Academies are also legally required to display the HSE-approved law poster or to provide every worker with a leaflet giving the same information. Care should be taken to ensure that any information, instruction and training is available in the worker's native language, to maximise understanding.

Particular focus should be given to the specific risks faced by any people with disabilities and new and expectant mothers.

Specific parental consent will be required for off-site activities involving a higher level of risk management or which take place outside school hours. The majority of off-site activities do not require written parental consent although parents should be informed where their child will be at all times.

Trusts must provide adequate and appropriate equipment, facilities and qualified first-aid personnel (Health and Safety (First Aid) Regulations 1981 (SI 1981/917)). Emergency procedures should be in place in the event of an incident and workers should be aware of the process to be followed (Management of Health and Safety at Work Regulations 1999 (SI 1999/3242)).

There are obligations under RIDDOR (Reporting of Injuries, Diseases and Dangerous Occurrences Regulations 2013 (SI 2013/1471)) to report certain serious workplace accidents, occupational diseases and specified dangerous occurrences known as 'near misses'.

Safeguarding

As with maintained schools, trusts have an obligation under the Education Act 2002 to safeguard pupils by ensuring that there are arrangements in place to ensure that they:

- carry out their functions with a view to safeguarding and promoting the welfare of children; and
- have regard to any guidance issued by the Secretary of State.

These requirements should be reflected in all policies and procedures in place in the trust.

Allegations against staff and volunteers

Any allegation must be reported immediately, generally to the head teacher, who will refer the matter for discussion with the LA Designated Officer (LADO).

Business continuity and disaster recovery plans

A business continuity or disaster recovery plan should be developed and maintained to provide a strategy in the event of a major disaster. This strategic recovery plan would ensure that disruption is minimised in the event of a disaster. Obviously, the likelihood of such an occurrence is small, but the impact would be significant, hence the need for a plan.

Having a plan that staff and trustees are familiar with will ensure that the response to any serious unforeseen event will be prompt and will help towards restoring normal operations.

COMMENT

Mark Taylor, Director of Lucas Fettes & Partners, explains the importance of business continuity planning:

'Whether it's a fire, flood, power failure, cyber-attack, or bullying case, all have the potential to pose a great threat to an academy's reputation and revenue. So it is essential to demonstrate your ability to act quickly and effectively in response to unexpected situations, highlighting that your primary concern is the wellbeing of pupils and staff.

The most effective method of protecting against any type of risk is to incorporate business continuity planning within your risk management strategy. Business continuity planning not only permits an academy to remain open in the event of disruption; it can also offer deeper insights into the running of the school, giving the opportunity to re-evaluate and improve internal operations. It can also help to increase competitiveness. If your academy is seen to be taking full and proactive responsibility for mitigating and resolving risks, levels of trust will increase, impacting positively on your reputation and revenue.'

Insurance

Under the Employers' Liability (Compulsory Insurance) Act 1969, trusts must secure employers' liability insurance which will cover the cost of any compensation payments granted to employees for any injuries or illness sustained as a result of their employment. This is a statutory requirement and a trust can be fined if they do not hold a current employers' liability insurance policy.

Other insurances are not compulsory but should be considered:

- trustee/governors' and officers' liability
- absence management, rehabilitation and supply cover
- buildings, contents and property damage – including accidental or malicious damage
- business interruption
- equipment breakdown for engineering and computer equipment, including statutory inspections of pressure, lifting and other plant
- public liability
- motor/minibus and occasional business use for teachers' vehicles;
- out-of-school clubs and holiday clubs
- pupils' personal accident
- pupils' personal effects including educational trips.

Care should be taken over the level of cover obtained and this should be kept under regular review to ensure that it is appropriate.

COMMENT

Mark Taylor, Director of Lucas Fettes & Partners explains the importance of an accurate valuation:

'Many schools insuring directly with insurers or via purchasing consortiums take their sums insured based on figures previously supplied by the LA. Often these figures are not a true representation of the cost of a full rebuild. The only way to achieve an accurate rebuild cost is to conduct a full valuation and update it every three to five years (because the cost of rebuilding will fluctuate over time as a result of many factors). This will ensure that you are fully covered in the event of a major disaster, and also that you are not paying too much for your insurances.'

Risk protection arrangement

The EFA has established a voluntary risk pooling scheme for trusts and free schools.

The risk protection arrangement (RPA) is not an insurance scheme, but a mechanism through which the cost of risks that materialise will be covered by government funds. The RPA will reimburse trusts in the event of a loss outlined in the 'Academies Risk Protection Arrangement Scope' document including:

- loss or damage to property (including minor works)
- increased cost of working following damage to property
- legal liability to pay compensation to employees for death or injury due to employment with the trust (including as a result of exposure to asbestos)
- legal liability to pay compensation to third parties for death, injury or property damage (including as a result of abuse or exposure to asbestos)
- loss of money and personal baggage whilst travelling on trust business in the UK
- loss of trust property due to employee dishonesty.

The RPA will not cover risks related to motor, overseas travel, statutory engineering inspections and works of art.

The DfE states that:

'As well as significant cost savings for school budgets, trusts that opt in to the RPA will avoid complex and time-consuming procurement of commercial insurance cover. Opting in to the scheme and updating cover is simple and quick.'

All trusts, whether SATs or MATs, including 'free schools, faith schools that are academies, special academies, alternative provision academies, university technical schools, studio schools and Private Finance Initiative (PFI) academy trusts', can choose to opt in to the RPA. Whilst there is no cost or premium to join the

RPA, a per-pupil deduction will be made from the trust's general annual grant (GAG).

Trusts that are part of a PFI scheme may be required to take out specific commercial insurance as part of their PFI contract and, therefore, will only be able to join the RPA for any non-PFI risks.

COMMENT

Mark Taylor, Director of Lucas Fettes & Partners:

'A great deal has changed in the world of insurance and risk management for academies since the last edition of this book was published, namely as a consequence of the introduction of the Department for Education's Risk Protection Arrangement, which was introduced in September 2014.

Is the RPA the right solution?

The Risk Protection Arrangement (RPA) is an attractive proposition for many academies, particularly now that proposals to reduce the GAG deduction from £25 to £20 per pupil have been accepted. However, there are a number of factors that academies should take into account before making a decision.

A GAG deduction of £20 or £25 can only deliver a very basic alternative to insurance that will be inadequate for many academies who require more bespoke consideration and covers that are not offered under the RPA – for example motor insurance, business interruption (loss of revenue) and international travel.

The DfE is gradually placing greater emphasis on risk management, which is a positive move, but what will this look like in practical terms? Good risk management should have school improvement at its core, and a formulaic approach, which assumes that one size fits all, will not achieve this – nor will it provide continuous review or the ongoing guidance and support of a dedicated adviser.

For some small academies, the RPA may become the only viable route. But for larger academies and multi-academy trusts in particular, it is prudent to undertake a cost/benefits comparison of the arrangement against commercial insurance alternatives.'

COMMENT

John Banbrook MA FCMI FNASBM, Business and Finance Director at the Faringdon Academy of Schools and elected Council Representative for the South East for ASCL:

'FAoS has not gone into the RPA arrangement at the present time as it was felt that it was an unproven scheme. There were concerns that if a school wasn't performing, a big claim would be the perfect opportunity for them to say that the school was a risk under the RPA.

Instead an individual policy has been obtained on a three-year deal. It was hoped that there would be positive feedback from the RPA scheme by then.'

Dealing with complaints

Under the Education (Independent Schools Standards) Regulations 2010 (SI 2012/2962), Schedule 1, Part 7 trusts are under an obligation to set out a formal, written complaints procedure. In practice, this means drafting and approving a complaints policy. The procedure must set out the way that complaints from parents or pupils will be handled and the timescales for the management of the complaint.

Complainants should, in the first instance, always be directed to the academy itself where the majority of complaints will be resolved. If this is unsuccessful, the complaint can initially be considered on an informal basis. The procedure should then involve a requirement for the complaint to be made in writing for formal consideration, initially by the academy head teacher/principal. If resolution is not achieved, a formal complaint hearing should be held. The panel constituted by the board must be made up of at least three people who were not directly involved in the matters forming the complaint and at least one of whom is independent of the day-to-day management and running of the academy, i.e. someone who is not a trustee.

If a complainant does not feel that their complaint has been satisfactorily resolved, they can, having exhausted the complaints procedure, appeal direct to the Secretary of State for Education through the EFA.

For converter academies, the funding agreement contains obligations relating to complaints arising in whole or in part in the 12 months prior to conversion to ensure that there is continuity and complaints are properly considered.

Although there is no legal requirement on trusts to have a complaints procedure in respect of any parties other than parents or pupils, trusts may wish to consider complaints made by other parties for the purposes of community cohesion. However, it will be for the board to decide.

Appeal panels

The process for permanent exclusion of a pupil follows that of a maintained school. It will occur only where there has been a serious or persistent breach of the trust's behaviour policy and allowing the pupil to continue in attendance would seriously harm the education or welfare of that pupil or others in the trust/

academy. The board must convene a panel to consider the exclusion and decide whether to uphold the decision or overturn it, in which case the pupil will be allowed to return to the academy.

Any subsequent request for a review of the decision must be presented to an Independent Review Panel within 15 days of such a request being made. In a trust, it will be for the board to convene the panel which must have either three or five members, all of whom must have received training on the process and have a clear understanding of the legal requirements. Independent Review Panels do not have the power to reinstate an excluded pupil.

A trust is its own admission authority and any appeal against a decision to refuse admission should be heard by an independent appeal panel composed of a chair and at least two other panel members. There must be:

- at least one person without any personal experience in the management of any school or provision of education in any school; and
- one person who has experience in education or who is a parent of a registered pupil.

The panel members and the clerk appointed to the panel must be appropriately trained.

In practice, many trusts/academies contract with another body (e.g. the local authority) to carry out the admissions functions on their behalf.

Review of board effectiveness

Having an effective board is central to the governance of the trust (see Chapter 14). It is good practice, therefore, to carry out regular reviews of the board and the governance structures in place to ensure that they are effective.

There are now numerous bodies offering external reviews at a cost. Most local authorities provide a service which can be part of wider school improvement services.

However, the board can carry out its own self-review and it is good practice for this to become a regular feature in the annual schedule of work for the board. Various self-audit tools are available.

In 2012, the All-Party Parliamentary Group on Education Governance & Leadership published 20 key questions for governing bodies to consider. These can be used as the basis of a self-review:

Right skills
Do we have the right skills on the governing body?
  1. Have we completed a skills audit of our governing body?
  2. Do we appoint governors on the basis of their skills, and do we know how to find people with the necessary skills?

Effectiveness
Are we as effective as we could be?
3. Do we understand our roles and responsibilities?
4. Do we have a professional clerk and run meetings efficiently?
5. What is our training and development budget and does every governor receive the support they need to carry out their role effectively?
6. Do we know about good practice from across the country?
7. Is the size, composition and committee structure of our governing body conducive to effective working?
8. Does every member of the governing body make a regular contribution and do we carry out an annual review of the governing body's performance?

Strategy
Does the school have a clear vision?
9. Have we developed long-term aims for the school with clear priorities in an ambitious school development plan which is regularly monitored and reviewed?
10. Does our strategic planning cycle drive the governing body's activities and agenda setting?

Accountability of the executive
Do we hold the school leaders to account?
11. Do we understand the school's performance data well enough to properly hold school leaders to account?
12. How effective is our performance management of the head teacher?
13. Are our financial management systems robust and do we ensure best value for money?

Engagement
Are we properly engaged with our school community, the wider school sector and the outside world?
14. How do we listen to and understand our pupils, parents and staff?
15. How do we report to our parents and local community regularly?
16. What benefit do we draw from collaboration with other schools and other sectors, locally and nationally?

Role of chair
Does our chair show strong and effective leadership?
17. Do we carry out a regular 360° review of the chair's performance?
18. Do we engage in good succession planning?
19. Are the chair and committee chairs re-elected each year?

Impact
Are we having an impact on outcomes for pupils?
20. How much has the school improved over the last three years, and what has the governing body's contribution been to this?

The All-Party Parliamentary Group on Education Governance & Leadership subsequently published 21 questions designed to help ensure that governance structures in MATs are fit for purpose.

A Governor Mark is a national award which gives an external evaluation of the quality of governance. It states that:

> governing bodies must have in place quality processes if they are to make a significant impact upon the achievements of schools. Intrinsic to this approach is a belief that if governing bodies have adopted such quality processes, the extent of their contribution and influence can make a real difference to the leadership and management of the school.

The Governor Mark Standards Document which sets out the framework criteria together with guidance is freely available on its website.

Following any review, it is essential that the board note the identified strengths and weaknesses and make an action plan for addressing any issues or areas for development.

The principles relating to board review should also be applied to the various committees.

COMMENT

Naureen Khalid, Vice Chair of Governors at Newstead Wood School, has developed a committee/governing body self-evaluation:

'I requested people who attend the committee I chair to complete an evaluation form. The reasoning behind this was that in order to see if the committee was functioning as effectively as it could, I needed to see what everyone thought of our practices. Such evaluations are important for governing bodies and committees in order to highlight areas for development which would then feed into how the identified concerns can be addressed. These evaluations will also show what is working well. It is just as important to acknowledge and appreciate what is working well as it is to highlight what is not.'

A copy of this self-evaluation form can be found in Appendix 9.

As well as a regular review, it is sensible for the board to formally adopt a code of practice. The National Governors' Association has a code of practice which 'sets out the purpose of the governing body and describes the appropriate relationship between individual governors, the whole governing body and the leadership team of the school'. It is good practice for the board to discuss the provisions of whichever code it chooses and formally adopt and sign it at the first meeting in the academic year.

Chair of the board

The role of chair is key to the governance function in any trust or academy and appropriate training and relevant experience is fundamental. The National College for Teaching & Learning offers a Chairs of Governors' Leadership Development Programme. Part of this involves a 360° review incorporating feedback from various sources such as the head teacher, other trustees/governors and the clerk. The review considers a number of aspects: leading strategically, leading services, self-management, leading in the community and leading people.

Incorporating some form of regular review into the annual schedule of the board is not only good practice from a governance point of view but it is also a learning opportunity for the chair.

COMMENT

Naureen Khalid, Vice Chair of Governors at Newstead Wood School, has developed a 360° review of the chair's performance based on various sources available online.

'360-degree feedback is a tool which can be used to provide valuable feedback about the performance of the chair. It is especially important for chairs to seek such feedback because it will give them an idea how their performance is viewed by fellow governors, the clerk, the head teacher and other members of the leadership team. If conducted properly, it helps the chair to understand his or her strengths and weaknesses and areas where professional development may be required. The feedback can help highlight a weakness which may not have been evident otherwise. I feel that in the present climate, where performance of school staff is under greater scrutiny than ever before, it is only fair that the performance of the chair be evaluated too.' A copy of the 360° review form used can be found in Appendix 10.

---

16 Policies

'Policies' are the overriding principles, rules and guidelines with 'procedures' setting out the detailed methods used. Together they provide the framework for the trust and/or academy to function smoothly and in accordance with agreed values and towards the vision embodied in the strategic plan. The policy should be a relatively short, high-level document with the detail contained in any connected procedures.

Statutory policies

All schools are required by law to have approved and adopted a number of policies and other documents. However, the list of 'statutory policies' and other documents that schools are obliged to have is fairly limited. The statutory policies and procedures required by a trust are:

- *Admissions arrangements*: Academies are their own admission authority (although the LA or another organisation can be contracted to carry out the tasks associated with the role). The admissions policy must comply with the requirements of the admission code and must be reviewed and adopted annually, irrespective of whether or not there are any changes. A formal consultation for a period of at least eight weeks between 1 November and 1 March must be carried out where any changes are required. Admissions-related information should be uploaded to the trust website.
- *Behaviour policy*: Every school should have a behaviour policy which includes the school rules and which covers:
  - screening and searching pupils (including identifying in the school rules items which are banned and which may be searched for);
  - the power to use reasonable force or make other physical contact;
  - the power to discipline beyond the school gate;
  - pastoral care for school staff accused of misconduct; and
  - when a multi-agency assessment should be considered for pupils who display continuous disruptive behaviour.
- *Charging and remissions*: The Education Act 1996 provides that parents and

pupils cannot be charged for any activity unless there is a policy in place. Charges per pupil cannot exceed the actual costs incurred so that no element of extra cost can be charged to cover pupils who cannot afford the activity or for a profit element. Charges for activities taking place during the normal school day can only be on the basis of voluntary contributions and pupils will be treated no differently whether they pay the contribution or not.

■ *Complaints procedure*: This sets out the process by which any complaint is dealt with. Complainants should, in the first instance, always be directed to the school itself where the majority of complaints will be resolved. If a complainant does not feel that their complaint has been satisfactorily resolved, they can, having exhausted the complaints procedure, appeal directly to the Secretary of State for Education through the EFA (see Chapter 15).

■ *Data protection*: Academies are 'data controllers' under the Data Protection Act 1998 and must have a policy outlining how and why any personal data is processed in order to comply with the provisions of the Data Protection Act. This applies to the processing of any personal data whether in electronic form or manually held data.

■ *Freedom of Information*: The Freedom of Information Act 2000 gives a right of access to information held by public bodies including academies. The Information Commissioner's Office has a model publication scheme which may be adopted without modification whereby a trust will commit to make information available to the public as part of its normal business activities.

■ *Equality information and objectives (public sector equality duty) statement for publication*: Academies must draw up equality objectives every four years which show how they will meet the aims of the general equality duty to:
  – eliminate unlawful discrimination, harassment and victimisation and other conduct prohibited by the Act
  – advance equality of opportunity between people who share a protected characteristic and those who do not
  – foster good relations between people who share a protected characteristic and those who do not.
  The protected characteristics are:
  – disability
  – gender reassignment
  – pregnancy and maternity (which includes breastfeeding)
  – race
  – religion and belief
  – sex
  – sexual orientation.
  Each trust must also publish information annually showing how the aims of the public sector equality duty are being met.

■ *Health and safety*: The Health and Safety at Work Act 1974 places a duty on trusts to take reasonable steps to ensure the health and safety of employees, pupils and visitors. Trusts must produce a policy and carry out a risk assessment.

- *Home-school agreement document*: This should be drawn up in consultation with parents and should apply to all pupils. Reasonable steps must be taken to ensure that parents sign the agreement confirming their agreement to participate in a partnership with the academy.
- *Sex and relationships education*: Trusts must have a policy which:
  - defines sex and relationship education;
  - describes how sex and relationship education is provided and who is responsible for providing it;
  - says how sex and relationship education is monitored and evaluated; and
  - includes information about parents' right to non-participation.
- *Special Educational Needs*: The Academies Act 2010 provides that academies must have regard to the SEN Code of Practice published by the DfE which includes adoption of a policy on SEN setting out the approach to meeting pupils' special educational needs whether with or without a statement.

Other documentation must also be kept:

- *Accessibility plan*: A plan or strategy must be put in place setting out how disabled pupils can participate in the curriculum and associated services, maximising access to the physical environment and written information provided to pupils.
- *Central record of recruitment and vetting checks*: Generally the responsibility for maintaining the record will be delegated to the principal who will ensure that it is dealt with in the normal administration of the academy. The record must contain details of DRB checks undertaken on members of staff. It is also a requirement of the articles of association that trustees undertake DBS checking. If they fail to do so, or if any information is disclosed which would 'confirm their unsuitability to work with children', then that person shall be disqualified as a trustee.
- *Minutes of, and papers considered at, meetings of the board of trustees body and its committees (including any local governing bodies)*.
- *Premises management documents*: Trusts have responsibility for ensuring safe management and maintenance of premises including health and safety, asbestos, compliance with the Disability Discrimination Act, fire safety, electrical testing and water hygiene (see Chapter 15). Documentation and certificates must be held and, where appropriate, displayed.
- *Register of pupils' admission to school*: Generally, the responsibility for keeping the register will be delegated to the principal who will direct appropriate trust staff to maintain it.
- *Register of pupils' attendance*: Similarly, the principal will generally have delegated responsibility for keeping the register which will be maintained by appropriate trust staff.

In addition, statutory guidance also recommends various other policies and procedures which should be in place (e.g. child protection policy and procedures, Early Years Foundation Stage (EYFS) and a statement of procedures). Although it is possible not to have all such policies, it will be necessary to show very good reasons for so doing. It is, of course, best practice to ensure that they are all in place.

The DfE website has a helpful list of 'policies and other documents that governing bodies and proprietors are required to have by law' which gives further details. However, it is worth noting that:

- drafting of school policies can be delegated to any member of school staff;
- not all policies need to be reviewed annually; and
- not all policies need to be approved by the board.

Reference must be made to the DfE's list providing information on the review frequency (which is often set by the relevant legislation/regulations) and the level of approval required for any policy or documentation. The DfE has stated its ongoing commitment to review the requirements relating to policy documentation and will endeavour to simplify the legal obligations on schools wherever possible.

Consideration must be given to any particular requirements contained in the funding agreement. Furthermore, the *Academies Financial Handbook* makes it a requirement that trusts have a whistleblowing procedure.

Nevertheless, trusts/academies have greater freedoms than maintained schools in relation to school policies and other documents.

In addition to the policies required by law or guidance, there are numerous others which should be considered and, where appropriate, adopted, such as:

- allegations of abuse against staff
- collective worship
- critical incident
- curriculum
- drugs
- first aid and administering medication
- governor/trustee visits
- homework
- lettings
- recruitment, selection and induction of staff
- staff appraisal
- staff discipline, conduct and grievance
- staff pay
- teaching and learning.

Policy drafting

There are many precedent policies available from LAs, corporate providers and member organisations. However, it is important that whatever model policies in use are tailored to the specific requirements of the trust.

The board of trustees is responsible for the strategic vision of the trust. The day-to-day practice and procedure must reflect this vision if it is to be realised. It is crucial that the policy establishes the overall framework for the management and operations in the trust. As a minimum, a trust is required to adopt each of the 'statutory' policies. However, trustees should give careful consideration to what other policies are required to ensure a coherent and effective approach.

In practical terms, the principal and staff will often do much of the detailed work on producing policies in relation to the educational aspects of running a trust. However, many other policies such as health and safety, equal opportunities or freedom of information may well sit better with a committee or an individual trustee with specific training or experience in that area.

Development of policies may, from time to time, involve consultation with those likely to be affected by them. An obvious example is the need to consult over pay and appraisal policies, which will involve negotiation with staff and unions. This means that the policy has the greatest possible chance of being successfully implemented and adopted by all!

There is no required format for a policy although it is useful to ensure that all trust policies follow a 'house style' with a consistency in the formulation. All policies should be written in 'plain English' and without the use of acronyms or abbreviations unless they are defined in the policy (no matter how well known these might appear to be). A policy should be a concise document which is likely to be a maximum of two sides of A4 paper – the detail should be included in the procedures.

Procedures deal with the day-to-day implementation of the policy and are more generally drawn up by the principal and executive in the trust. This may not always be the case, particularly in a MAT where a particular consistency of approach is required across a number of individual academies each headed up by their own senior leadership team.

Policies in MATs

The board will generally wish to adopt a consistency of approach across a MAT. As one legal entity it is important to have a single policy based on the overall vision; it is also far more practical! Policies relating to staff, for example, must be the same across all schools, as all staff are employed by the MAT. Some level of flexibility may be required in the procedures put in place to realise the policies – the procedure applied in a secondary school may not be appropriate in an infant school within the same MAT.

COMMENT

Liz Holmes is Vice Chair of the Faringdon Academy of Schools, a multi-academy of eight schools including one secondary, five primary, one junior and one infant school:

'A multi-academy trust will require a hierarchy of policies which reflects those which must be applied across all the academy's member schools and those which are school specific.

A comprehensive list of all the policies in existence at each member school at the point at which the multi-academy trust is formed should be collated and used to inform the scope of work to be done to develop a unified approach to policies across all member schools. As new schools join, their joint information should be added to the collated information.

Most of the decisions around what must become a single academy-wide policy will be determined by looking at the list of statutory policies required of any academy or maintained schools.

Single academy-wide policies will in most instances be required where:

- the academy may be held to account;
- a statutory requirement or employer/employee duty exists;
- consistency across all member schools is an academy requirement; or
- consistency of actions taken or decisions made need to be demonstrated or evidenced.

When drafting an academy policy for all the schools within a multi-academy trust, the need to separate out procedural steps from policy aims or objectives is very important.

A policy's aims and objectives should, whilst satisfying all statutory requirements and legal duties, be applicable to all member schools.

The procedures which support the application of a policy in a multi-academy trust must allow for variances in organisational and/or operational structures within member schools to be appropriately reflected.

Academy policies must be agreed by the trust's board for subsequent adoption and use within individual member schools.

It is also necessary to ensure systems are in place to ensure an academy policy has been adopted by a member school and that all publication duties are being complied with.

Clear guidance should be provided around which academy committees are responsible for the promotion and review of academy policies.

Additional guidance may be required around application of parts of a policy (i.e. where a pay policy requires an annual Pay Committee to be convened and responsibility for this has been devolved to each member school, some of the questions it must ask should be specified as should how the local governing body will report back to the appropriate academy committee).'

Access to policies

Aside from any legal requirement to publish policies it is important, for practical reasons, that easy access is given for staff, trustees and parents as appropriate. Consideration should be given to the particular policy or procedure and the needs of the school and options include:

- uploading all policies onto the website or VLE;
- including policies in a staff handbook issued to all staff;
- providing hard copies in community languages or for the visually impaired; and
- holding a master file in the school office.

Review

Policies should be reviewed on a regular basis, although it is not necessary that they are all reviewed on an annual basis. Care should be taken to identify any statutory or recommended review periods.

An efficient process for managing policies must be established. It is not a good use of board time to consider the detail of policies and it is only rarely that a policy will need to be approved at that level. A better structure is for responsibility for policy review and approval to be delegated to the relevant committees which will then report back to the board to confirm that the delegated authority has been exercised. Trusts will have a significant number of policies in place and sharing policies amongst the committees/LGBs avoids it being an onerous task.

A centrally held schedule is a good idea, setting out the relevant review dates and the party or committee responsible. A simple schedule could be:

Policy	Committee/Individual responsible	Date approved	Date for review

The schedule can be expanded to include a note of where the policy is held, e.g. website, staff handbook, etc., so that all versions can be replaced whenever the policy is reviewed and updated.

Regular monitoring should be carried out to ensure that the policy is embedded in practice and to establish whether it is achieving what was intended. Much of that monitoring will be done by the board considering reports from the principal and staff. Schools are used to ongoing monitoring, not least because of the tracking and monitoring that is done on pupil progress. Therefore, the principal will be in the strongest position to ensure that evidence is gathered and evaluated for presentation to the board.

Trustees should also undertake their own monitoring and it is useful to put in place a schedule of visits identifying the areas or subjects that will be the subject of the monitoring visit. However, it is important to remember that trustee visits are not to consider or comment on the quality of teaching and learning taking place and should never attempt to make Ofsted-style judgements. It is crucial that there are clear protocols regarding trustee visits in place which should cover:

- how visits will be arranged (e.g. according to a schedule agreed by the principal);
- scope of the visit (e.g. subject area);
- the nature of the visit (e.g. observation of class or collective worship, or meeting with subject leader);
- who trustees will meet (e.g. staff, pupils); and
- reporting back to the board (e.g. initial discussion with principal prior to reporting back via committee structure).

There should also be a standard trustee visit form setting out the purpose of the visit, the trustee's comments and any key issues arising.

Trustee visits are useful not only because of the evidence that can be used to generate debate or inform decision making by the board, but because a well-structured programme of visits will give trustees a better understanding of the day-to-day operation of the trust as well as fostering good working relationships with staff.

Evaluation of the impact of policies can also be undertaken through the use of comparative data such as RAISEonline (a tool which provides an interactive analysis of school and pupil performance data).

Social media

All schools now routinely use technology. Many schools have suites of netbooks or iPads that can be used wirelessly in the classroom, whilst other schools have started to issue iPads to all new pupils. Some teachers use blogging or social media to encourage pupil engagement and independent learning.

Therefore it is important to consider the use of social media, noting any potential risks and setting appropriate policies for adherence by pupils and teachers.

COMMENT

Peter Wright, solicitor and managing director of DigitalLawUK:

'Social media

Why social media is important in a school
Social media is changing the way that people communicate and how business works and is arguably the biggest change to the economy since the Industrial Revolution. People's movements and comments on social media can be used as evidence in courtrooms, while for employers, a lack of proficiency on social media can be a disadvantage when recruiting staff. Conversely, employees around the world are fired every day for inappropriate comments or use of social media. In educating the workforce of tomorrow, social media is an issue that can't be ignored in schools today.

Social media can be used to create a positive online view of a school
A decade ago prospective pupils and their parents would attend an open day and perhaps review a brochure when making a choice on which school they should attend. However, with the advent of social media, first-hand experience from those attending a school is now available at the touch of a button on Facebook, Twitter and other platforms. A well-organised and run corporate account on Twitter or Facebook for your school will speak volumes to those looking for more information about an establishment than that contained on a website or in a brochure. Achievements in terms of awards for the institution or staff could be publicised, as could notable charitable fundraising. However, institutions should refrain from showing pictures of any pupils on social media, in particular those under 16. Consent should be sought from any individual featured in any photographic content, including adults, prior to it being uploaded.

Important to pupils in their future careers

Social media is of crucial importance for pupils. In their professional careers they will be expected to develop their professional networks of contacts using systems like LinkedIn, while they may also be expected to use systems like Twitter in a professional capacity. Their knowledge of new and developing social media networks will give them an advantage in the recruitment market, and it will not be in the interests of the school for its pupils to be in any way disadvantaged compared to those from other institutions.

Majority of pupils are engaged on social media platforms and have smartphones

The majority of pupils will most likely already have their own smartphones and be active on social media networks of some sort, despite networks like Facebook making it clear that their systems are for use by adults only. Consequently, their use is a matter for a school to regulate.

School corporate social media use

It has been known for schools to operate corporate social media accounts in the name of the institution. Issues to be aware of are:

- No photos of anyone below the age of 16 to be uploaded to social media accounts.
- Permission to be obtained from anyone featured in a photograph before it is uploaded.
- Have guidelines in place for acceptable use in terms of comment and content. Comment on sensitive subjects such as politics or religion may be specifically prohibited.
- Ensure that any corporate accounts do not follow or are not in any way linked to any other content, accounts or pages that could be inappropriate.
- Consider having clear guidelines in place on how and when the social media account is to be updated (e.g. only to be updated from a laptop or desktop machine rather than a mobile device to ensure the security of the account and to remove the possibility of inappropriate corporate social media use outside normal work hours by a member of staff who has been entrusted to update the account).

Social media use by staff

Social media use by staff in any organisation is extremely important when it comes to managing reputation. It is of particular importance in a school, but for other reasons in addition to those that may appear obvious:

- Staff should not be connected on social networks to any of their pupils below the age of 16. Connecting with pupils who are leaving/have left following GCSEs or A levels should be permissible at the discretion of the member of staff.
- There should be a clear social media policy in place governing interaction between staff on social media. Organisations with no employee social media policy can be held liable in any instance of cyber bullying by one member of staff to another.
- The school may wish to have a policy governing the use of social media by staff during work hours, both on equipment provided by the school and on mobile devices owned by staff themselves. Persistent documented use of mobile devices such as tablets and smartphones by staff in some organisations to engage on social media has led to dismissal.
- Staff should consider having rigorous privacy settings on any social networks they are active on such as Facebook, so that pupils cannot identify any of their teachers, or see them in a social setting in any

photographs or exchanges of comments with social friends that may be inappropriate. Social media content is usually searchable by search engines like Google and staff must be aware of images leaking online if not properly monitored.

■ Staff should refrain from uploading comments or photos to either their own social media accounts or accounts belonging to a class or school. In the United States, one teacher was dismissed for uploading a photograph of a pupil restrained to a chair using tape. The teacher alleged the restraint was a prank carried out by the pupils themselves and that it was uploaded online in a moment of jollity in the classroom, but the local press and school governors took a more unfavourable view. Clear guidance and training on social media should be provided to all staff.

Social media use by pupils

■ Consider prohibiting pupils from using mobile devices either during school hours or on school grounds. This could be a time-consuming resource-intensive step, but it should be considered against staff time engaged in investigating unsuitable social media use or interaction by pupils.

■ Pupils should be made aware that bullying online – inside or outside of school hours – is as unacceptable as bullying on school premises and will not be tolerated.

■ Repeated online bullying and harassment can be an offence under the Protection from Harassment Act 1997. Threats of violence or intimidating criminal acts can breach the Communications Act 2003 and can lead to a criminal record and custodial sentences. Such behaviour is not tolerated in society and should not be acceptable in a school. This should be made clear to pupils from an early age.

■ A Code of Conduct on social media may be considered as being appropriate.

■ Pupils approaching school leaving age should be given guidance on the use of professional social media sites like LinkedIn in the same way that pupils will receive guidance on CV drafting before entering the workplace.'

17 Information management

Website

There are now requirements for significant amounts of information to be uploaded to the trust/academy website. Unfortunately, the requirements do not come from one single source and there is no published DfE guidance which covers all requirements.

It is essential to undertake regular website reviews to ensure compliance (see Appendix 12). Apart from the need for compliance, the website is likely to be the first port of call for an Ofsted inspector intending to visit.

Information that must be uploaded includes:

- the funding agreement, memorandum and articles of association;
- the annual report and accounts;
- a statement of the trust's/academy's ethos and values; and
- details of any childcare services available.

The academy contact details should include the academy name, postal address and telephone number as well as the name of the member of staff who deals with queries from parents and other members of the public.

Admissions

The academy's admission arrangements should be published or details given of how the arrangements may be obtained through the local authority. Information should explain how applications are considered for every age group, including:

- arrangements in place for selecting the pupils who apply;
- oversubscription criteria (how places are offered if there are more applicants than places); and
- an explanation of the process parents need to follow if they want to apply for their child to attend the academy.

The timetable for organising and hearing admission appeals must also be published by 28 February each year.

Curriculum

The content of the curriculum the academy follows in each academic year for every subject must be uploaded. This should include the names of any phonics or reading schemes used in Key Stage 1 and the content of, and approach to, Key Stage 4 qualification options, where applicable. Details on how additional information relating to the curriculum can be obtained must be included.

Pupil performance and results

The funding agreement contains provisions requiring the publication of certain information on the trust's website. Information must be updated as soon as possible after any change and at least annually. Responsibility for meeting the requirement and authority to approve the content may be delegated to a committee, an individual trustee or the head teacher.

Earlier versions of the funding agreement may not have this requirement, but it remains good practice to do so.

Specific information should be published on the website regarding pupil achievement and attainment at Key Stage 2 and Key Stage 4, as appropriate.

Pupil premium

The pupil premium is additional funding given to schools to raise the attainment of disadvantaged pupils and close the gap between them and their peers. A plan giving details on the pupil premium allocation for the current academic year together with how it will be spent must be uploaded. A report must also be uploaded showing how the previous academic year's allocation was spent and the impact on educational attainment of those pupils for whom it was allocated.

PE and sport premium

The PE and sport premium is granted to primary schools, and is designed to help improve the quality of the PE and sport activities they offer their pupils. The website must include details of the PE and sport premium allocation for the current academic year and how it will be spent. A report must be prepared on how the previous academic year's allocation was spent and the impact on PE and sport participation and attainment of those pupils for whom it was allocated.

SEN report

A report on the trust's policy for pupils with SEN which complies with section 69(2) of the Children and Families Act 2014 and regulation 51 and schedule 1 of the Special Educational Needs and Disability Regulations 2014 must be uploaded and include details of:

- the admission arrangements for pupils with SEN or disabilities;
- the steps taken to prevent pupils with SEN from being treated less favourably than other pupils;

- access facilities for pupils with SEN; and
- the accessibility plan written in compliance with paragraph 3 of schedule 10 to the Equality Act 2010.

Policies
It is only obligatory to upload a limited number of policies:

- behaviour policy, including discipline, exclusions and anti-bullying which must comply with section 89 of the Education and Inspections Act 2006
- charging and remissions policy, including the activities for which the school will charge parents and the circumstances where an exception will be made on a payment you would normally expect under the policy
- safeguarding, including child protection policy.

Although not legally required, it would make practical sense to make sure that various other policies are uploaded to the website so that they are easily accessible by parents of pupils and by staff.

Company information
As a company, trusts must include certain information on their website or be liable to a fine. The requirements are:

- company registration number;
- place of registration (i.e. registered in England);
- registered office address; and
- the information must be in legible characters.

This information must also be included on 'business letters' and electronic documents such as e-mails. It does not need to appear on every page and on websites can easily be included in the 'About us' or 'Contact' pages.

Governance arrangements
The *Academies Financial Handbook* requires that trusts must publish details of their governance arrangements on their website in a 'readily accessible format'. The details should be kept up to date and must include:

- the structure and remit of the members, board of trustees, its committee and LGBs, and the full names of the chair of each;
- for each member who has served at any point over the past 12 months, their full names, date of appointment, date they stepped down where applicable, and relevant business and pecuniary interests including governance roles in other educational institutions;
- for each trustee and local governor who has served at any point over the past 12 months, their full names, date of appointment, term of office, date they stepped down where applicable, who appointed them, any positions of

responsibility such as chair or vice-chair and relevant business and pecuniary interests including governance roles in other educational institutions;
- if the accounting officer is not a trustee, their relevant business and pecuniary interests;
- for each trustee, their attendance records at board and committee meetings over the last academic year; and
- for each local governor, their attendance records at local governing body meetings over the last academic year.

The details in the governance statement must include the scheme of delegation for governance functions setting out what the board has delegated to its committees and, in the case of MATs, to LGBs.

An annual statement of issues faced and addressed by the board of trustees over the last year must include an assessment of the impact of the board on the trust. An assessment of governance should also be included, incorporating a review of the composition of the board in terms of skills, effectiveness, leadership and impact.

Register of interests

This must contain relevant business and pecuniary interests of members, trustees and senior staff and details of any other educational establishments they govern.

Equality duty

Trusts must comply with the public sector equality duty created under the Equality Act 2010. The trust draws up equality objectives every four years that show how it will meet the aims of the general equality duty to:

- eliminate unlawful discrimination, harassment and victimisation and other conduct prohibited by the Act;
- advance equality of opportunity between people who share a protected characteristic and those who do not; and
- foster good relations between people who share a protected characteristic and those who do not.

The protected characteristics are:

- disability
- gender reassignment
- pregnancy and maternity (which includes breastfeeding)
- race
- religion and belief
- sex
- sexual orientation.

Each trust must also publish information annually showing how the aims of the public sector equality duty are being met. The regulations are not prescriptive about how the equality information is published and it will be for the trust to decide how best to publish the information to ensure that it is accessible.

Gender pay gap reporting

All companies, including trusts, with more than 250 employees must publish details of the difference in the pay of men and women in their organisation. The information must be compiled on 30 April and published annually on the website, and include:

- the mean and median pay for men and women in the trust, which should include basic pay, paid leave, maternity pay, sick pay, shift premium pay and certain over allowances, but not overtime;
- the average bonus paid to men and women over the preceding 12 months; and
- the number of men and women working in each salary quartile of the trust.

It is not necessary to explain the numbers, although trusts may do so to provide context.

Slavery

Any commercial organisation that supplies goods or services in the UK and has an annual turnover of £36m or more (including its subsidiaries – wherever based) are now required by the Modern Slavery Act 2015 to publish an annual slavery and human trafficking statement on its website in respect of each financial year. Government guidance indicates that charities or charitable companies engaging in commercial activities will not be exempt from the requirement if they fulfil the relevant criteria (regardless of their purpose for which profits are made). Furthermore, legislation has now extended the requirement to specifically include 'public bodies'. For MATs meeting the criteria, it makes sense to comply with the requirement.

The statement must describe the steps the trust has taken during the financial year to ensure modern slavery and human trafficking is not occurring in any part of the trust or academies. The statement must be approved by the board and signed by a trustee before being published.

Edubase

All trusts must provide details of individuals involved in the leadership and management of the trust to the DfE. In particular, the trust must notify the DfE of the appointment and vacating of the positions of:

- member, trustee and local governor in a MAT; and
- chair of trustees, chairs of LGBs, accounting officer and chief financial officer.

All details for the named individuals must be completed and direct contact details provided for the latter category.

All notifications should be made within 14 days of any change through the governance section of the DfE's Edubase, which is accessed via Secure Access.

Freedom of Information Act 2000

As trusts are recipients of public funding, they are required to provide public access to information by reason of the Freedom of Information Act 2000. This transparency is to ensure that trusts are accountable for their actions and can demonstrate the best use of public funds.

Information could include printed documents, computer files, letters, e-mails, photographs and sound or video recordings. It is not limited to formal documents but can include drafts, notes and letters received or other information provided by a third party. The Act only covers information that is already held in recorded form so it is not necessary to create documentation in response to a request.

Information held on behalf of the trust will also be covered even if the documentation is physically held off-site (e.g. by solicitors or someone acting as company secretary). Any documentation which contains purely private or trade union information will not be covered.

It is important that trusts adopt good records management practice so that information can be easily retrieved. The Code of Practice, issued under s. 46 of the Freedom of Information Act, sets out good practice. All trusts should:

- have in place organisational arrangements that support records management;
- have in place a records management policy, either as a separate policy or as part of a wider information or knowledge management policy;
- ensure they keep the records they will need for business, regulatory, legal and accountability purposes;
- keep their records in systems that enable records to be stored and retrieved as necessary;
- know what records they hold and where they are and that they remain usable for as long as they are required;
- ensure that records are stored securely and that access to them is controlled;
- define how long they need to keep particular records, dispose of them when they are no longer needed and be able to explain why records are no longer held;
- ensure that records shared with other bodies or held on their behalf by other bodies are managed in accordance with the Code; and
- monitor compliance with the Code and assess the overall effectiveness of the programme.

There should be a publication scheme (i.e. a policy) which sets out:

- the information that is published;
- how and where that information is published; and

- whether the information is available free of charge.

The Information Commissioner's Office has a model publication scheme which may be adopted without modification whereby a trust will commit to make information available to the public as part of its normal business activities.

Publication of information

Trusts must proactively publish certain information so that members of the public can access it at will. The board must agree the classes of information that are safe to disclose and which will be set out in the publication scheme. Examples of information that is likely to be covered include policies and procedures, minutes of meetings and supporting documentation, annual reports, financial information and examination results data. Some of this information may also be available via other websites such as Companies House or Ofsted.

Ideally, the information should be disclosed on the website so that it can be accessed immediately. However, it should also be available 'promptly and automatically' to anyone who asks for it. In addition, it is good practice to make the publication scheme itself available on the website so that the classes of information available are clear.

Requests for information

In addition, members of the public are entitled to request information that is not listed in the publication scheme. An applicant does not need to give a reason for wanting the information and all requests should be treated equally irrespective of whether they come from the parent of a pupil or a journalist. Information should generally be disclosed unless there is good reason for it to be confidential as recognised by the Act.

A request must be in writing but does not need to make reference to the Freedom of Information Act or be directed to a designated member of staff. Any letter or e-mail sent to the trust requesting information is a request falling within the remit of the Act. Nevertheless, most correspondence will be handled in the normal administration of the trust without recourse to the formal mechanisms of the Act unless:

- the requested information cannot be provided immediately; or
- the request specifies that it falls under the Freedom of Information Act.

Normally a trust must respond to a request within 20 school days or 60 working days if this is shorter (e.g. if the request is received over the summer holiday period). Working days will be any day other than a Saturday, Sunday or public holidays and bank holidays.

A charge to cover the costs of communication such as printing, photocopying and postage may be made subject to a limit set by the Act. Such fees are, however, rarely levied and information will often be provided in electronic form, removing such costs.

A request can be refused if:

- it would cost too much or take too much staff time to handle the request;
- the request is vexatious (i.e. the request is likely to cause a disproportionate or unjustifiable level of distress, disruption or irritation); or
- the request is a repeat of a previous request from the same person.

The Freedom of Information Act also contains a number of exemptions which mean that information does not necessarily need to be released. However, the majority of the exemptions are unlikely to apply to trusts. The most likely exemptions will relate to disclosures which would be 'likely to endanger the physical or mental health or the safety of any individual', complying with the request would be a breach of confidence or where someone requests their own personal data which should be sought as a 'subject access request' under the Data Protection Act.

Most of the exemptions set out in the Act require a 'public interest' test to be applied when considering whether information should be disclosed: the public interest considerations in favour of withholding the information should outweigh the public interest considerations in disclosing it. Exempt information would include information:

- contravening the Data Protection Act;
- which could endanger the physical/mental health or safety of an individual;
- given in confidence;
- intended for publication in the future; and
- available by other means.

Some documents may include parts which are exempt from disclosure. Despite this, they should be produced in a 'redacted' form with the exempt elements edited or obliterated.

If in doubt about information which should be provided following a request, trusts are advised to seek professional help.

COMMENT

Peter Wright, solicitor and managing director of DigitalLawUK:

'Freedom of Information Act
Academy schools are subject to the Freedom of Information Act 2000 (FOIA) and need to have appropriate systems in place to deal with requests. Requests can come from anywhere, but are particularly common from journalists and authors in search of statistics and raw data.

Institutions subject to a FOIA request have 20 working days to respond and can be fined by the Information Commissioner's Office (ICO) for handling requests in a dilatory manner or not responding with sufficient disclosure to the request.

There are certain issues that a school should consider in order to make it easier to process and respond to FOIA requests:

- The majority of school data and material will be stored securely either on a server or online securely in the Cloud. By storing data electronically, it can be searched, securely retrieved, reviewed and disclosed quickly and cheaply.
- Be aware of the main exemptions under which material can be withheld. Personal data referring to a third party, such as the names of a pupil or teacher or anything that allows them to be identified such as an address, photograph, audio or video recording, national insurance number or pupil number, should be redacted and on no account should be disclosed.
- Commercially sensitive details such as contracts with suppliers, payroll data, financial records etc. can also be withheld under the Act.
- Disclosure following a FOIA request can be made electronically via encrypted CD, USB or securely online. If made in hard copy, it should be sent securely via recorded delivery or courier.
- Consider the use of an online document management service for records to be securely reviewed, redacted and disclosed.
- Consider obtaining legal advice from a law firm. Some firms offer a fixed fee service to review each FOIA request and may turn out to be more cost effective than using staff time.
- Charges can be levied under the FOIA for making requests.'

Data protection

The Data Protection Act 1998 provides for 'the regulation of the processing of information relating to individuals, including the obtaining, holding, use or disclosure of such information' and is based on eight data protection principles, which state that personal data must be:

1. processed fairly and lawfully;
2. processed only for the specified and lawful purposes;
3. adequate, relevant and not excessive;
4. accurate and, where necessary, kept up to date;
5. not kept for longer than is necessary;
6. processed in accordance with the rights of data subjects;
7. protected from unauthorised or unlawful processing and against accidental loss or destruction or damage; and
8. not transferred to a country or territory outside the European Economic Area without adequate protection.

Every trust must register with the Information Commissioner's Office as they are 'data controllers'. In fact, trusts process vast amounts of 'personal data' in respect of pupils and staff and great care should be given to ensuring that processing, whether by electronic or computerised means or in a structured manual filing system, fulfils the requirements of the legislation.

In addition, it is necessary to show that one of the following conditions has been satisfied in order to permit processing:

- The data subject has consented to the processing.
- The processing is necessary for the performance of a contract or to enter into a contract with the data subject.
- Processing is necessary because of a legal obligation.
- Processing is necessary to protect the data subject's 'vital interests' (i.e. in the case of life or death).
- Processing is necessary for the administration of justice, or for exercising statutory, governmental or other public functions.
- Processing is in accordance with the 'legitimate interests' condition.

Stricter conditions apply when the information is 'sensitive'. Examples of this kind of information include:

- ethnic background
- political opinions
- trade union membership
- religious beliefs
- health
- sexual health
- criminal records.

Individuals are able to make a subject access request to see any personal information that is held on them. The request should be made in writing and the data controller may require payment of a fee subject to a maximum depending on the circumstances and verification of the identity of the data subject making the request.

A response to a subject access request should be provided within 40 calendar days of receiving it.

There are very limited circumstances when information can be withheld, for example in connection with:

- the prevention, detection or investigation of a crime;
- national security or the armed forces;
- the assessment or collection of tax; and
- judicial or ministerial appointments.

Great care should be exercised when dealing with requests in connection with pupil data which are likely to be made by those with parental responsibility for the child. Consideration should be given to whether the child is mature enough to understand their rights and, as they are the data subject, the response should be made to them rather than a parent or guardian. Particular consideration should be given to:

- the child's level of maturity and ability to make decisions;
- the nature of the personal data;
- any court orders relating to parental access or responsibility that may apply;
- any duty of confidence owed to the child or young person;
- any consequences of allowing those with parental responsibility access to the child's or young person's information, especially if there have been allegations of abuse or ill treatment;
- any detriment to the child or young person if individuals with parental responsibility cannot access this information; and
- any views the child or young person has on whether their parents should have access to information about them.

The Information Commissioner can serve a data controller with an 'information notice' requiring certain information to be provided within set time limits. Failure to do so is a criminal offence. If the Commissioner concludes that there has been a breach of the Act, then an 'enforcement notice' may be served preventing future processing. Failure to comply with an enforcement notice is also a criminal offence. Resultant fines may be unlimited, but the threat of being prevented from processing personal data is a far greater deterrent as a trust would be unable to operate.

Trustees or members of the senior leadership team may also be found to be personally criminally liable if the offence has been committed with their consent, connivance or neglect.

Detailed consideration of the way that data is handled, processed and stored by the trust is absolutely essential, and should encompass the following areas:

- cloud storage
- back-up, disaster plan and disaster recovery
- remote working/travel
- devices/laptops/phones
- Bring Your Own Device
- destruction of IT hardware
- e-mail encryption and security/data rooms
- administration system/finance and accounts systems/payroll/regulatory
- website, privacy, cookies and website backup
- social media, personal data and confidentiality
- password security
- CCTV/hearing loop/recording of calls
- office procedures/file storage/desk storage
- archived files/destruction/confidential waste
- post/confidential post/DX/fax.

Compliance with data protection legislation is a necessity. Detailed practical guidance on the issues that need consideration, setting out the principles and examples of mistakes made by other organisations (along with the fines that they received) can be found in Appendix 11. The cases serve to illustrate why the practical steps outlined are being recommended and that they are not just examples of over-zealous regulation being implemented with no purpose.

COMMENT

Peter Wright, solicitor and managing director of DigitalLawUK:

'Data protection
Academy schools need to be aware of the catastrophic risk that they carry from being susceptible to a data protection breach. By their very nature, schools hold huge amounts of personal data, everything from pupil attendance data, staff salary and payroll information, pupil qualifications, addresses, dates of birth, health screening records – the list goes on. All it takes is for some of this data to be transmitted to an incorrect recipient, stolen from an office or the car or home of a member of staff and a school could be facing a fine of up to £500,000 from the UK Information Commissioner's Office (ICO). The regulatory regime also applies should a school's IT system be compromised and data taken.

 Schools should consider the following:

■ The security of the IT system, be it on a server or a cloud-hosted network.
■ Having a workable disaster recovery plan in place should the school be inaccessible or key staff be unable to attend work.
■ Remote access issues created by staff working out of school, including at home or during travel.
■ Security risks from staff working on mobile devices, smart phones and laptops.
■ The need for a rigorous Bring Your Own Device (BYOD) policy or prohibition.
■ Ensuring the secure destruction of IT equipment belonging to the school including hard drives.
■ Putting systems in place to ensure the secure transmission of personal data including encrypting email and the use of secure online data rooms if applicable.
■ Proving the security of any third party-supplied systems such as finance, administration and payroll systems, in particular those that are hosted on the cloud.
■ The security of any school website, including the use of an accurate cookie policy and website backup.

- The need for a comprehensive social media policy, ensuring the confidentiality of personal data will be preserved online.
- Having a system in place to ensure that any passwords used for systems at the school are sufficiently complex, that different passwords are used for different systems and that they are regularly changed.
- Ensuring the security of any records from CCTV systems, hearing loops and recorded calls.
- Putting policies in place to ensure that there are minimal security risks in the workplace through having a clear desk policy to make sure cleaning or security staff do not have access to confidential data, and limiting access to confidential records only to those who need to use them to fulfil their roles.
- Having a clear method for archiving files and their secure destruction.
- Making sure personal data is not sent via first class post or unsecure fax but is sent by approved methods such as recorded delivery or courier only.
- Ensuring that all members of staff receive adequate data protection training, including all new starters, and that this is repeated regularly to ensure compliance, along with spot checks to ensure rules and policies are being followed in practice.

Finally schools need to be aware that the law relating to data protection is always evolving, and that a data protection professional should be consulted regularly to make sure the school is up to date with the latest risks and security measures.'

Risk management

The modern digital age brings many benefits and opportunities for trusts as well as for their employees and pupils. However, it also brings significant risks which must be considered and managed (see Chapter 15).

Mark Taylor, Director of Lucas Fettes & Partners:

'Cyber breaches and attacks are on the rise and schools are by no means immune from threat. It is critical that schools consider the various ways in which they – and their pupils – could be exposed, and build this into their risk register and risk management plan. Purchasing cyber liability insurance is one way to mitigate the risk, but it only offers financial recompense in the event of a claim. It is critical to have in place measures to try and prevent a claim from occurring, particularly given the potential impact a breach can have on an academy's reputation.'

Appendix 1: Example registers

Register of members

Surname:	
Forenames:	
Former names:	
Address:	
Date of entry as a member:	
Expiry of term:	
Consent to act:	

Register of secretaries

Surname:	
Forenames:	
Former names:	
Service address:	
Date of appointment:	
Date of resignation:	

Register of directors/trustees

Surname:	
Forenames:	
Former names:	
Service address:	
Business occupation:	
Other directorships:	
Nationality:	
Date of birth:	
Date of appointment:	
Expiry of term:	
Date of resignation/removal:	

Register of directors'/trustees' addresses

Surname:	
Forenames:	
Address:	

Register of interests

Name	Name of business	Nature of interest	Self/partner/ close relative	Date registered

Register of gifts, hospitality and entertainment

Name	Date of declaration	Description of gift, hospitality or entertainment	Value

PSC register

An example PSC register can be downloaded from the gov.uk website.

Appendix 2: Skills audit

Skills audit and training needs

Name ....

Please add any other skills you feel you have to offer:

Your skills	High level of skills and qualifications	Medium level of skills	Some skills	Would like to develop skills in this area
Financial management				
HR				
Facilities management				
Teaching and learning				
SEN				
Data analysis				

Royal Wootton Bassett Academy Governing Body Skills Audit Form

NAME _____ DATE _____

How would you rate your knowledge/ understanding/competence in the broad skill/experience areas listed in the table?

Skills/experience	Very good	Good	Adequate	Poor
Commercial/Strategic Development				
Marketing				
Pastoral experience				
Working as part of a team				

Communication skills:
  Written
  Oral				

Administrative/Organisational				
Mediation				
Strategic planning				
Problem solving				
Project management				
Procurement				
Public speaking				
Chairing meetings				
Taking minutes				
Monitoring, reviewing, and evaluating school performance				
School finances				
School curriculum				
School policies				
Human resources/staffing				
Equality and diversity issues				
Health and safety, including safeguarding				
Building maintenance/facilities management				
Information technology/computers				
School data analysis (e.g. RAISEonline)				
Special educational needs				
Marketing/publicity/public relations				
Performance management/appraisals				

Skills/experience	Very good	Good	Adequate	Poor
Education				
PR				
Charity fund raising				
Further and Higher Education experience				
Risk assessment				
Quality assurance				
Director experience				
Legal experience				
Governor experience				
Business links/Community relations				
Others (details of any skills/ experiences not listed):–				

Training needs analysis

Name _____

Responsibility	No previous knowledge	Some knowledge	A lot of knowledge
Roles and responsibilities of a board			
Teaching and learning			
SEN			
Financial management			
Understanding school data			
Health and Safety			
Safeguarding			
Performance management			
HR			
School improvement planning			
Monitoring performance			
Accountability			

Appendix 3: The minute-taker's reminder checklists

Before you begin scanning the lists, please remember the following with respect to each one:

The 'before' list

This list covers a wide range of activities in connection with pre-meeting preparation. You should review this list *well in advance*; some of the activities require a longer lead time for completion, whereas others will relate to activities on the day of the meeting itself.

The 'during' list

This list covers all the points which need to be considered in relation to the meeting itself. However, it is unlikely that you will be sitting in the meeting attempting to take the notes while at the same time pondering the contents of the reminder checklist! So, the best approach is to consider the points prior to the meeting as a form of preparation and then review them again following the meeting as a form of evaluation. In time, the points will become well embedded in your mind and you will naturally reflect on some of these points *during* the meetings you minute.

The 'after' list

This list covers all the activities which follow the meeting. Some relate to activities which should be undertaken straight after the meeting, some to the writing of the actual minutes and others to self-development activities and self-reflection. The conclusions you draw from your review of this list will naturally feed into your preparation activities for the meeting that follows.

The minute-taker's reminder checklist: before the meeting

Tick the following as completed:

- [ ] Do I clearly understand the meeting cycle for this meeting?
- [ ] Have I created a timeline plan to show how this meeting cycle dovetails with those for the other meetings I attend?

☐ Am I expected to contribute at this meeting in addition to taking the minutes?

☐ If I am expected to contribute for one item only, have I made arrangements for someone else to take the minutes for that one item?

☐ If I am expected to be the minute-taker and full meeting contributor, have I explained to everyone that the minutes will be more concise than usual with the emphasis on noting action points? Have I explained to the chairperson that a summary would be appreciated at the end of each item?

☐ Am I fully aware of the layout and style of the minutes required in respect of this meeting?

☐ Do I fully understand all the procedural matters in relation to this particular meeting?

☐ Have I confirmed all the necessary administration arrangements for the meeting?

☐ Have I checked that all equipment is in good working order?

☐ Has the meeting room been arranged in the way the participants have requested?

☐ Have I read thoroughly the minutes of the last meeting?

☐ Have I read and fully understood the agenda?

☐ Have I read and understood all the supporting papers?

☐ Is there any additional information that I need to read and understand in order to be fully prepared?

☐ If I need help, what should my approach be for this particular meeting?
  - Speak to the participant(s) before the day?
  - Speak to the participant(s) before the meeting?
  - Speak to the chair in advance of the meeting?
  - Seek clarifications afterwards?
  - Talk to the chair during the meeting?
  - Interrupt during the meeting?

☐ Have I copied up all the necessary papers for the meeting including the minutes of the last meeting?

☐ Do I have enough copies?

☐ Is the chair required to sign the minutes? Do I have a copy for this purpose?

☐ With respect to this meeting, do I know who the chair is?

☐ If I have not worked with the chair before, what can I do to establish a professional relationship?

☐ Have I arranged a pre-meeting briefing session with the chair?

☐ If a briefing is not possible prior to the day of the meeting, have I arranged for a short discussion with the chair just prior to the commencement of the meeting?

☐ Have I made arrangements to sit next to the chair at the meeting?

☐ If it is not possible to sit next to the chair what arrangements can I make to ensure that the quality of my note-taking is not compromised?

☐ Have I created an attendance list for circulation at the meeting?

☐ Is all my paperwork well arranged and in good order?

☐ Have I created a minute taking template that I am comfortable with?

☐ If I am using loose-leaf sheets of A4, have I numbered the pages in advance?

☐ Do I have enough spare writing paper?

☐ Have I noted all the abbreviations, technical terms and jargon that may be used by participants at this meeting?

☐ Do I have all the pens and pencils I need including a choice of colours?

☐ Do I have my highlighter pens?

☐ Have I allocated time to undertake an initial review of my notes immediately following the meeting?

☐ Have I arranged to arrive a little earlier at the venue to check the final arrangements and converse with participants?

☐ Is my personal appearance appropriate for this particular meeting occasion; is it professional?

☐ Is my clothing comfortable?

☐ Have I eaten foods that will help to maintain my energy and concentration levels throughout the meeting?

☐ Have I brought a bottle of water to help maintain hydration levels?

☐ If I need to interrupt for clarifications, have I practiced my voice projection and assertiveness techniques to enable me to do so with confidence?

☐ Have I prepared a personal checklist for all the above points?

The minute-taker's reminder checklist: during the meeting

Tick the following as completed:

☐ Have I entered the room confidently?

☐ Does my body language give evidence that I am a professional person with every right to be at the meeting, in order to fulfil an extremely important role, or does it suggest that I am a second-class citizen who is attending the meeting only to perform the onerous task of note-taking?

☐ Have I taken the opportunity to mix and converse with participants in order to build rapport?

☐ Have I placed my papers on the table and arranged my working space in a neat and orderly fashion?

☐ Have I spoken to the chair just prior to commencement to clarify any last-minute points of concern?

☐ Has everyone seen and signed the attendance list?

☐ Do I have a complete and accurate record of all apologies?

☐ Am I sitting properly with good back support?

☐ Is my writing arm positioned so as to minimise the stress on the wrist?

☐ Have I put all distractions out of my mind and am I fully focused on the meeting?

☐ For each item, am I formulating in my mind an idea as to the main emphasis of the discussion and the possible decisions, from the chair's opening summary?

☐ Am I working with the chair to ensure that all participants who want to contribute are able to do so?

☐ Am I getting the sense of the *message* or am I focusing too much on the actual words?

☐ Am I isolating the key points from each speaker's contribution?

☐ Am I relating the key points to the central matter under discussion?

☐ Am I tending to record the arguments verbatim or am I employing my personalised form of shorthand?

☐ From the discussion, am I clearly extracting and recording all the decisions and action points?

☐ For the action points, have I made a note of who is responsible and the deadline date for completion?

☐ Where points are unclear am I asking for appropriate clarifications?

☐ Am I maintaining concentration or is my mind beginning to wander?

☐ Am I checking periodically that my handwriting is still legible?

☐ Am I tending to write sentences or am I mastering the use of bullet points and abbreviations?

☐ Am I setting out my bullet points clearly and legibly in a vertical format with plenty of space in between, or am I tending to bunch them together in clusters?

☐ If a problem arises regarding understanding and it is inappropriate at that point to seek clarification, have I clearly highlighted this (perhaps with a different colour pen) in my notes?

☐ Am I moving my writing hand too much (thus contributing to tiredness) or am I moving the *paper* to create the writing space I need?

☐ Am I maintaining eye contact with the speaker in order to improve the quality of my listening or do I seldom look up from my notes?

☐ Am I being influenced or distracted by the voice tone of the speaker, the manner of delivery or the emotional nature of the contributions, or am I still focusing on the key points, actions and decisions?

☐ Although my notes will be structured to a greater degree during the writing-up stage, am I trying to keep the key points to the fore in my note-taking?

☐ Am I intervening confidently and assertively when required or am I a little 'backward in coming forward'?

☐ Am I helping the chair to keep the meeting on track and, where necessary, to observe procedural conventions?

☐ When I am contributing to an item on the agenda, do I ask the chair to summarise the discussion in the interest of an accurate set of minutes?

☐ Am I *listening* effectively, remembering to employ the different forms of listening in order to create a rounded out understanding?

☐ Am I allowing anything to influence my listening in a *negative* sense, such as bias, prejudice, cynicism, indignation or vested interests?

☐ Have I clearly noted the time, date and place of the next meeting?

☐ Before the participants disperse, am I taking the opportunity to speak to anyone I need to in order to seek necessary clarifications?

▨ The minute taker's reminder checklist: after the meeting

Tick the following as completed:

☐ Have I taken the trouble to shake hands with and say goodbye to all the participants or have I remained in my seat with my head in my notes?

☐ Have I taken the time, after everyone has left, to analyse my notes and check understanding and legibility?

☐ Have I made sure that all the key points are highlighted while my memory is still fresh?

☐ Have I thanked the chair?

☐ Have I discussed any pertinent points with the chair prior to leaving the meeting room?

☐ Have I asked the chair to sign the minutes of the previous meeting (if necessary) so that they can be filed and archived?

☐ Have I started writing up the draft minutes as soon as possible after the meeting?

☐ Am I using the correct format and style having regard to the nature of the meeting and the level of formality or informality required?

☐ Am I using an appropriate numbering system?

☐ Am I using the passive voice and correct verbs, particularly where the minutes are of a formal nature?

☐ Have I checked the *level of detail* required for this particular meeting? Is the recording of decisions and actions enough or do I need to incorporate the 'flavour' of the discussion?

☐ When summarising the discussions, am I being crisp and concise, perhaps consolidating certain discussion points into one sentence or is the minute tending to be too drawn out and 'wordy'?

☐ Have I carefully *proofread* the minutes before sending them to the chair for approval?

☐ I am aware that the draft minutes need to be returned on time to adhere to the meeting cycle, but have *I given* the chair a clear deadline for their approval?

☐ When sending the minutes have I clearly highlighted the action points for the individual participants?

☐ Which background papers do I need to file with the minutes?
☐ From my perspective as minute-taker, what went well at the meeting and what areas need to be worked on?
☐ What exercises can I undertake to practice my listening and note-taking skills?
☐ At the next meeting, what can I *personally* do to make it even more effective?

This is an excerpt from ICSA Publishing's book, *Effective Minute Taking*, reproduced with the authors' permission.

Appendix 4: Finance processes for month-end reporting

		Sep-13		
	Finance processes for month-end reporting	**Done by**	**Date**	**Comments**
	Mid-month			
1	Run supplier invoice payment run for invoices falling due. Record transactions in the finance system. Process banking and ensure all completed correctly.			
2	Review dummy payroll. Reconcile to budget, overtime claim forms etc. Ensure all changes correctly reflected. Follow up any differences. Update budget if necessary; consider if material and take appropriate action.			
3	Review credit card transactions. Ensure copy invoices attached to statement. Book expense to finance system.			
	Last week of the month if not before			
4	Review live payroll. Ensure in line with expectations; any changes from dummy are understood and queries resolved.			
5	Journal/upload payroll entries.			
6	Enter all invoices and credit notes.			
7	Complete all banking – enter all paying in slips, nominally receipt any remittances direct to the bank account, reflect direct debits and payroll cashbook entries and any other transactions.			

	Finance processes for month-end reporting	Done by	Date	Comments
	At month end			
8	Perform bank reconciliation – make any adjustments as necessary.			Dependent upon the number of transactions the school may wish to do this weekly, fortnightly or at least monthly.
9	Review all purchase ledger accounts and reconcile to statement. Request copy invoices and action as appropriate – if invoices missing from finance system book to finance system. Process further invoice payment runs as necessary.			
10	Post any sales invoices and reconcile any debtor balances.			Significance of this item will depend upon the activities of the academy.
11	Review all transactions in the month – check nominal codes and cost centres are correct – if not raise a journal. File journal and supporting documentation.			
12	Review trial balance. Ensure that income/ expense amounts look right and reconcile balance sheet accounts. Investigate any errors or omissions.			
13	Review outstanding purchase commitments and ensure all goods received have been correctly reflected in the accounts.			

	Finance processes for month-end reporting	Done by	Date	Comments
14	Check Capex booked to the correct ledger codes.			
15	Process month-end journal to correct any items identified above.			
16	Run VAT reports and reconcile. When satisfied correct process VAT reclaim.			
17	Prepare month-end reports to include actuals in the month and year to date against budget; bank balances and cashflow forecasts. Significant variances from budget should be explained and corrective action taken/reforecasts made.			

Thanks to Sarah Chambers FCA.

Appendix 5: Board of Directors (BoD) Decision Planner

KEY	
	Level 1: Decision to be taken by full Board of Directors
	Level 2: Decision to be delegated to a committee of the Board of Directors
	Level 3: Decision to be delegated to an individual Director
	Level 4: Decision to be delegated to Headteacher
	Level 5: Headteacher day-to-day management

Column blank: Action could be undertaken at this level.
Column blocked off: Function cannot be legally carried out at this level.
Column with lighter shading – not recommended at this level.

			Decision Level				
For Secretary	Key Function	Tasks	1 Board of Directors	2 Committee	3 Individual Director	4 Delegate to Headteacher	5 Headteacher Day-to-day
	Curriculum	To ensure National Curriculum (NC) is taught to all pupils (monitoring curriculum)				X	
	Curriculum	To consider any disapplication from National Curriculum for pupil(s)				X	
	Curriculum	To draft curriculum policy				X	
	Curriculum	To agree or reject curriculum policy			X		
	Curriculum	To implement curriculum policy					X
	Curriculum	To monitor and review implementation of the curriculum policy		X			
	Curriculum	To ensure that the school meets for 380 sessions in a school year.				X	
	Curriculum	To set the times of school sessions and the dates of school terms and holidays	X				
	Curriculum	To ensure that the curriculum contributes to community cohesion		X			
	Curriculum	To decide which subject options should be taught having regard to resources, and implement provision for flexibility in the curriculum (including activities outside school day)		X			
	Curriculum	To ensure that only approved external qualifications and syllabuses are offered to pupils of compulsory school age				X	
	Curriculum	To monitor standards of teaching					X
	Curriculum	To take responsibility for individual child's education					X

For Secretary	Key Function	Tasks	Decision Level				
			1 Board of Directors	2 Committee	3 Individual Director	4 Delegate to Headteacher	5 Headteacher Day-to-day
	Curriculum	To make and keep up to date a written policy on Sex Education		X			
	Curriculum	To prohibit political indoctrination and ensuring the balanced treatment of political issues				X	
	Curriculum	To set and publish targets for pupil achievement		X			
	Curriculum	To review and amend curriculum policies				X	
	Curriculum	To ensure that the school appoints a Special Educational Needs Coordinator (SENCO)				X	
	Curriculum	To review (amend) and monitor the school's SEN policy.		X			
	Curriculum	To discharge other duties in respect of pupils with special educational needs.				X	
	Curriculum	To review (amend) and monitor the Board of Directors' other policies to ensure inclusion (in regard to gender, social disadvantage, race equality and disability discrimination).		X			
	Curriculum	To ensure that the Headteacher sends the Early Years Foundation Stage Profile assessments and Key Stage 1 teacher assessments results to the DfE.				X	
	Curriculum	To monitor pupil achievement against set targets.		X			
	Curriculum	To approve off-site visits and activities of up to 1 day				X	
	Curriculum	To approve off-site visits and activities of more than 24 hours or which involve a hazardous pursuit or journey by air or sea.		X			
	Religious Education	To provide RE in line with school's basic curriculum. (Implementation)				X	
	Religious Education	To ensure provision of RE in line with school's basic curriculum. (Monitoring)				X	
	Collective Worship	Ensure that all pupils take part in a daily act of collective worship (after consulting BoD).				X	
	Collective Worship	To make application to the Standing Advisory Council for Religious Education (SACRE) to disapply the Christian requirements for collective worship (after consulting BoD).				X	
	Collective Worship	To make arrangements for collective worship in schools without religious character (after consulting BoD).				X	
	Behaviour	To decide a discipline policy.		X			

For Secretary	Key Function	Tasks	Decision Level 1 Board of Directors	2 Committee	3 Individual Director	4 Delegate to Headteacher	5 Headteacher Day-to-day
	Behaviour	Headteacher has powers to search, with or without consent a pupil whom they reasonably suspect is carrying a knife or other weapon.					X
	Behaviour	To exclude a pupil for one or more fixed terms (not exceeding 45 days in total in a year) or permanently					X
	Behaviour	To review the use of exclusion and to decide whether or not to confirm all permanent exclusions (and fixed term exclusions where necessary)		X			
	Behaviour	To direct reinstatement of excluded pupils		X			
	Behaviour	To review the overall pattern and use of exclusions within the school.	X				
	Behaviour	To monitor and review pupil attendance				X	
	Behaviour	To set attendance targets		X			
	Behaviour	To decide whether parenting contracts should form part of the school's		X			
	Behaviour	To implement parent contracts				X	
	Pupil Welfare	To decide the content, presentation, and cost of school food, and where there is a cash cafeteria system, set the standard meals allowance for those entitled to free meals.		X			
	Pupil Welfare	To ensure that school policy and procedure for Looked After Children are consistent with measures set out in the statutory guidance.		X			
	Pupil Welfare	To decide whether to appoint a designated Director for Safeguarding Children or to retain as a full Board of Directors task	X				
	Pupil Welfare	To carry out annual review of Safeguarding Children and Child Protection policy and procedures and report to the BoD.		X			
	Parents	To publish the School Prospectus.	X				
	Parents	To approve and publish the School Profile annually.	X				
	Parents	To plan and coordinate strategies by which the Board of Directors can demonstrate its accountability and consult parents and community.	X				
	Parents	To adopt and review home-school agreements.		X			
	Parents	To ensure that school lunch nutritional standards are met.				X	

For Secretary	Key Function	Tasks	Decision Level				
			1 Board of Directors	2 Committee	3 Individual Director	4 Delegate to Headteacher	5 Headteacher Day-to-day
	Community	To consider matters relating to the role of the school in the community, including public relations.	X				
	Community	To ensure that the school contributes to community cohesion.		X			
	Extended Schools	To research and review the opportunities/challenges arising from extended school provision (from a pupil learning perspective).	X				
	Extended Schools	To research and review the opportunities/challenges arising from extended school provision (from a premises and resources perspective).		X			
	Extended Schools	To decide to offer additional activities under extended schools provision – or to cease provision.				X	
	Extended Schools	To put into place additional services provided.				X	
	Extended Schools	To ensure delivery of services provided.				X	
	Planning	To ensure that recommendations following OFSTED inspection are incorporated into the School Business and Development Plan/School Improvement Plan.	X				
		To prepare and review a strategy for school improvement on the following outcomes: • Stay safe • Be healthy • Enjoy and achieve • Achieve economic well-being • Make a positive contribution.	X				
	Planning	To agree priorities for the School Improvement Plan	X				
	Planning	To approve School Improvement Plan	X				
	Planning	To monitor School Improvement Plan overall	X				
	Staffing	To develop, review and oversee implementation of the Board of Directors' personnel policies (with reference to Employment Law and HR guidance).		X			
	Staffing	To appoint Headteacher (on recommendation of selection panel).	X				
	Staffing	To appoint Deputy Headteacher/Assistant Headteacher (on recommendation of selection panel).	X				
	Staffing	To appoint other teachers		X			
	Staffing	To appoint teachers to leadership group (as defined by agreed staffing structure).				X	
	Staffing	To appoint non teaching staff outside the leadership group.				X	
	Staffing	To draft/amend and review whole school pay policy.		X			
	Staffing	To decide on recommendations relating to the pay of all members of staff.		X			

For Secretary	Key Function	Tasks	Decision Level				
			1 Board of Directors	2 Committee	3 Individual Director	4 Delegate to Headteacher	5 Headteacher Day-to-day
	Staffing	To implement disciplinary procedures.					X
	Staffing	To agree disciplinary/capability procedures NB *Based on model policy as agreed with unions.*		X			
	Staffing	To dismiss Headteacher (BoD must act through Dismissal Committee		X			
	Staffing	To dismiss other staff (BoD must act through Dismissal Committee but normally delegated to Headteacher).				X	
	Staffing	To suspend Headteacher.			X		
	Staffing	To suspend staff (except Headteacher).				X	
	Staffing	To end suspension (Headteacher).		X			
	Staffing	To end suspension (except Headteacher).			X		
	Staffing	To determine staff complement.	X				
	Staffing	To approve applications for early retirement, secondment and leave of absence not covered by local agreements.		X			
	Staffing	To establish and maintain a performance management policy.		X			
	Staffing	To implement the performance management of staff				X	
	Staffing	To implement the performance management of Headteacher.		X			
	Staffing	To draft and review a policy on absence management.				X	
	Staffing	To agree and monitor a training strategy for teachers, support staff and Directors.				X	
	Premises	To obtain buildings insurance.		X			
	Premises	To develop a school buildings strategy (including budgeting for repairs etc.) and contributing to Asset Management Planning arrangements		X			
	Premises	To procure and agree a maintenance strategy for new buildings including developing a properly funded maintenance plan.		X			
	Premises	To review security of school premises and equipment.		X			
	Premises	To agree level of maintenance service the school will buy from service providers.			X		
	Premises	To research and be involved in drawing up an Accessibility Plan for the school.			X		
	Premises	To recommend a hiring policy to the Board of Directors and to oversee its implementation.				X	
	Premises	To approve hiring policy and charges		X			
	H & S	To implement health and safety arrangements					X

For Secretary	Key Function	Tasks	Decision Level				
			1 Board of Directors	2 Committee	3 Individual Director	4 Delegate to Headteacher	5 Headteacher Day-to-day
	H & S	To monitor health & safety arrangement			X		
	H & S	To ensure that suitable risk assessments are prepared and action taken to minimise risk.				X	
	H & S	To monitor accident book and agree appropriate action.			X		
	Admissions Academy	To implement Admissions Policy.	X				
	Admissions All schools	To appeal against Local Authority directions to admit pupil(s).		X			
	Organisation	To draw up instrument of government and any amendments thereafter.	X				
	Organisation	To agree proposals to change category of school.	X				
	Organisation	To consider forming, joining or leaving a federation	X				
	Organisation	To appoint (and remove) the chair and vice-chair of a permanent or a temporary Board of Directors.	X				
	Organisation	To appoint and dismiss the clerk to the Directors.	X				
	Organisation	To appoint and remove Directors.	X				
	Organisation	To appoint and remove associate members.	X				
	Organisation	To set up a Register of Directors' Business Interests.	X				
	Organisation	To approve and set up an Expenses Scheme.		X			
	Organisation	To consider whether or not to exercise delegation of functions to individuals or committees.	X				
	Organisation	To regulate the BoD procedures (where not set out in law) e.g. Standing Orders	X				
	Organisation	To establish and Review Committees annually.	X				
	Organisation	Agree a policy and protocol for Director visits to the school.		X			
	Finance	See attached Financial Regulations Manual					
	Finance	To set a charging and remissions policy.		X			
	Finance	To ensure provision of free school meals to those pupils meeting the criteria.				X	

Thanks to Rush Common Primary School.

Appendix 6: Example strategic objectives and key indicators

1. Our aim is to be the best multi-school academy in southern England	
Performance Indicators	Target Date
All Academy Schools to have an Ofsted outstanding rating	April 2017
All Academy Schools to consistently achieve progress and attainment standards within the top 25% nationally (KS1 – KS5)	April 2017
Satisfaction survey with stakeholders and if possible benchmark against other schools	Half Yearly

Notes
How can we measure and directly contribute to improvements in attainment? This is not just about actual results but also perceptions, image and other subjective criteria.

2. We want to achieve seamless progression across all key stages	
Performance Indicators	Target Date
Implement a 'through-life' teaching and learning strategy	April 2017
Create a rich and motivating curriculum acknowledged through student and parental 'voice' feedback; and independent verification	Annually at year end

Notes
What will help us to achieve an enhanced educational experience for our students? How can we assess 'seamless progression' at each key stage transition?

3. Maximise engagement with students, their families and the local community to achieve a vibrant community dimension	
Performance Indicators	Target Date
Produce an Academy Community Strategy document, detailing development of all key partnerships and interactions	July 2017
Annually audit the Academy's delivery of a 'safe, creative and ethical environment' with staff, parents and the local community	Easter term annually

Notes
What are the key areas for community engagement and how can they be measured? This also includes wider development of our students to help develop 'responsible, capable and confident young people who are active citizens in the 21st Century'.

4. Build a viable and sustainable long term Faringdon Education Strategy	
Performance Indicators	Target Date
Produce and publish a Faringdon Education Development Plan (10 year vision) linked to the Faringdon Neighbourhood Plan	April 2017
Proactively support the conversion of Faringdon Partnership schools to Academy status with feedback via the Headteacher Steering Group	November 2017

Notes

How can we keep a strategic perspective on the wider development of education locally?

5. Ensure that our Academy proactively adds value to member schools	
Performance Indicators	Target Date
Academy Board to subjectively assess the quality of approved 'Added Value Projects' being successfully implemented each year; and/or assessment by Local Governing Bodies using questionnaires with ratings on added-value progress	September Annually
Additional investment made available per year by becoming a Multi-school Academy – whether derived via economies of scale or other savings (measured as absolute quantum or % of total budget)	June Annually

Notes

Given that we need to add value to each school (above what was being achieved previously), what approach should we take to ensure that the sum is greater than the parts?

Copy kindly provided by Faringdon Academy of Schools. Reproduced with permission.

Appendix 7: Risk assessment form

Category	Specific	Probability	Impact	Score	Controls	Residual Probability	Residual Impact	Residual Score
Data Security and Integrity	Loss of up-to-date student information re students' past / present education, behaviour, medical or domestic situation or contact details				Tight controls in place. Acceptable usage policy – all staff have to read and sign.			
	Protection of confidential data – failure to maintain confidentiality of data on various media (print, data sticks, laptops, emails)				Tight controls in place. Training given to all staff. IT security. Acceptable usage policy signed by all staff.			
IT Hardware	Catastrophic failure of IT equipment impacting on teaching/ learning, management and support systems				New back-up and servers in place with APSs. New ICT vanilla network in place. Cco in with G4S for more power into server room.			
	Impact of crisis financial constraints on support systems (IT, H&S, medical care, parent information systems, website maintenance/ development)				Crisis financial constraints no longer in place.			
	Failure to develop ICT infrastructure needed to keep RWBA ahead of the curve				Recognised as high priority by school. Plan in place. Allocate annual budget.			
Financial Risk	Loss of financial control				Quality Finance Manager (Accountant) Headteacher line manages. Overview F&P			
	Insufficient income (core and additional) to maintain planned Teaching and Learning				Increasing numbers. Advertising. Recruitment drive. Proactive in other schools. Curriculum choice wider.			
	Fraud by employees, Governors or third parties				System in place, signatures etc.. Over £50,000 requires 3 tenders etc. Insurance – theft/fraud. External Audit			
	Theft of property by employees, governors, pupils, or third parties				Buildings locked and secure from 4pm. Theft is negligible?			

Category	Specific	Probability	Impact	Score	Controls	Residual Probability	Residual Impact	Residual Score
	Unknown liabilities, not covered by PFI contract				Headteacher leading with PFI contract. Link governor and chair of F and P heavily involved.			
	Underestimate of cost of outsourcing to replace WCC				All costings checked before outsourcing is bought			
Governance and Strategy	Failure to develop a clear aim and strategy for WBS (and to engage all staff in its achievement).				There are clear aims and they are being revisited. (Job of LT and Headteacher and Governing Body)			
	Failure to manage financial, operational, compliance and H&S risks				Checks in place for finance and new Finance Manager. Other issues less likely but all are covered on Governor Committees and standing items on Full Governing Body agenda. External audit			
	Failure to establish, maintain and comply with a framework of governance (roles, authorities, terms of reference, delegated powers etc.)				Follow Academy Handbook. All procedures set up and followed External Audit Reviewer			
	Suboptimal outcomes of change projects due to incomplete evaluation of options and analysis of risk and/or ineffective decision making and project management				Extensive consultation with governors happening all the time. Checks and tendering process does exist for items over £80,000. Formal project management training being looked into for a member of team.			
Long-term loss of staff	Staff leave the school or profession due to pressures of resource constraints or changing Terms and Conditions				Replace them. No one irreplaceable. May require short-term replanning. We have already shown we can manage this risk with a huge variety of people leaving including Deputy Headteacher			

Category	Specific	Probability	Impact	Score	Controls	Residual Probability	Residual Impact	Residual Score
Short-term loss of staff	Loss of large number of staff at one time due to strike, illness, accident, transport problems...causing loss of teaching and learning time				Always short-term. Planned time, work given. Time made up			
Loss of Buildings	Risk of damage to buildings – fire accident, loss of power/heat/water, poor maintenance, environmental causes				G4 sort out any problems			
	Lime Kiln development reduces access for RWBA to sports and other facilities				New campus proposed if not Lime Kiln will be refurbished.			
Pastoral Care	Failure to engage parental support against absence/truancy				Truancy call. EWO input. Student Managers phone home. Tutors phone home after 2 days. Electronic registration. Appointed our own EWO.			
	Pupil behaviour standards erode through gradual slippage/contagion				Outstanding T&L. Quality Assurance. Behaviour policy – stages, B15 etc... Outstanding C, G, S.			
	Risk that students/parents are not given appropriate guidance leading to students embarking on wrong course.				Outstanding IAG. Interviews. Aim Higher. Information evenings. Personalised curriculum. ECM days. Outside agencies			
	Failure to work with outside agencies (social care/policy/healthy minds/primary schools etc.) leading to insufficient "not joined up" support				School contracts outside agencies constantly. MAF. MA meetings. TWC meetings. Cluster CPD			
	Press Level' school incident (site damage, financial error, violence, drugs etc.) leading to loss of student numbers, inability to recruit high calibre staff				Press training for LT (Headteacher has had this). Many incidents dealt with in past			

Category	Specific	Probability	Impact	Score	Controls	Residual Probability	Residual Impact	Residual Score
	Accidents with school				Risk Assessment. Meet G4S. H&S Policy. Outstanding T&L. Outstanding Safeguarding. Annual staff training			
	Ineffective risk assessment on school trips				Forms completed before you go. Signed off and checked			
	Inadequate visitor control/ supervision				Outstanding safeguarding procedure. CCTV			
Student Numbers varying from plan	Higher = pressure on staff and buildings (6th Form Centre, in particular)				Constant review of numbers in and out of school. LT awareness of numbers and potential impact. AHT curriculum looking into this rooming and timetable impact.			
	Lower = pressure on finances				Constant recruitment in primary and secondary schools for Years 7-12 entry			
Teaching Quality and Standards	Fall in quality of teaching delivered				Quality Assurance. 1-2-1. Professionalism. Outstanding T&L			
	Failure to maintain performance in GCSE/A-level and resulting loss of outstanding status leading to inability to attract pupil numbers and high calibre staff				Quality Assurance. 1-2-1. Professionalism. Outstanding T&L. Recent Ofqual interference in English gradings has made this even more crucial. Curriculum change ahead. Porgress checked in all years against targets. Intervention as necessary.			

Thanks to Royal Wootton Bassett Academy.

Appendix 8: Example risk register

Risk ID	Risk (description)	Date Raised	Academy affected	Risk owner	Probability	Impact	Severity	Aggravating factors	Mitigation measures	Status	Date Reviewed	Date closed
	Governance and Legal											
G1												
G2												
	Strategic											
S1												
S2												
	Financial											
F1												
F2												
	Human resources											
HR1												
HR2												
	Health and safety											
HS1												
HS2												
	Other legal and operational											

Continued overleaf

Risk ID	Risk (description)	Date Raised	Academy affected	Risk owner	Probability	Impact	Severity	Aggravating factors	Mitigation measures	Status	Date Reviewed	Date closed
LO1												
LO2												
	Educational											
E1												
E2												

Copy provided by Cabot Learning Federation. Reproduced with permission.

Appendix 9: Committee self-evaluation

Committee Self-Evaluation   Name:

	Agree. Evidence	Neither agree nor disagree. Steps we could take to improve	Disagree. Steps we could take to improve
I understand the purpose and goals of the Committee			
The committee has help and support of the key stakeholders			
Meetings are planned well in advance			
Meetings begin and end on time			
I know how to contribute to the agenda			
I prepare and send out papers supporting my agenda items			
Agenda is clear and self explanatory			
The time devoted to each agenda item is proportionate to its importance			
All paperwork is sent out well in advance			

	Agree. Evidence	Neither agree nor disagree. Steps we could take to improve	Disagree. Steps we could take to improve
I read the paperwork before the meeting			
We have an agreed policy for "Any other business"			
I note down the Action I am responsible for and report back in the agreed time frame			
When I speak I feel listened to and my comments are valued			

What do you like most about our meetings?

What would you like to see improve in our meetings?

What would you consider to be the main achievements of the committee this academic year?

Thanks to Naureen Khalid.

Appendix 10: 360° review of chair's performance

Name:

The chair understands the role of the committee and communicates it effectively to other governors.			
Strongly Agree	Agree	Disagree	Strongly Disagree
Comments			

The relationship between the chair and the deputy head and other members of SLT who attend the committee meetings is that of a supportive and critical friend and is not 'cosy'.			
Strongly Agree	Agree	Disagree	Strongly Disagree
Comments			

The chair understands the difference between the role of the committee and the role of the SLT and seeks to ensure that the committee has a strategic focus.			
Strongly Agree	Agree	Disagree	Strongly Disagree
Comments			

The chair encourages the committee to review its processes and practices.			
Strongly Agree	Agree	Disagree	Strongly Disagree
Comments			

The chair ensures that meeting agendas and the work of the committee focus on school priorities.			
Strongly Agree	Agree	Disagree	Strongly Disagree
Comments			

All governors and members of SLT feel they can contribute to meetings and feel that their views are listened to.			
Strongly Agree	Agree	Disagree	Strongly Disagree
Comments			

Meetings are well organised and run to time. Decisions are clear and are minuted.			
Strongly Agree	Agree	Disagree	Strongly Disagree
Comments			

The chair has a good understanding of the school and its ethos.			
Strongly Agree	Agree	Disagree	Strongly Disagree
Comments			

Interpersonal Skills: The chair is friendly, approachable and accepts effective criticism.			
Strongly Agree	Agree	Disagree	Strongly Disagree
Comments			

Communication skills: The chair is a good communicator and listener.			
Strongly Agree	Agree	Disagree	Strongly Disagree
Comments			

Leadership: The chair encourages teamwork and delegates appropriately.			
Strongly Agree	Agree	Disagree	Strongly Disagree
Comments			

The chair has your confidence.			
Strongly Agree	Agree	Disagree	Strongly Disagree
Comments			

For the following, please give an answer rather than using the above scale.

1. What do you like best about the way I chair the committee?

2. Is there anything you would want to change in the way I chair the committee?

Thanks to Naureen Khalid.

Appendix 11: Data protection

The material in this Appendix has been compiled by Peter Wright, solicitor and managing director of DigitalLawUK.

Academies should comply with the Data Protection Act. What does that mean?

- If you have a breach – what do you do? It is now a matter of when, not if, you are breached.
  - Keep quiet?
  - Tell those involved not to do it again?
  - Inform the parents of pupils that are affected?
- Should you tell the Information Commissioner's Office (ICO)? There is no legal requirement to do so (*at present*), however:
  - Full and frank disclosure to those involved will be taken into account by the ICO should it issue a monetary penalty notice, which can be of the value of up to £500,000, following a Data Protection Breach
  - An academy is classed as the data controller for holding the data of its staff and pupils, and as the data controller and it is the data controller that is fined. An academy cannot delegate this responsibility. By the same token, academies can be fined for services they may have outsourced.

1. 'Cloud' storage
Principles
Andrew Jonathan Crossley (ACS Law) (10 May 2011)
- Firm specialised in pursuing copyright infringement on behalf of holders.
- Massive data requests sent to ISPs for 1,000s of IP addresses, ISPs would return requests with name and address data for each IP address. Would be saved to CMS by ACS.
- Some of those pursued would provide information about being elderly or infirm with chronic or serious illnesses or mental health issues, whereupon ACS would enter into compromise agreements. These could contain sensitive data including medical records or bank account and credit card info.
- AJC asked junior paralegal to find a new web hosting company as current one not fit for purpose. Neither AJC nor paralegal had IT qualifications. Carried out search and found web hosting company with 'home' package at £5.99 pcm. Not intended for business use. No guarantees given regarding personal data storage.

- High-profile litigation led to a targeted attack from activists to server. Server went offline and file containing ALL e-mails from ACS account made available online allowing spreadsheets and e-mails to be accessed. 6,000 sets of personal details leaked.
- ACS reported to ICO, stopped using cloud host, obtained report with 20 suggestions to improve security including a firewall and access control. Spent £20,000 as a result of incident, suffered loss of revenue and had to make 14 of 16 staff redundant.
- Breach of Principle 7 – Appropriate measures shall be taken against unauthorised or unlawful processing of personal data and against accidental loss, destruction or damage to personal data.
- No professional IT advice taken, had not followed guidance on BSO/IEC 27001.
- ICO felt that as a lawyer, the data controller should have been fully aware of his obligations under the Data Protection Act.
- Issued Monetary Penalty Notice of £200,000 as reasonable and proportionate.

Practical guidance
Cloud computing: Reasons not to do it:
- Still some unknowns.
- Lack of control.
- Security.

Reasons why you should do it:
- Exceptionally versatile.
- Less expensive and cumbersome than on-site servers.
- It is the future of data storage.

List of 10 questions to ask cloud service providers:
1 What is the reputation of the vendor? Are they well known or a new start up that could be 'here today gone tomorrow'? If possible, obtain references from other lawyers that use the same system.
2 Will I have unrestricted access to my data? The lawyer must have full unfettered access to data. Can be ensured through off-site back-up. Alternatively, have a secondary back-up in case provider restricts access for any reason.
3 What will happen when I stop using vendor's service – what will happen to data? Ensure all data can be recovered, ideally in a non-proprietary format such as .csv. If relationship ends in dispute (e.g. non-payment of bills) will you still have access to the data or have it returned? Some cloud providers are explicit on this point that users will still have access and have data returned even in event of non-payment of bills. You also do not want the vendor to retain any of your data, even as a back-up, after you have stopped using the service.

4   Are passwords required to protect access to data? Will two-stage verification be used and will this be using a RSA token or text message system? You may also be logged out after a period of inactivity to prevent unauthorised access.

5   What is the provider's policy for the handling of confidential data? You need to know how the vendor's employees will treat data to preserve confidentiality. You may want to ensure that the provider notifies you if they receive a request to provide your data (e.g. to the police as part of an investigation).

6   Does the vendor use encryption? Data movement should be covered by secure socket lawyers (SSL) encryption of at least 128 bit. Data is encrypted and authenticated with the recipient. Many vendors use 256 bit. Web addresses will display as 'HTTPS' if SSL is being used and a padlock icon should appear on the browser. Data should remain encrypted while at rest on vendor's server.

7   What measures will vendor take to back-up data? You need daily back-up to multiple locations including physical removal from vendor's primary location. Even if vendor has back-up, you should have your own back-up system. If vendor offers regular ability to export or download your data, ensure that this is done and logged to a secure location.

8   How does the provider protect the security of the network? There should be firewalls, virus detection systems and the provider should be able to easily provide you with documentation about this. There should be regular scans of the system and ports to detect any unauthorised access.

9   How does the provider protect physical security of the data centre?
    ■ Where is the centre located?
    ■ What is the security? Is there video monitoring and verification?
        – Are there uninterrupted power supplies and a generator?
        – Redundant climate systems to maintain systems?
        – Fire detection and suppression including offsite alarm and monitoring?
        – 24 × 7 system monitoring?

Few cloud providers have their own data centre, so try to insist on it and if they outsource, still find answers to these questions.

10 What are the vendor's terms of service? Review terms and any licence agreements. Look for terms about confidentiality, security and data ownership
    ■ Train staff.
    ■ Verify regularly.

Do not rely on the cloud 100%.

2. Back-up, disaster plan and disaster recovery
Principles
Buncefield (11 December 2005)
■ Damaged 30 nearby buildings

Boston alcohol warehouse fire (14 July 2011)
- Massive fire led to huge response from emergency services, massive cordon around hazard due to risk of further explosion. Who knows if an illegal business is being operated from a nearby unit?

Sheffield flood (2007)
- Heavy persistent rainfall led to massive flood and attendant issues.

A disaster does not have to be a terror attack or emergency incident in your office or building. It could be something as mundane as a gas or water leak preventing access to your office, or a limited fire in a derelict building some distance away leading to the police restricting access to your office. Or even a power cut. What would you do if access to your office and systems were limited, even if just for an hour or two? This could be enough to prevent a major transaction or event.

Practical guidance
Rule of one's exemplified
- Have a back-up of all data. Daily back-up and weekly back-up. Have a back-up register completed by staff.
- Have a back-up of your back-up. Consider large monthly back-up after end of month procedures followed.
- Test and verify your back-up regularly.

Scenarios to consider:
#1 IT system goes down
- Have paper back-up of all crucial data such as payroll, HR and pupil records at the academy but in a secure fireproof and waterproof safe
- Had a digital file of all raw data in a .csv format that could then be used in any other system. Copy kept updated with all off-site digital back-ups.

#2 Rain in the academy – flood from roof leak above
- All papers in office scanned when they came in onto digital files and backed-up offsite.
- All original documents kept in fire and waterproof safe or an inexpensive hazard-resistant cabinet.

*Once you have a system, **USE IT** – then no need to worry in future.

3. Remote working/Travel
Principles
Jala Transport Ltd (26 September 2013)
- Small money-lending business. Owner driving to work when thief leaned through window and stole briefcase from seat of car. Briefcase contained external hard drive and documents.

- Hard drive protected by password but unencrypted. Contained all details of 250 clients including ID proof.
- £5,000 fine but far greater damage from loss of reputation and bad publicity.

Practical guidance
So it happens – be smart
Electronic
- Encrypted/secure access only.
- Monitored access so can identify who, when and where.
- Training staff on when and how to use (i.e. not using unsecure WiFi hotspots to access your secure academy server).
- Lock devices and keep as few data files on remote devices as possible.
- Encrypted USB drives using products like Trucrypt.
- Where – who can see your screen?
- What can people see?
- How you protect data:
  - first class travel;
  - never leave unattended;
  - work with redacted travel files.

Paper
- Use locked cases
- Who can see your papers? (How often have you seen others working on trains and been able to tell that they are working on confidential papers!)
- Never leave unattended. (Remember criticism of David Cameron leaving Red Box unattended on train.)

Use specific redacted files put together to be taken out of the office for this specific purpose that do not contain any sensitive personal data.

4. Devices/Laptops/Phones
Principles
Ealing & Hounslow Council (4 February 2011)
- Ealing operated 'Out of Hours' service with staff working from home in the evening and supplied staff with phones and laptops so that they could work remotely.
- Opportunistic theft at home of one of workers, two laptops stolen. Sensitive personal data on both machines, none of it encrypted. Breached Ealing's own professed data protection policy by not being encrypted. Staff received data protection training at induction, but staff member had been there for 12 years.
- Home working policy existed but management had not checked out of hours team was actually following it. No quarterly assessments carried out, despite being supposed practice.

- Hounslow subcontracted out-of-hours cover to Ealing as well. Contract had no details about security to be followed by Ealing as it would contain data on Hounslow users. No procedure for Hounslow to monitor if Ealing was in compliance with Data Protection Act. Hounslow itself had no security policy in place, just a series of 'Do's and Don'ts'.

Ealing kept its work from Hounslow, but would your clients stay with you after such a breach?

Practical guidance
- Anti-virus on phones and tablets.
- Careful of other apps on devices.
- Have Bluetooth off by default on all mobile devices. Only activate when necessary.
- Be aware of using open wifi networks in public locations like cafés.
- Ensure any site that is interacted with uses HTTPS not unencrypted HTTP connections. If you don't, anyone nearby can use Firesheep to see what you are doing.
- Easier to think about securing devices if they are perceived differently. Devices are mini vaults of vital information and portals to more vital information via remote access – treat them that way.
- Encryption
- Passwords
- Screen locks
- Anti-virus software – Can even download free anti-virus as a start, but better premium anti-virus apps are available.
- Limit the mixing of business and personal use on devices.
- Protect them like you would a million pound cheque. They are not to be left in a cab, bar, train or unattended car overnight.

Have a home working policy in place.

5. Bring Your Own Device
Bring Your Own Device (BYOD) is the use by staff of their own personal devices such as smart phones or tablet PCs to access academy related e-mails, contact lists, applications and data, including accessing remote working systems. However it is a practice that is fraught with risk:
- Evaluate – is it worth it?
- Reduced cost to academy in short term in having staff easily contactable and more productive.
- Therefore greater flexibility for staff **BUT** greatly increased risk of security breach.
- Increased chances of misuse of personal confidential data.

Don't do it or have very clear guidelines, policies and training with support on work-based applications on devices from IT support. Cannot be treated in a cursory or casual manner.

6. Destruction of IT hardware
Principles
Brighton & Sussex University Hospitals NHS Trust (1 June 2012)
- Destruction of hard drives. Contractor used sub-contractor to destroy drives for free. No contract directly between hospital and sub-contractor. Basic checks carried out against sub-contractor.
- Sub-contractor only occasionally accompanied on site.
- Generic certificate of destruction provided for all drives. Should have individual certificated containing serial numbers for each drive.
- Drives found for sale online on eBay – still contained medical records. Easily available info for anyone familiar with MS Access, no encryption.
- Hospital unable to confirm how large volume of drives were removed from their site without their knowledge.
- No audit trails or logs of destruction undertaken by sub-contractor.
- Fined hospital £325,000.

NHS Surrey (12 July 2013)
- Sub-contractor assured NHS IT that drives would be destroyed using industrial guillotine for free.
- Destruction certificates provided, but disposal process not observed. No written contract in place, but written assurances given.
- Public began buying refurbished PC equipment online containing hard drives that held medical records and other data.
- Certificates had been provided for these supposedly destroyed hard drives.
- Fined £200,000.

The largest fines to date by the Information Commissioner (ICO) have been for organisations that had large amounts of IT hardware, including hard drives, to be destroyed. This task was outsourced and led to hardware being found for sale online, despite the organisation being assured that the correct procedures had been followed and that the hardware had been destroyed. Generic destruction certificates had been supplied rather than specific ones and contractors had not been constantly supervised at all times. While the contractor had been at fault, it was the organisation that was fined and suffered negative publicity.

Practical guidance
Phones
- Probably the lowest security risk but still a risk – particularly smart phones which are themselves mini-computers.
- Destroy SIM cards.

- Ask providers to wipe phone memory and confirm with spot-checks.
- Safest? Destroy the phone yourself.

Tablets
- As risky as computers.
- If you have them recycled or destroyed, verify method and obtain a destruction certificate for each device.
- Safest – destroy them yourself.

Computers (Desktop and Laptop)
- Do not try to have them recycled or donated. Good intention but not a risk you can afford to take.
- If you have them destroyed by a third party, verify method and obtain destruction certificate for each device. Observe destruction.
- Safest – destroy hard drives yourself.

7. E-mail encryption and security/data rooms
Principles
Academies store large volumes of personal data. There can also be commercial and confidential data for commercial contractors. Spreadsheets of confidential data along with other documents can often be in use across a school. Any personal data includes:
- Full names
- Date of birth
- Address
- NI number
- Photograph or video footage
- Bank account details (e.g. sort code, account, IBAN)
- Biometric data – fingerprints, retina scans, height & weight measurements
- Personal e-mail addresses
- Passwords.

Personal data should not be sent via unencrypted e-mail. If a parent or other party refuses to comply with measures taken to encrypt communication, make it clear that data will not be sent and they will be charged to receive it special delivery or can collect from the academy if they show ID and sign for it. They should be pleased with the measures that you are taking to protect their data!

Practical guidance
All e-mail systems you use should be encrypted 64 bit.

Password access to the academy e-mail system should be via two-stage identification.

If you are encrypting individual files attached to e-mails, send a separate e-mail containing the encryption key after the encrypted data has been sent to the recipient and receipt of the encrypted data has been confirmed by the intended recipient.

Consider using a **secure** cloud site to share data with client (Virtual Data Rooms) – same safeguards as discussed under Cloud providers above

Confidentiality notices on e-mails:

■ Best practice for an academy to use in all correspondence.

■ Consider an additional notice when first sending an e-mail to a new recipient at the top of e-mail (e.g. as when hard-copy mail is sent private and confidential).

Doesn't work if all sensitive data and information is laid out BEFORE the warning is given in an e-mail footer. Consider having 'Protect: Personal Data' at the top of any e-mails.

There are numerous encryption systems from free applications like Winzip to encrypt individual attachments through to premium encryption that are less time consuming and more secure.

8. Administration system/Finance and accounts systems/Payroll/Regulatory
Principles
There are numerous time-saving systems on the market. However consider whether they are secure. Do they store data on your server or at their own facility? If so, ensure that the data is stored in the UK and enquire as to how it is transmitted to and from your school.

Practical guidance
■ Who has access to any data? How can it be accessed?

■ Contracts with any IT suppliers should allow for systems to be available for regular inspection and data protection audits.

■ Ask the questions. Is the system secure? How secure?

■ On-site, cloud or another system?

■ Password access.

■ Monitor and tracking of access by staff.

■ Limit who is able to act as an administrator.

■ Firewall options to lock out staff that are leaving.

■ Consider giving department access only to specific parts of system that they require to fulfil their duties.

■ Test back-ups regularly – at least monthly.

■ Consider hard copy back-up printed once a month (e.g. after invoicing).

■ Keep in fire/ hazard-proof safe.

■ Where is system located?

■ How is data transmitted?

■ Consider RSA token or similar access.

9. Website, privacy, cookies and website back-up
Principles
Cookies are items that a website installs on a user's machine when they visit the site. It can tell the website where the user is based and what pages they looked at. Products like Google Analytics install cookies on user's machines. More sophisticated cookies track a user's search patterns while they visit other sites, so that when a user returns, the site will display advert banners based on searches carried out by that specific user previously.

The ICO requires that all websites that use cookies need to have a privacy policy that makes it clear what cookies are used by the site, what data they collect and how a user can turn them off. This privacy policy is not generic – it must be specific to the site. It must be easily identifiable from the home page. The 'consent' button is not strictly required, but it is nonetheless good practice. It is likely that if your academy has a website, it will have cookies and the privacy policy must accurately reflect this.

Practical guidance
Limit access through website
■ Data collected from viewers
■ Limit information shared on website
  – Should all staff be on website – is it necessary?
  – Should internal policies and procedures be on the site?

Train staff on web surfing, cookies and downloading anything from web.

Search engines build search profiles of individual users from search history. Consider using 'DuckDuckGo' which does not store search data as Google and others do.

Have a 'consent to cookies' button installed on the homepage for a 'belt and braces' approach.

10. Social media, personal data and confidentiality
Principles
Many academies have engaged on social media, with their own pages on Facebook and/or LinkedIn along with a Twitter feed. This needs to be handled carefully. How should the 'corporate' social media accounts be updated? One business gave this task to a junior member of staff as they were felt to be the most comfortable with the technology. They proceeded to set up the corporate Twitter account so that it could be updated from their phone as they were more comfortable with this, only to forget that the phone was still enabled over the weekend. During an evening out, a friend picked up the phone and sent a 'joke' tweet, only for it to go

out on the corporate Twitter account. The member of staff lost their position due to this error, as they were still on their initial probationary period.

On personal accounts, academy staff must consider how much information they give out on social media. For example, 'Going to London for a meeting' is acceptable, as is 'Going to London for a conference' … 'Meeting Mr & Mrs X to discuss Pupil Y' is not. This may seem obvious, but a quick look at news related to social media shows that users reveal confidential personal data all the time without considering the consequences.

Staff in organisations have also been known to talk about information relating to clients, customers, patients or other staff. If this continues with no policy or guidance from an employer, the employer can be held liable for any online bullying that takes place between staff members.

Make sure management are aware how to access any corporate social media accounts. Remember HMV, who made much of their head office staff redundant before realising one of those losing their job was in charge of the Twitter feed. Several tweets were sent under the #HMVxfactorfiring hashtag before the account was closed, leading to the story featuring in the national press.

Should staff be updating social media from their own devices during work hours? Staff at the DVLA have been disciplined for updating social media accounts from their own devices during work hours.

Practical guidance
- Make a proper appointment for an individual responsible for the corporate social media feed, or contract with a supplier. Don't just pick the first person in the office below the age of 30 and presume that they are comfortable with the technology.
- Have clear policies for how the firm is to use social media.
- Provide guidance for staff on how the corporate account should be updated – from what device, appropriate content etc.
- Guidance on who should be connected to, or followed, on social media – should staff be connecting with parents on LinkedIn or other networks?
- What should staff be saying about their employment and experience on a LinkedIn profile?
- Remind staff that their work is highly confidential and their pupils rely on their discretion
- Clear policy not to discuss work on social media
- Even technically savvy staff can make inadvertent mistakes. One US lawyer checked in on Foursquare at a location before confirming in the narrative that they were attending to take witness evidence. Given that their field was defending professional negligence it was clear who they were representing and what the meeting was in connection with. In such circumstances, a lawyer is very close to breaching their duty of client confidentiality

- Two-stage social media account authorisation (e.g. enter login, password and a unique token supplied via e-mail or SMS to the user).
- Avoid using services such as Foursquare that require location information.
- Advise staff to remove DOB from social media profiles and to be aware of what is posted online about them by their 'friends' such as being tagged in inappropriate photographs.
- Own your own social media accounts. Don't let a member of staff take your corporate Twitter feed and hard-won followers with them when they leave. It is up to you as an employer to make it clear what proprietorial right, if any, is exerted over social media contacts.

11. Password security
Principles
Social media accounts, e-mail accounts and other applications like remote access, virtual data rooms and document management systems often all require password authentication. This can lead to a plethora of passwords. However, if a password is easy to guess – and over 50% of passwords are apparently 'password1' – they can be hacked easily. Multi-nationals like McDonalds and Jeep have all had their corporate social media accounts hacked. This can lead to reputational damage, not to mention the loss of thousands of carefully acquired followers.

Practical guidance
- Two-stage social media account authorisation.
- Don't use same password across multiple accounts.
- Regularly change passwords (have a system for this).
- Mixture of upper and lower case, numbers and non-alphanumeric characters.

Change regularly, ideally monthly.

12. CCTV/Hearing loop/Recording of calls
Principles
Many CCTV systems record and store their footage to a server. A restaurant was fined by the ICO for having their CCTV footage stored on a server where it was unencrypted and could be accessed remotely. As more and more academies have rudimentary CCTV at their entrances or in reception areas for security purposes, consider the damage from a breach where the details of who had visited the school revealed the identities of pupils and parents. Security is advisable and can be provided at an increasingly lower cost as the technology becomes more widespread.

Many academies are also using hearing loops for pupils and parents who may be hearing impaired. While this should be encouraged, ensure that the system is secure – could it be accessed remotely? Is the audio recorded and stored? This could present a risk.

Some academies routinely record calls. Some parents have been known to request that calls are recorded. If calls are recorded, participants need to be aware of this and message should be played to all callers so that they are fully aware of this practice.

Practical guidance
- Check positioning of CCTV cameras. What is being recorded?
- Where is footage or audio stored? Is it over-written, logged or backed-up? Server or cloud?
- Ensure appropriate level of security applied to data.
- Ensure data kept for no longer than is necessary.

13. Office procedures/file storage/desk storage
Principles
Schools historically had large numbers of hard-copy administrative files, many of which stay on a desk while they are worked on over several days; they may pass from teaching staff to secretarial, admin staff or accounts. They often find their way onto the corner of a desk, in a large pile on the floor by the desk, under the desk, on top of cupboards and stacked on shelves as well as their intended home in filing cabinets or lockable cupboards. These are often kept unlocked or in cupboards that are never actually closed and locked. While this allows for easy access, it also leaves an academy dangerously at risk from a data protection breach. Cleaning or maintenance staff may have access to areas out of hours or when staff are absent, while security staff may also have the run of the entire building. Should their access to certain areas be limited?

Have clear procedures that MUST be followed

Practical guidance
Use the basic principle that if you can see it without unlocking, entering a password or other security hurdle, then others can see it too.
- Where are administrative files stored?
  - How are they accessed?
  - Who can access them (paper and digital)?
- How secure are your storage or archive rooms?
- Third parties present in office (parents, guests, health visitors, cleaners, security, maintenance)
  - Can they see administrative files +/or personal data on a desk, on shelves, or on the screen of a PC or device?
  - Can third parties access file storage, server rooms or other facilities from near reception areas (e.g. if visitor is directed to where the toilets are?)
  - Can third parties access data if they use your Intranet, or access your WiFi network?

'Clear desk' policy
- Before seeing third parties in an office.
- At the end of the day before leaving the school.
- All staff must comply – needs the academy leadership to lead for all to follow.
- Consider having certain rooms clearly marked 'Do not enter' and restricting access to all except those members of staff who truly need access to them to fulfill their roles.

Consider having key fob access to areas where administrative staff work and data is stored and even having specific fobs for specific areas.

14. Archived files/Destruction/Confidential waste
Principles
Scottish Borders Council (11 Sept 2012)
- Council digitised pension records. No contract in place with processor carrying out the digitising.
- Public noticed paper recycling bank overflowing with discarded files containing personal data – files handed to police.
- Council unaware after it received digitised images exactly what was happening to the old files.

Fined £250,000.

Practical guidance
The basic principle of filing and archiving. File archives are easily accessible. If material can be viewed by you without any security steps being taken, then someone else could see it too. It is not an excuse to blame a lack of security on needing to have regular access to the archive.
- Locked and secure archive storage. Don't assume out of sight out of mind.
- Review security regularly.
- Train staff and spot check to ensure that they are following procedures.
- Repeat training regularly.

Destruction
- On-site
  - Storage prior to destruction must be as secure as during archive.
  - Cross-cut, shred or incinerate (strip-shred is not enough).
  - Recycling is not an option unless documents are near pulp.
- Off-site
  - Storage before pick up to be as secure as during archive.
  - Have strong secure contract with destruction supplier that is up to date, valid and current and allows for regular audit. Any problems and YOU will be fined, not contractor.
- Verify that destruction is undertaken as they claim. Ideally can be shredded by contractor at your premises using their equipment and resources.

15. Post/Confidential post/DX/Fax

Principles

Bank of Scotland PLC (30 July 2013)

- Member of public received details of BoS customer's mortgage by fax in error.
- 1 digit difference between internal fax number and actual recipient's fax.
- Error repeated consistently over a period of time, despite remedial action having been taken with individuals involved.
- Recipient, tired with continuing to receive faxes from BoS, stopped contacting BoS about them and just referred matter to ICO. Supplied ICO with 60 faxes containing personal data, including ID.
- Faxes sent from multiple different locations in BoS but all intended for same internal department.
- Further breaches continued after notification to controller that ICO was investigating matter. Probable that it was not mis-dialling, but incorrect pre-programming of numbers into fax machine.
- Majority of faxes sent with no fax cover sheet which contained disclaimer.
- Fined £75,000.

Nursing & Midwifery Council (12 February 2013)

- DVDs and evidence sent to Fitness to Practice (FTP) hearing to be held at hotel. Instructions given for package to be sent securely via courier.
- Package delivered and opened at hearing but DVDs not inside. No encryption applied to DVDs. Contained interviews with witnesses. No policy in place requiring that such data be encrypted.
- DVDs never found. No evidence package was tampered with.
- Fined £150,000.

Plymouth City Council (22 November 2012)

- Council sent additional social work report pages from third-party matter to family. Contained sensitive details of child neglect.
- Human error and no system in place to check correct documents being sent to recipients. In this instance report picked up from printer containing correct report and three additional pages from another report. All pages then packaged and sent out.
- Revealed single printer was in use by five members of staff in a single 15-minute period. Created risk of reports and papers being picked up by other users.

Practical guidance

- Staff must be well trained.
- Best practice – consider that all post could be marked 'Private & Confidential'.
- Have a procedure for packaging sensitive/personal data; double skinning envelopes etc.

■ Fax cover sheets to be used at all times. Follow-up call to ensure received by correct recipient; call to be logged.

■ System for unintended recipients to be able to report receipt and for issue to be dealt with promptly, efficiently and sensitively.

■ Have individual printers for each department and do not have large numbers of staff all using the same printer. If a specific department or staff member regularly prints sensitive, personal data, consider providing them with their own printer.

■ Consider having an ID for individual users to key into printer that has to be entered before their document can be printed.

16. Data protection policy and training

All of these principles and procedural steps need to be codified for your organisation into a data protection and security policy which can form a large part of your school's employee handbook. This can provide real guidance and change the way that your academy operates.

This can only be done with good practical training for all staff and incorporation into the training given to all new members of staff joining the school.

For the policies to work, they need to be regularly audited and spot-checked. They need to be adopted from the top, with the academy leadership taking a lead and showing an example for others to follow.

It must not be a document that just sits on a shelf gathering dust. It will need regular review and updating, ideally on an annual basis. Refresher update training should also be provided to staff. A one-off training session is not an end in itself.

Training should not just be 'death by Powerpoint'. Allow staff to understand the risks and the possible damage to the business. Allow them to input and if they think of a way of implementing something that is sufficiently rigorous but allows them to get the work done more efficiently, consider their input and modify or implement accordingly. Have assessments or 'informal quizzes' where staff are questioned about different scenarios and asked what the appropriate action would be. Ask them for examples from their daily activity too and continually assess risks to your business as it evolves and changes.

17. Relations with the ICO

There is a vast amount of information on the ICO website including check lists. Use it. Use the ICO helpline, consult on any extraordinary issues. Make sure you are registered as a data controller. If you are unsure about a procedure your academy is following, call and query it with the ICO. See what established best practice should be.

Have a proactive relationship with the regulator, which can help if you subsequently do have a data breach.

18. Data protection changes in immediate future

New EU Data Protection regulation could come in imminently. They would not require implementation at UK level with an Act of Parliament, so the Data Protection Act 1998 will be replaced immediately.

In its current draft form, businesses would have to report breaches within 24 hours. Would need measures in place to detect and report such breaches quickly.

Regulators may be able to fine based on percentage of turnover rather than on fixed rate, as currently set at £500,000.

Regularly consult a specialist in data protection for clear guidance on new regulatory matters to be aware of and any changes in the law that could affect your school.

Appendix 12: Website review

Key: 1 – In place 2 – Partially compliant / Not known / Not yet found 3 – Not in place	1	2	3
Company information ■ Company registration number ■ Place of registration (ie Registered in England) ■ Registered office address			
Academy contact details ■ Academy name ■ Academy postal address ■ Academy telephone number ■ Name of the member of staff who deals with queries from parents and other members of the public			
Admission arrangements *Either*: publish the academy's admission arrangements, explaining how applications are considered for every age group, including: ■ Arrangements in place for selecting the pupils who apply ■ Oversubscription criteria (how places are offered if there are more applicants than places) ■ An explanation of the process parents need to follow if they want to apply for their child to attend the school *Or*: publish details of how parents can find out about academy's admission arrangements through local authority			
Admission Appeal arrangements The timetable for organising and hearing admission appeals must be published by 28 February each year.			
Ofsted reports ■ *Either*: Publish a copy of the most recent Ofsted report ■ *Or*: Publish a link to the most recent Ofsted report			
Exam and assessment results **Most recent key stage 2 (KS2) and key stage 4 (KS4) results** Information on attainment and progress of pupils			

	1	2	3
Performance tables Link to the DfE school performance tables website			
Childcare Provision Details of any childcare services available.			
Curriculum ■ The content of the curriculum the school follows in each academic year for every subject (see analysis of specific subjects below) ■ The names of any phonics or reading schemes used in KS1 ■ How additional information relating to the curriculum can be obtained.			
Policies ■ Behaviour Policy including discipline, exclusions and anti-bullying which must comply with section 89 of the Education and Inspections Act 2006. ■ Charging and Remissions Policy including the activities for which the school will charge parents and the circumstances where an exception will be made on a payment you would normally expect under the policy. ■ Safeguarding including child protection policy			
Pupil premium ■ Pupil premium allocation for the current academic year ■ Details of how the allocation will be spent in the current academic year ■ Details of how you the previous academic year's allocation was spent ■ The impact on educational attainment of those pupils for whom it was allocated			
PE and sport premium ■ PE and sport premium allocation for the current academic year ■ Details of how the allocation will be spent in the current academic year ■ Details of how you the previous academic year's allocation was spent ■ The impact on PE and sport participation and attainment of those pupils for whom it was allocated			
SEN Report Report on the trust's policy for pupils with SEN which complies with section 69(2) of the Children and Families Act 2014 and regulation 51 and schedule 1 of the Special Educational Needs and Disability Regulations 2014			

	1	2	3
The report must include details of: ■ The admission arrangements for pupils with SEN or disabilities ■ The steps taken to prevent pupils with SEN from being treated less favourably than other pupils ■ Access facilities for pupils with SEN ■ The accessibility plan written in compliance with paragraph 3 of schedule 10 to the Equality Act 2010			
Values and ethos A statement of the trust's ethos and values.			
Trustee information For each trustee who has served at any point over the past 12 months ■ Full name ■ Category of trustee ■ Date of appointment ■ Date of resignation (if applicable) ■ Which body appointed them ■ Term of office ■ Names of any committees each trustee serves on ■ Details of any positions of responsibility, such as chair or vice-chair of the board of trustees or a committee of the board. ■ Attendance records at board and committee meetings over the last academic year			
Member information For each member who has served at any point over the past 12 months ■ Full name ■ Date of appointment ■ Date of resignation (if applicable)			
Register of governors' interests ■ Relevant business and pecuniary interests of members and trustees and details of any other educational establishments they govern ■ Any relationships between trustees and school staff including spouses, partners and relatives			
Annual Report and Accounts			
Governance information ■ The structure and remit of the members, board of trustees, the committees and full names of the chair of each			

	1	2	3
■ Annual statement of issues faced and addressed by the board of trustees over the last year including assessment of the impact of the board on the trust			
Equality Duty			
Gender Pay Gap Reporting Trusts more than 250 employees			
Slavery Trusts with an annual turnover of £36m or more			

Glossary

Academy State-funded schools, independent of Local Authority control.

Academy chain Any collaboration between academies whether that is done through a legal structure (i.e. MAT or umbrella) or a more informal approach (e.g. collaborative agreement).

Accounts A statement of the academy's financial affairs which can refer to published accounts or internal management accounts.

ACMF Academies Capital Maintenance Fund (now closed and replaced by CIF).

Annual return A return of information that all companies must make to the registrar of companies within every 12-month period providing a snapshot of the company including its directors, principal business activities and registered office (now replaced by an annual confirmation statement).

ARD Accounting reference date – the date that marks the end of a company's accounting year end for the purposes of preparation and filing of statutory accounts.

Articles of association The trust's main constitutional document which prescribes the internal management, decision making and running of the academy trust and its liability.

BME Black and Minority Ethnic.

Board of trustees The collective term for the trust's trustees acting together as the governing body of the company, having the powers and authorities that are bestowed upon it by the company's constitution.

Board meeting A formal meeting of the board of trustees.

Board resolution A formal resolution or decision of the board of trustees.

CA 2006 Companies Act 2006.

CEO Chief executive officer (in a MAT).

Charitable company A company set up and run solely for non-profit-making purposes with the proceeds only to be used for the purpose of the charity.

CIF Condition Improvement Fund.

Companies House An executive agency of the Department for Business Innovation and Skills, Companies House is the registry for companies incorporated in the UK.

Company limited by guarantee A company where the liability of the members is limited to a fixed amount that each member agrees to contribute to the assets of the company in the event of a winding up.

Company secretary An officer of a company with no legally defined role but who generally has responsibilities with regard to the administrative, governance and compliance aspects of a company's affairs.

Confirmation statement A return of information that all companies must make to the registrar of companies within every 12-month period providing a snapshot of the company including its directors, principal business activities and registered office.

Connected person Persons who are considered to be connected with a trustee such as a spouse or civil partner, any other person whom the trustee lives with in an enduring family relationship, the trustee's children and stepchildren, the trustee's parents and a body corporate in which the trustee has an interest in at least 20% of the share capital.

Corporate director A company which acts as a director of another company.

Corporate governance Principles and best practice concerning the way in which companies are run and directed. There is no one definition of what corporate governance is, in the broader view it also encompasses issues relating to corporate social responsibility and business ethics.

Date of Incorporation The date on which a company was formed.

DBS Disclosure and Barring Service – replaces Criminal Records Bureau (CRB).

De facto director A person acting as a director/trustee who has not been formally or validly appointed.

Derivative claim A claim brought by a member of a company against a director on the academy's behalf in accordance with the procedure set out in the Companies Act 2006.

DfE Department for Education.

Directors' general duties Seven general duties of directors which are set out in the Companies Act 2006.

Disqualification order A court order preventing a person from, among others, acting as a director of a company without the consent of the court for the period of time specified in the order. Breach of a disqualification order is a criminal offence.

DPA Data Protection Act 1998.

Duty of skill and care One of the seven codified general duties of directors set out in the Companies Act requiring directors to exercise reasonable care, skill and diligence.

EAG Earmarked Annual Grant – paid in respect of either recurrent expenditure or capital expenditure for specific purposes agreed between the Secretary of State and the academy.

EFA Education Funding Agency – an executive agency of the DfE.

Electronic communication A communication sent in electronic form such as by e-mail, text or on a disk.

Electronic filing A form or document filed with Companies House in electronic format using either approved software or the Companies House WebFiling service.

Executive director A trustee who is a full-time employee with management responsibility within the company. Not to be confused with an executive head teacher/principal, which refers to a person occupying the role of CEO in a MAT.

EYFS Early Years Foundation Stage.

FASNA Freedom and Autonomy for Schools – National Association – a national forum for self-governing primary, secondary and special schools and academies.

FE Form Entry (as in 2FE).

FE Further Education.

FFT Fischer Family Trust.

Filing The process of submitting or presenting documents or information to Companies House.

FMGS Financial Management and Governance Self-Assessment.

FMSiS Financial Management Standards in Schools (now replaced by FMGS).

FOI Freedom of Information.

Free school An academy set up by a 'proposer group' such as parents, teachers, charities or other groups.

FS Foundation stage.

FSM Free school meals.

GAG General annual grant – funding paid to cover the normal running costs of the academy such as salary and administration costs.

General meeting A formal meeting of a trust's members.

HSE Health and safety executive.

ICSA The Institute of Chartered Secretaries and Administrators.

Incorporation The process by which a company is created, also referred to as 'formation' and 'registration'.

INSET In-Service Education and Training.

KS1 Key Stage 1, age 5–7 'Infants'.

KS2 KS2 age 7–11 'Juniors'.

KS3 KS3 age 11–14.

KS4 KS4 age 14–16.

LA Local Authority.

LAAP Local Authority Associated Persons.

LADO Local Authority Designated Officer.

LGB Local Governing Body.

LGHA Local Government and Housing Act 1989.

LGPS Local Government Pension Scheme.

Maintained school A school funded by central government via the local authority.

Management accounts Accounts produced by an academy for internal decision making and monitoring purposes.

MAT Multi-academy trust – a single legal entity formed by a number of schools combining to form a single trust.

Member A person or corporate body whose name is entered in the trust's register of members.

Memorandum of Association Document confirming the three 'subscribers' who wish to form the company/trust and become its members. The memorandum has no ongoing significance once a company/trust has been incorporated.

Minutes A formal record of the proceedings of a meeting and the decisions made.

Model Articles The standard form articles for trusts prescribed by the Secretary of State under powers granted by the Companies Act. There are various model articles available to suit the particular governance structure.

Natural director A director who is a real person.

NGA National Governors' Association.

Non-executive director A director who is not a full-time employee involved in the management of the company.

NOR Number of pupils on roll.

Officer A director, manager or secretary of a company (under s. 1173 of the Companies Act 2006). In the case of an 'officer in default' this is broadened to include any person who is to be treated as an officer of the company for the purposes of the provision of the Companies Act in question.

OFSTED Office for Standards in Education.

Ordinary resolution A decision/resolution requiring approval by a majority of a company's members.

PAN Published admission number.

Poll vote A vote by way of a ballot, generally by completing a slip or paper in secret.

PPG Pupil premium grant – additional funding provided to support disadvantaged pupils and pupils with parents in the armed forces.

Principal regulator Responsible for overseeing the compliance of exempt charities with charity law. For academy trusts, the principal regulator is the Secretary of State for Education.

PROOF 'Protected online filing' – an agreement between a company and Companies House that the company will always file certain information electronically.

PSC People with Significant Control.

Quorum In relation to a board meeting or a members' meeting, the minimum number of directors or members respectively who must be present in order for the meeting to be validly constituted.

RAISEonline Reporting and analysis for Improvement through School Self-evaluation (online).

RAP Raising achievement plan.

Ratification Formal approval of something that has been considered or agreed by somebody else, in order that it can become valid or operative. Can be used to validate an otherwise invalid act by retrospectively confirming or approving it.

Registered office A company's official address at which legal and other documents can be validly served and at which certain company records must be kept if not kept at a SAIL. For a single academy trust this is likely to be the school itself.

Remuneration Payments and benefits that an employee is entitled to in respect of services provided by the employee to a trust.

Resolution A formal decision of trustees or members.

Risk assessment The process of identifying risks, the persons affected by them, the severity of the likely injuries or loss that might result from them, whether the control measures in place are adequate and any further measures needed to control them.

SAIL Single alternative inspection location – a location at which certain company records can be kept as an alternative to keeping them at the registered office.

SAT Single academy trust.

SCR Single Central Record of DBS.

SDP School Development Plan (see also SIP).

SEN Special educational needs.

SENCo Special educational needs coordinator.

SEND Special educational needs and disability.

Service address An address for correspondence that directors/trustees must provide to Companies House which can, and ideally should, be different from their residential address. Generally this is the trust's registered office address.

Shadow director A person who has not been appointed as a director but who directs or gives instructions to a company's true directors.

SIP School improvement plan.

SLT Senior leadership team.

SORP Statement of Recommended Practice.

Special resolution A members' resolution requiring a majority in favour of 75% or over.

Sponsor A body responsible for the performance and finances of a trust.

Stakeholder A person or group of persons with an interest in a trust or academy or who are in some way affected by a trust or academy's activities.

Statutory registers Books/registers containing information relating to company directors, members, etc which must be maintained in accordance with the Companies Act.

TPS Teachers' pension scheme.

TUPE Transfer of Undertakings (Protection of Employment) Regulations 2006.

Umbrella trust An academy chain whereby the over-arching academy, or umbrella, is a charitable trust in its own right and each of the individual schools is a single academy.

UIFSM Universal Infant Free School Meals.

UTC University technical college.

VA Voluntary aided – a maintained school with a majority of the board of governors appointed by a foundation or trust, usually a religious body, which may also own the land and contribute financially.

VC Voluntary controlled – a maintained school with a quarter of the board of governors appointed by a foundation or trust, usually a religious body. The foundation may own the land, but will have less direct influence than in a VA school.

VLE Virtual learning environment.

WGA Whole of Government Accounts.

Written resolution A document setting out one or more proposed resolutions that is circulated to a company's members for approval as an alternative to holding a general meeting.

Y5 Year 5.

Directory

Charity Commission
www.charitycommission.gov.uk

Companies House
www.companieshouse.gov.uk

Department for Education
www.gov.uk/government/organisations/department-for-education

DigitalLawUK
@DigitalLawUK
www.DigitalLawUK.com

Disclosure and Barring Service
www.gov.uk/government/organisations/disclosure-and-barring-service

FASNA (Freedom and Autonomy for Schools – National Association)
www.fasna.org.uk

GLM Partnership – Governor Mark
www.glmpartnership.org/governor-mark

Good Governance Code
www.governancecode.org

Health and Safety Executive
www.hse.gov.uk

HM Revenue and Customs
www.hmrc.gov.uk

Inspiring the Future
www.inspiringthefuture.org

Local Government Pension Scheme
www.lgps.org.uk

National Association of School Business Management
www.nasbm.co.uk

National College for Teaching and Leadership
www.nationalcollege.org.uk

National Governors' Association
www.nga.org.uk

New schools network
www.newschoolsnetwork.org

Teachers' pensions
www.teacherspensions.co.uk

The Information Commissioner
www.ico.org.uk

The Institute of Chartered Secretaries and Administrators
www.icsa.org.uk

The Registrar of Companies for England and Wales (Companies House)
www.companies-house.gov.uk

Whitley Stimpson
www.whitleystimpson.co.uk

Index

Academies
  application for status 2–3
  continuing obligations 5
  development 1–3
  origin 1–2
Academies Financial Handbook
  application 68
Academy trust 3–5
Accounting officer 178
Accounting reference date 177
Accounts 197–218
  approval 212
  dormant 217–218
  filing 212–215
  financial statements 210
  governance statement 202–207
    capacity to handle risk 205
    purpose of system of internal
      control 204
    review of effectiveness 206–207
    risk and control framework
      205–206
    scope of responsibility 202
  group 211–212
  independent auditor's report on
      financial statements 208
  independent auditor's report on
      regularity 208–209
  multi-academy trusts 211
  new academies 215
  reports 199–207
  statement of financial activities for the
      year 210–211

  statement of trustees'
      responsibilities 208
  statement on regularity, propriety and
      compliance 207
  strategic review 200–202
  subsidiary companies 211–212
  trustees' report 199–200
  whole of government 216–217
Advisory councils/bodies 24
Annual accounts and audit 69
Annual general meeting 123–125
  notice 94–95
Annual return 85
Annual report 198–199
Appeal panels 255
Apprentices 185–186
Articles of association 77–89
  accounts 85
  annual report 85
  annual return 85
  avoiding influenced company status
      86–89
  chairman of trustees 82
  changes to 89
  chief executive officer 84
  clerk/secretary to trustees 81–82
    committees 82–83
  conflicts of interest 82
  delegation 83–84
  general meetings 80
  honorary officers 85
  indemnity 85–86
  meetings of trustees 84

members 78–79
minutes 82
notices 85
objects 77–78
patrons 85
power of trustees 82
principal 84
rules 86
seal 85
trustees 80–81
vice-chairman of trustees 82
Auditors 215–216
removal 106–107

Becoming an academy 31–46
Board
role of 127–128
Board meetings
adjournments 158
agenda 147–150
annual schedule of business 151
attendance 145–146
calling 145–152
chair, role of 154–155
clerk to board 156–157
conflicts of interest 156
documentation 151
effectiveness 161
Local Governing Bodies 161
managing 151–153
quorum 153–154
notice 146–147
reports 151
telephone/video conferencing 157
voting 155–156
written resolutions 160–161
Board meetings 165–166
Board of Directors Decision Planner
299–304
Borrowing powers 70
Bring Your Own Device 324–325
Budgeting 186–187

Capital funding 187–190

Catholic schools 26–27
Centralised services 48–49
Chair of the board 142
Chairman of trustees 82
Chair's performance
360 degree review 315–318
Charity status 6–8
trustee 8–9
Chief executive officer 80, 84, 231
Church of England schools 27–28
Church schools 25–6, 49–50
land transfer 43–44
Clerk/secretary to trustees 81–82
Clerk to the board 235–238
Cloud storage see Data protection
Cluster governing bodies 24
Collaborative arrangements 10–14
Committee self-evaluation 313–314
Community governors
process for recruiting and
appointing 136
Companies House 96–110
accounts 102–103
annual report 102–103
appointing director/trustee 104
appointment of company
secretary 105
change of trustee's or secretary's
details 106
change of registered office
address 103–104
change to accounting reference date
103
duties 109
filing hard copies 98–99
late filing 109–110
Monitor 100
notification of SAIL 106
powers 109
PROOF 100
public record 97–98
removal of auditor 106–107
special resolutions 108–109,
126

termination of appointment of trustee or secretary 105–106
Web Filing 99
Company registers 96–97
Company secretary 238–239
Condition Improvement Fund 187–188
Conflict of interest 225–228
Conversion process 37–39
  following opening 39
  pre-application 37–38
  prepare to open as academy 39
  set up or join academy trust 38
  start of 38
  transfer responsibilities to academy 38–39
Corporate governance 219–242
  chief executive officer 231–232
  Code of Governance 223
  committees 229–230
  CPD 242
  ensuring cohesion 235
  governance professional 239–240
  independent trustees 221–222
  mechanisms 220–224
  Ofsted 222–223
  performance management 242
  principal 231–232
  professional recognition 240–242
  self-regulation 223–224
  strategy 232–235
  trust name 235
  vision 232–235
CPD 242

Data protection 279–283, 319–335
  administration system 327–328
  archived files 332
  back-up 321–322
  Bring Your Own Device 324–325
  CCTV 330–331
  changes in immediate future 335
  cloud storage 319–321
  confidential post 333

confidential waste 332
confidentiality 328–330
cookies 328
desk storage 331–332
destruction 325–326, 332
devices 323–324
disaster plan 321–322
disaster recovery 321–322
DX 333
e-mail encryption 326–327
fax 333
file storage 331–332
finance and accounts systems 327–328
hearing loop 330–31
laptops 323–324
office procedures 331–332
password security 330
payroll 327–328
personal data 328–330
phones 323–324
policy 334
post 323
principles 279
privacy 328
pupil data 280–281
recording of calls 330–331
relations with ICO 334
remote working 322–323
security/data rooms 326–327
sensitive information 280
social media 328–330
training 334
travel 322–323
website 328
website backup 328
Delegation of authority 229–232
Director decision making see Board meetings
Directors 129–133 see also Trustees
  de facto 139–140
  disqualification 138–139
  duties 131
  eligibility 130–131

LAAPs 141–142
liability 140–141
member appointments 132
shadow 139–140
staff 132
Due diligence 51–59
areas to consider 53–55
MATs, for 55–59

Edubase 275–276
Example registers 285–286
Exempt charity status 179

Finance processes for month-end
reporting 296–298
Financial and accounting
requirements 68–70
Financial management 177–196
governance self-assessment, and
195–196
Financial monitoring 190–196
internal scrutiny 193–195
management, and 191–193
Financial records 69
Formula funding 188–189
Free schools 29, 31–32
Freedom of academisation 5–6
Freedom of Information Act 2000
276–279
publication of information 278
requests for information 277–278
Funding agreement 61–75
access by Secretary of State's
officers 72–73
acquiring or disposing of publicly
funded assets 69
admission requirements 65
annexes 73–74
annual accounts and audit 69
assessment 66
budgeting for funds 68–69
carrying forward of funds 69
charging 64
complaints 70

curriculum 65–66
designated teacher for looked after
children 63
Disclosure and Barring Service
checks 62
duration of school day and year 62
exclusions agreement 65
general obligations 62
governance 62
information 72
MATs 74–75
notices 73
pupil premium 64
pupils 63
school meals 64
staff 63
teachers 63
termination 70–72
change of control 71–72
effect 72
notice of intention 71
warning notice 70–71
transactions outside usual planned
range 70

General meetings 80, 117–123
adjournment 120
chair 120
convening 118–119
decision making at 120–121
minutes 125–126
notice 119–120
proxies 123
quorum 120
voting 121–122
written resolutions 125–126
Gift Aid 180
Glossary 341–346
Governance and delegation 23–25
Governance structures 17–30
Governors 142–143
link 143
Grants to be paid by Secretary of
State 66–67

capital grant 66–67
earmarked annual grant 67
general annual grant 67

Health and safety 246–250
hazards 249

ICSA Code for Good Boardroom
        Practice 158–160
Independent schools 29
Information management 271–283
Investment policies 181–183

Key indicators 275–276

Land clauses 70
Land transfer 43–44
  church schools 43–44
  land held by trust or foundation that is
        not diocese 43
  land owned by foundation or trust or
        governing body 43
  land owned by local authority
        43
Local authority
  Role of 45–46
Local Governing Bodies 23, 24, 161

Marketing 42
Members
  appointment 112–113
  ceasing to be 116–117
  derivative claims 115–116
  MATs 111–113
  protection against unfair
        prejudice 115
  remedies 114
  removal 117
  resignation 117
  responsibilities 114
  rights 114
  termination 116
  two-tier management system 111
Memorandum of association 77

Mergers and acquisitions 46
Minute-taker's reminder
        checklists 290–295
Minutes of trustees' meetings
  action points 173–174
  any other business 172
  apologies 168
  appointment of chair and vice
        chair 169
  chair's welcome 168
  close of meeting 174–175
  confidential items 175
  correspondence 172
  declaration of interests 168–169
  drafting 166
  heading 166
  introduction 168
  items of business 172
  matters arising 170
  minutes of last meeting 169–170
  next meeting 185
  practical considerations 163–165
  preparation 175–176
  reports 171
  resolutions 172
  storing 176
  quorum 167–168
Multi-academy trusts (MATs) 19–20,
        36–37
  accounts 211
  advantages 5–6, 37
  converting to 36–37
  disadvantages 37
  due diligence, and 47–60
  expansion 60
  governance structure 21
  members 111–113
  policies 263–265
  staff 60

National Governors' Association 14
National Leaders of Education 9–10

Ofsted 14–15, 222–223

Parent trustees 131–132
Pension schemes 40–41
Performance management 242
Performance tables 51
PFI academies 190
PFI schools 44–45
Policies 259–269
  access to 265
  drafting 263–265
  MATs 263–265
  review 265–266
  social media 266–269
  statutory 259–262
Procurement 190

Regional Schools Commissioners 9
Register of directors/governors 285
Register of directors/governors
      addresses 286
Register of directors/trustees 92
Register of directors'/trustees'
      interests 92
Register of directors'/trustees' residential
      addresses 92
Register of gifts, hospitality and
      entertainments 94–95,
      286
Register of interests 274, 286
Register of members 91, 285
Register of people with significant
      control 95–96
Register of secretaries 91, 285
Register of trustees 92
Reserves policy 183
Risk assessment
  form 307–310
Risk management 243–258
  allegations against staff and
      volunteers 250
  appeal panels 255
  business continuity and disaster
      recovery plans 251
  chair of board 258
  dealing with complaints 253–254

Faringdon Academy of Schools
      Model 245
  health and safety 246–250
  insurance 251–253
    risk protection arrangement
      252–253
  review of board effectiveness 255–258
  safeguarding 250
Risk register 311–312

SAIL
  notification 93–94, 106
Salix funding 189
Scheme of delegation 24–25
Single academies 17–19, 35–36
Single academy trust
  converting to 35–36
Skills audit 135, 287–289
Social media 266–269
  importance 267
  pupils, use by 269
  school corporate use 268
  staff, use by 268–269
Sponsors 34–35
Staff 60
Staff directors 132
Stakeholder management 41–42
Statutory policies 259–262
  admissions arrangements 259
  behaviour policy 259
  charging and remissions 259–260
  complaints procedure 260
  data protection 260
  equality information and
      objectives 260
  freedom of information 260
  health and safety 260–261
  home-school agreement
      document 261
  sex and relationship education 261
  Special Educational Needs 261
Statutory registers 91–93
  inspection 94
Strategic objectives 305–306

Structure of trust 128
Studio schools 29–30
Subsidiary trading companies 179

Tax relief 180–181
Teaching schools 10
Training needs
  analysis 135
Trust 3–4
Trustees 8–9, 80–81, 144 *see also*
      Directors
  appointment 131–133
  diversity 133
  finding right person 133–135
  induction and training 135
  payment 137
  power 82
  sponsor/foundation appointments 133
  termination of office 137–138
TUPE 39–40

Umbrella trust 4, 28–29
University technical colleges (UTCs) 30,
      32–33

Value added tax 184–185
Vice-Chairman of trustees 82

Website 271–275, 336–339
  admissions 271
  company information 273
  curriculum 272
  equality duty 274–275
  gender pay gap reporting 275
  governance arrangements 273–274
  PE and sport premium 272
  policies 273
  pupil performance and results
      272
  pupil premium 272
  register of interests 274